Short Order CROOKS

CREATED BY
CHRISTOPHER SEBELA
GEORGE KAMBADAIS
LESLEY ATLANSKY
HASSAN OTSMANE-ELHAOU &
KELLY SUE DECONNICK

ONI PRESS

AN ONI PRESS PUBLICATION

Short Order CROOKS

SCRIPT: CHRISTOPHER SEBELA
LINE ART: GEORGE KAMBADAIS
COLORS: LESLEY ATLANSKY
LETTERS: HASSAN OTSMANE-ELHAOU
LOGO: DYLAN TODD
EDITED BY: JIM GIBBONS
COLLECTION EDITED BY: JASMINE AMIRI
COLLECTION DESIGNED BY: SONJA SYNAK
COVER BY: GEORGE KAMBADAIS

ONI-LION FORGE PUBLISHING GROUP, LLC.

James Lucas Jones, president & publisher • Charlie Chu, e.v.p. of creative & business development • Steve Ellis, s.v.p. of games & operations • Alex Segura, s.v.p of marketing & sales • Michelle Nguyen, associate publisher • Brad Rooks, director of operations • Amber O'Neill, special projects manager • Margot Wood, director of marketing & sales • Katie Sainz, marketing manager • Tara Lehmann, publicist Holly Aitchison, consumer marketing manager • Troy Look, director of design & production • Angie Knowles, production manager • Kate Z. Stone, senior graphic designer • Carey Hall, graphic designer • Sarah Rockwell, graphic designer • Hilary Thompson, graphic designer • Vincent Kukua, digital prepress technician • Chris Cerasi, managing editor • Jasmine Amiri, senior editor • Shawna Gore, senior editor Amanda Meadows, senior editor • Robert Meyers, senior editor, licensing • Desiree Rodriguez, editor • Grace Scheipeter, editor • Zack Soto, editor • Ben Eisner, game developer • Jung Lee, logistics coordinator • Kuian Kellum, warehouse assistant

Joe Nozemack, publisher emeritus

1319 SE Martin Luther King Jr. Blvd.
Suite 240
Portland, OR 97214

onipress.com

First Edition:
October 2021

ISBN 978-1-63715-005-4

eISBN 978-1-63715-006-1

Library of Congress Control Number:
2021934308

1 2 3 4 5 6 7 8 9 10

1: IN THE WEEDS

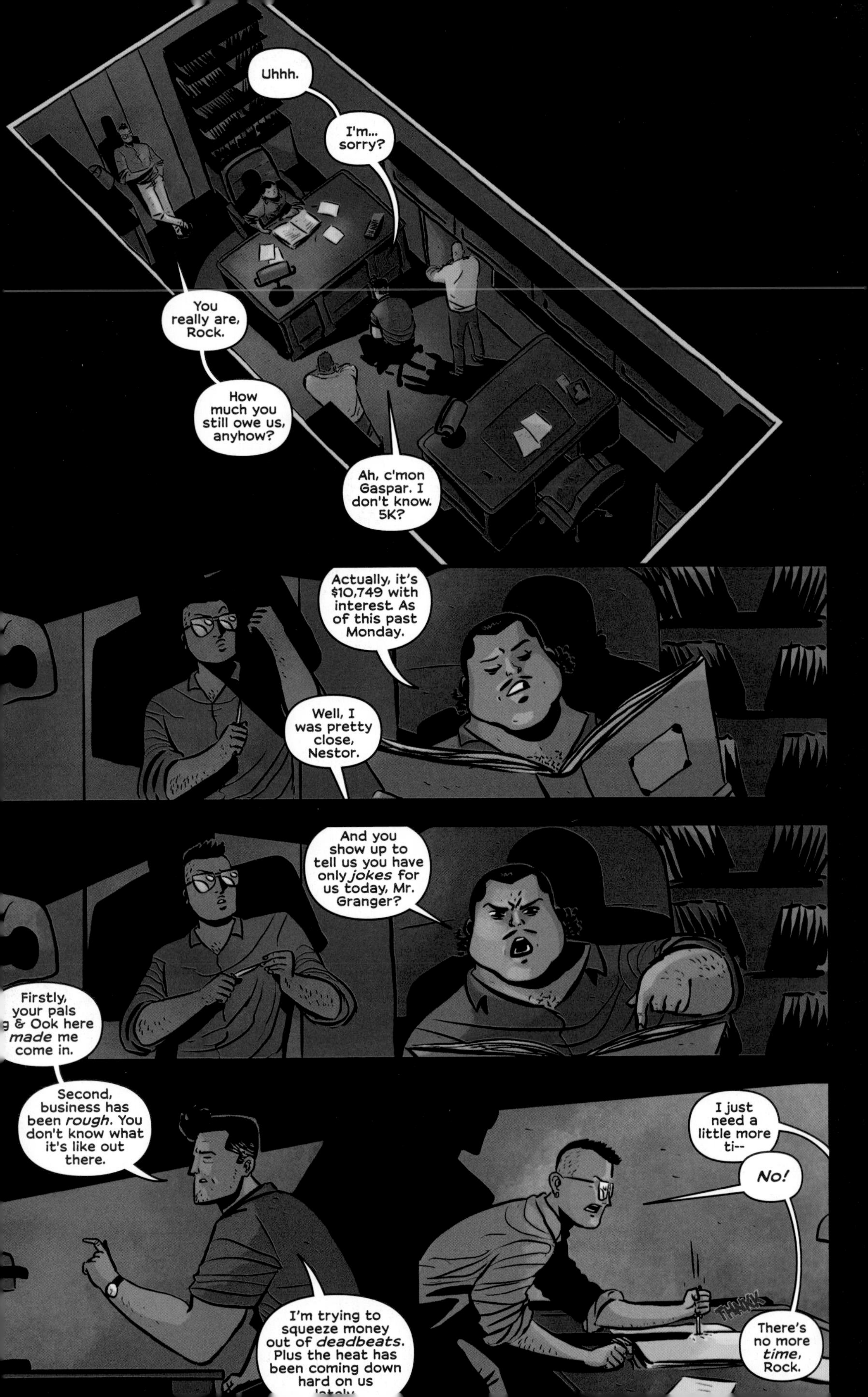

Uhhh.
I'm... sorry?
You really are, Rock.
How much you still owe us, anyhow?
Ah, c'mon Gaspar. I don't know. 5K?
Actually, it's $10,749 with interest. As of this past Monday.
Well, I was pretty close, Nestor.
And you show up to tell us you have only *jokes* for us today, Mr. Granger?
Firstly, your pals & Ook here *made* me come in.
Second, business has been *rough*. You don't know what it's like out there.
I'm trying to squeeze money out of *deadbeats*. Plus the heat has been coming down hard on us
I just need a little more ti--
No!
There's no more *time*, Rock.

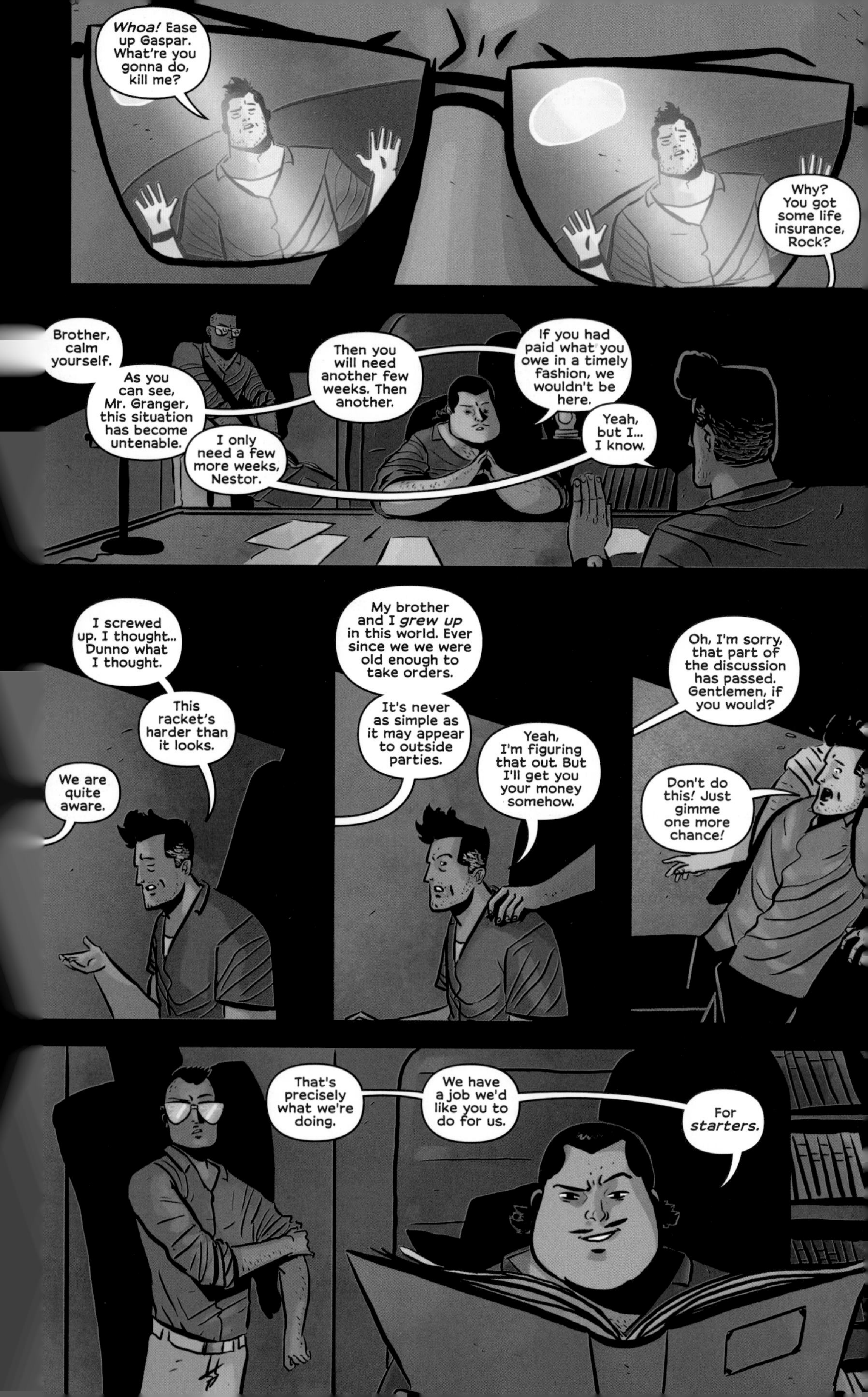
Whoa! Ease up Gaspar. What're you gonna do, kill me?
Why? You got some life insurance, Rock?
Brother, calm yourself.
As you can see, Mr. Granger, this situation has become untenable.
I only need a few more weeks, Nestor.
Then you will need another few weeks. Then another.
If you had paid what you owe in a timely fashion, we wouldn't be here.
Yeah, but I... I know.
I screwed up. I thought... Dunno what I thought.
This racket's harder than it looks.
We are quite aware.
My brother and I grew up in this world. Ever since we we were old enough to take orders.
It's never as simple as it may appear to outside parties.
Yeah, I'm figuring that out. But I'll get you your money somehow.
Oh, I'm sorry, that part of the discussion has passed. Gentlemen, if you would?
Don't do this! Just gimme one more chance!
That's precisely what we're doing.
We have a job we'd like you to do for us.
For starters.

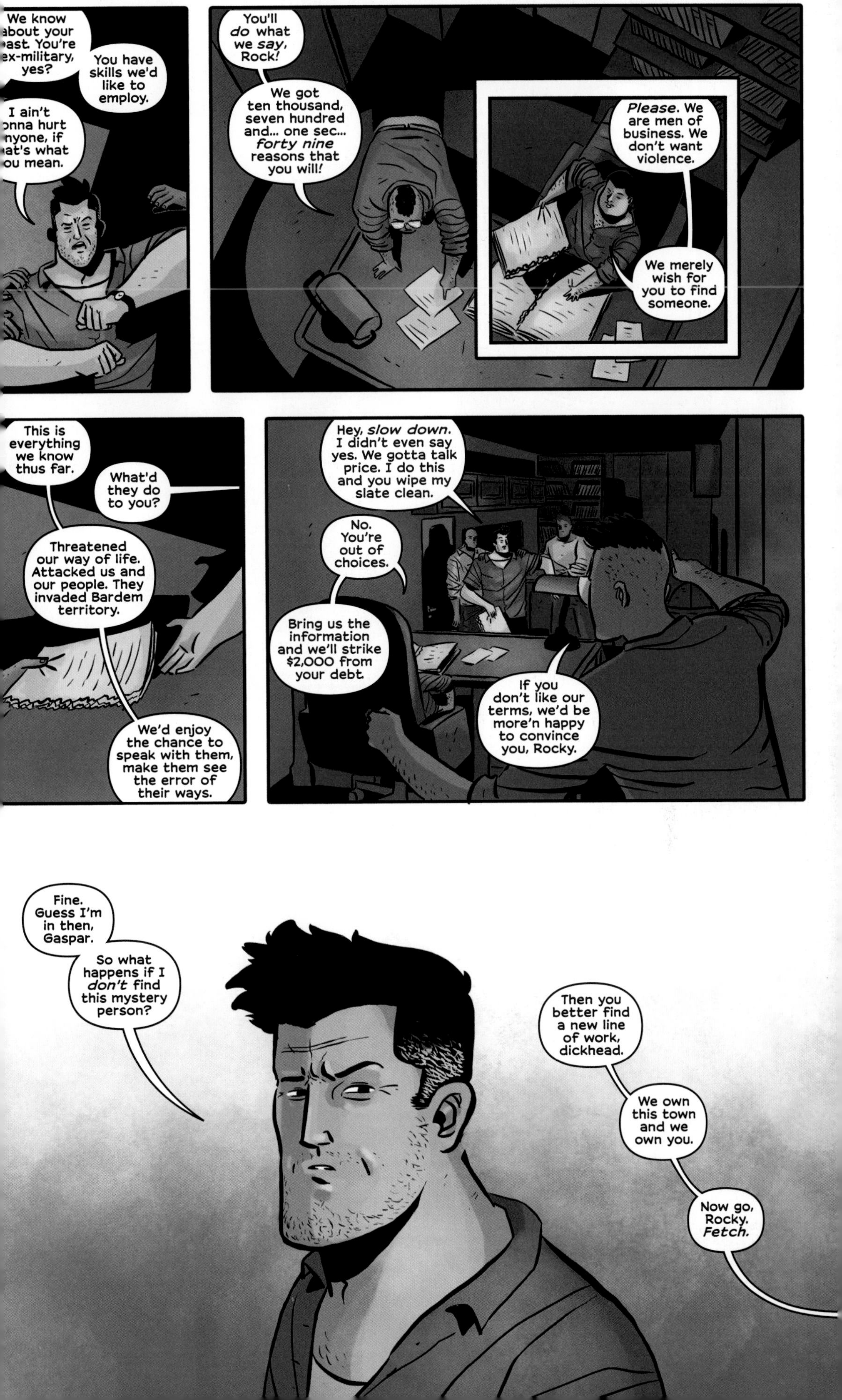
We know about your past. You're ex-military, yes?
You have skills we'd like to employ.
I ain't gonna hurt anyone, if that's what you mean.
You'll *do* what we *say*, Rock!
We got ten thousand, seven hundred and... one sec... *forty nine* reasons that you will!
Please. We are men of business. We don't want violence.
We merely wish for you to find someone.
This is everything we know thus far.
What'd they do to you?
Threatened our way of life. Attacked us and our people. They invaded Bardem territory.
We'd enjoy the chance to speak with them, make them see the error of their ways.
Hey, *slow down*. I didn't even say yes. We gotta talk price. I do this and you wipe my slate clean.
No. You're out of choices.
Bring us the information and we'll strike $2,000 from your debt.
If you don't like our terms, we'd be more'n happy to convince you, Rocky.
Fine. Guess I'm in then, Gaspar.
So what happens if I *don't* find this mystery person?
Then you better find a new line of work, dickhead.
We own this town and we own you.
Now go, Rocky. *Fetch.*

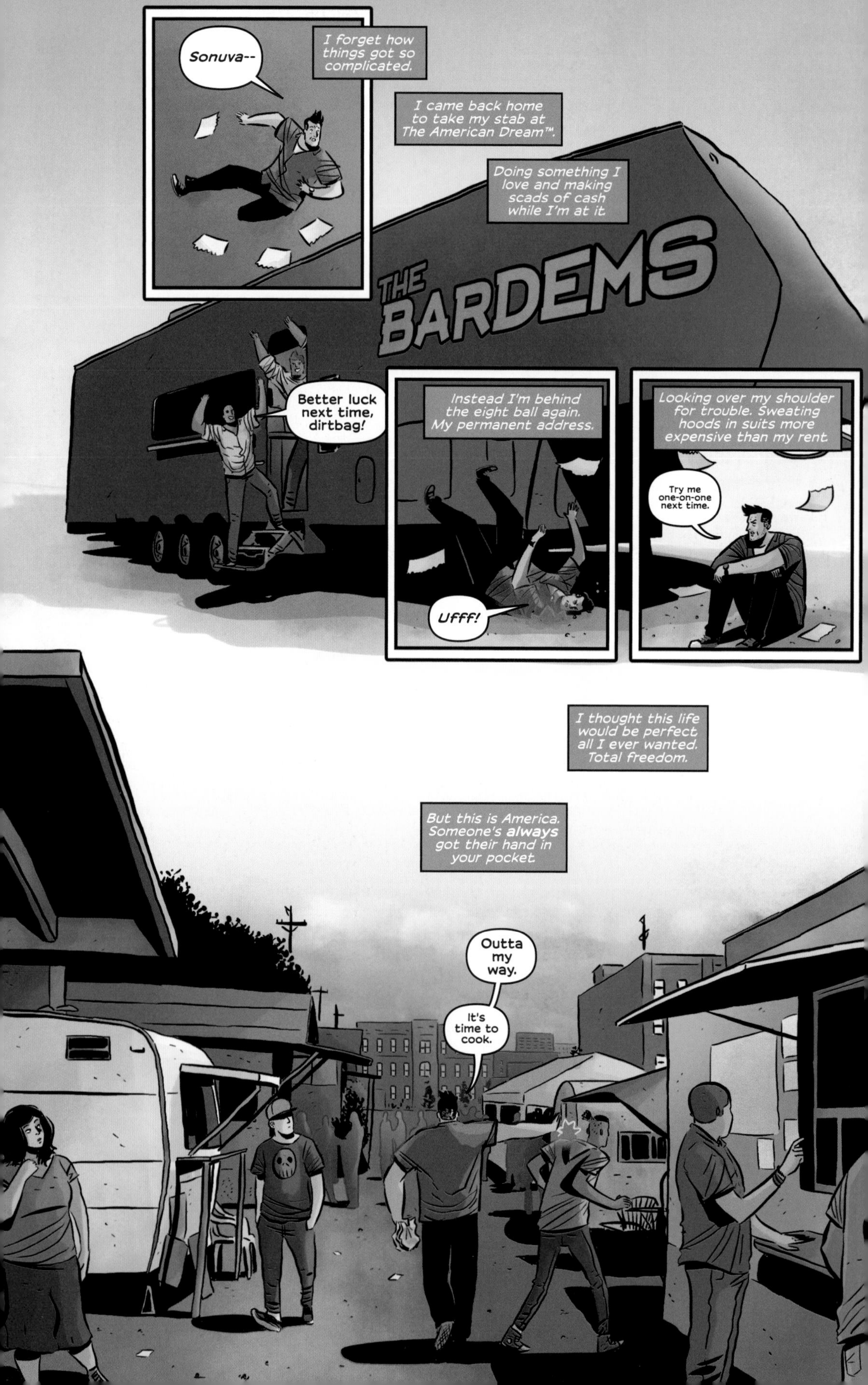
Sonuva--
I forget how things got so complicated.
I came back home to take my stab at The American Dream™.
Doing something I love and making scads of cash while I'm at it.
THE BARDEMS
Better luck next time, dirtbag!
Instead I'm behind the eight ball again. My permanent address.
Ufff!
Looking over my shoulder for trouble. Sweating hoods in suits more expensive than my rent.
Try me one-on-one next time.
I thought this life would be perfect. all I ever wanted. Total freedom.
But this is America. Someone's **always** got their hand in your pocket.
Outta my way.
It's time to cook.

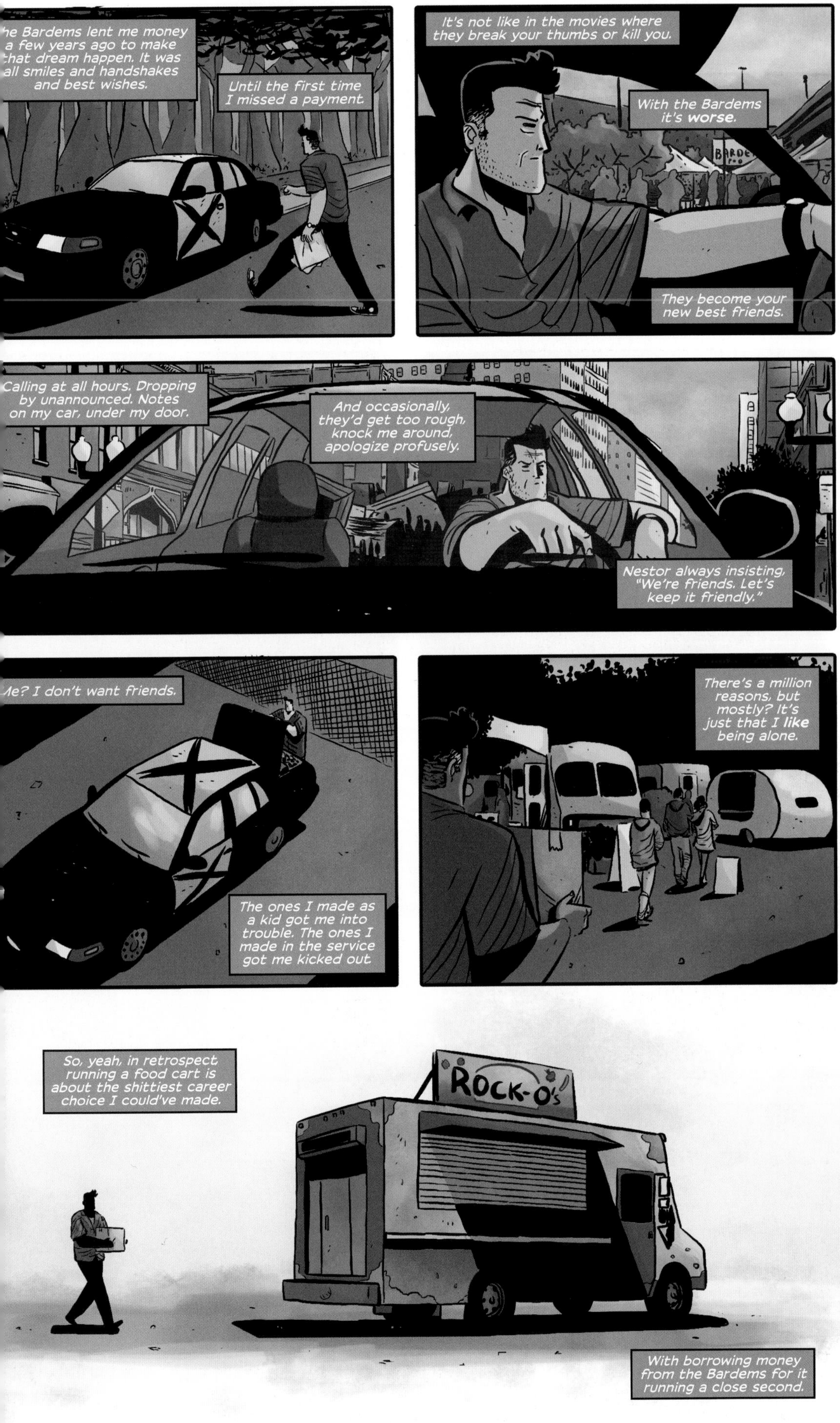
he Bardems lent me money a few years ago to make that dream happen. It was all smiles and handshakes and best wishes.
Until the first time I missed a payment.
It's not like in the movies where they break your thumbs or kill you.
With the Bardems it's **worse.**
They become your new best friends.
Calling at all hours. Dropping by unannounced. Notes on my car, under my door.
And occasionally, they'd get too rough, knock me around, apologize profusely.
Nestor always insisting, "We're friends. Let's keep it friendly."
Me? I don't want friends.
The ones I made as a kid got me into trouble. The ones I made in the service got me kicked out.
There's a million reasons, but mostly? It's just that I **like** being alone.
So, yeah, in retrospect running a food cart is about the shittiest career choice I could've made.
ROCK-O's
With borrowing money from the Bardems for it running a close second.

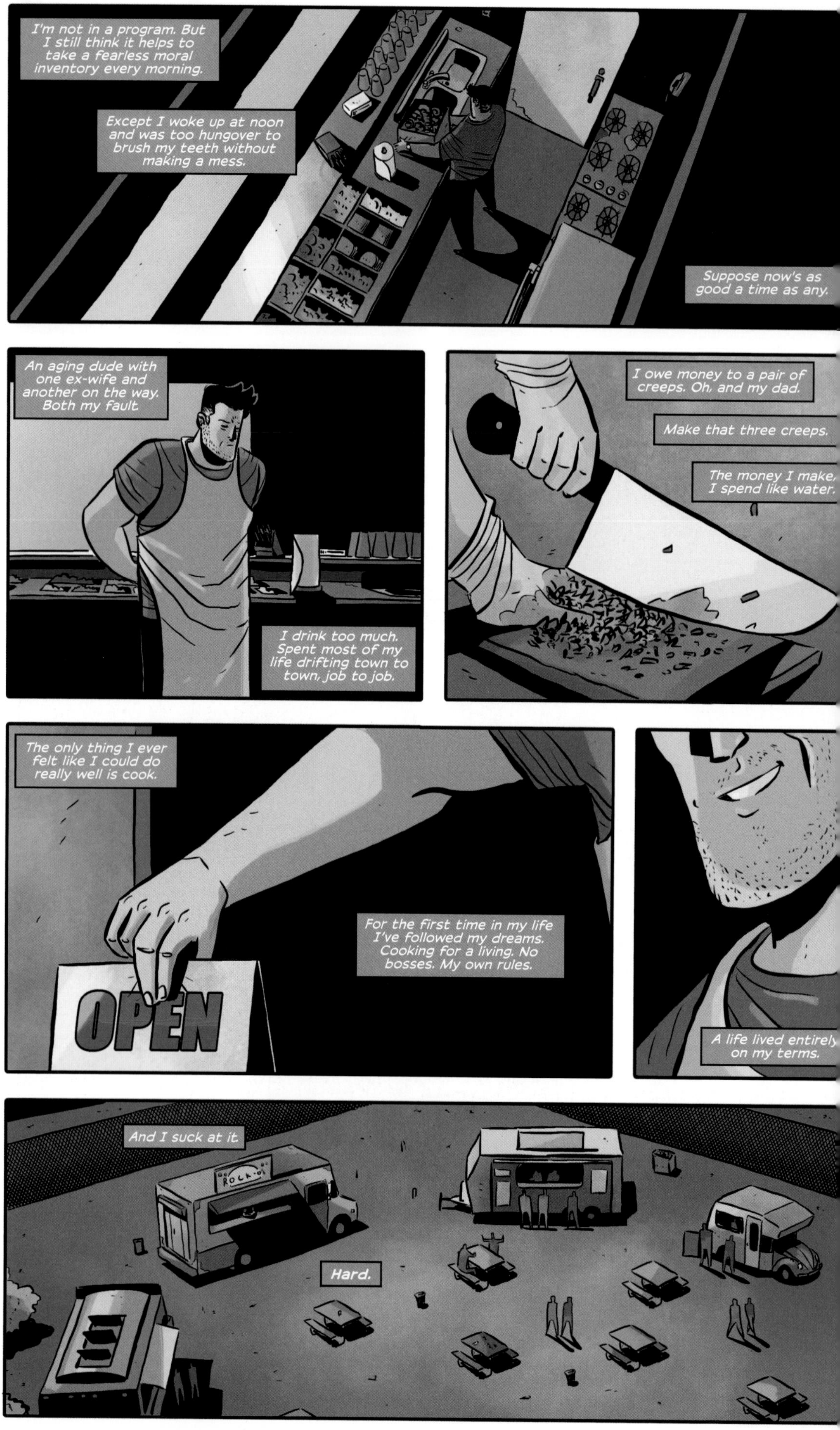
I'm not in a program. But I still think it helps to take a fearless moral inventory every morning.
Except I woke up at noon and was too hungover to brush my teeth without making a mess.
Suppose now's as good a time as any.
An aging dude with one ex-wife and another on the way. Both my fault.
I drink too much. Spent most of my life drifting town to town, job to job.
I owe money to a pair of creeps. Oh, and my dad.
Make that three creeps.
The money I make, I spend like water.
The only thing I ever felt like I could do really well is cook.
OPEN
For the first time in my life I've followed my dreams. Cooking for a living. No bosses. My own rules.
A life lived entirely on my terms.
And I suck at it.
ROCK-O'S
Hard.

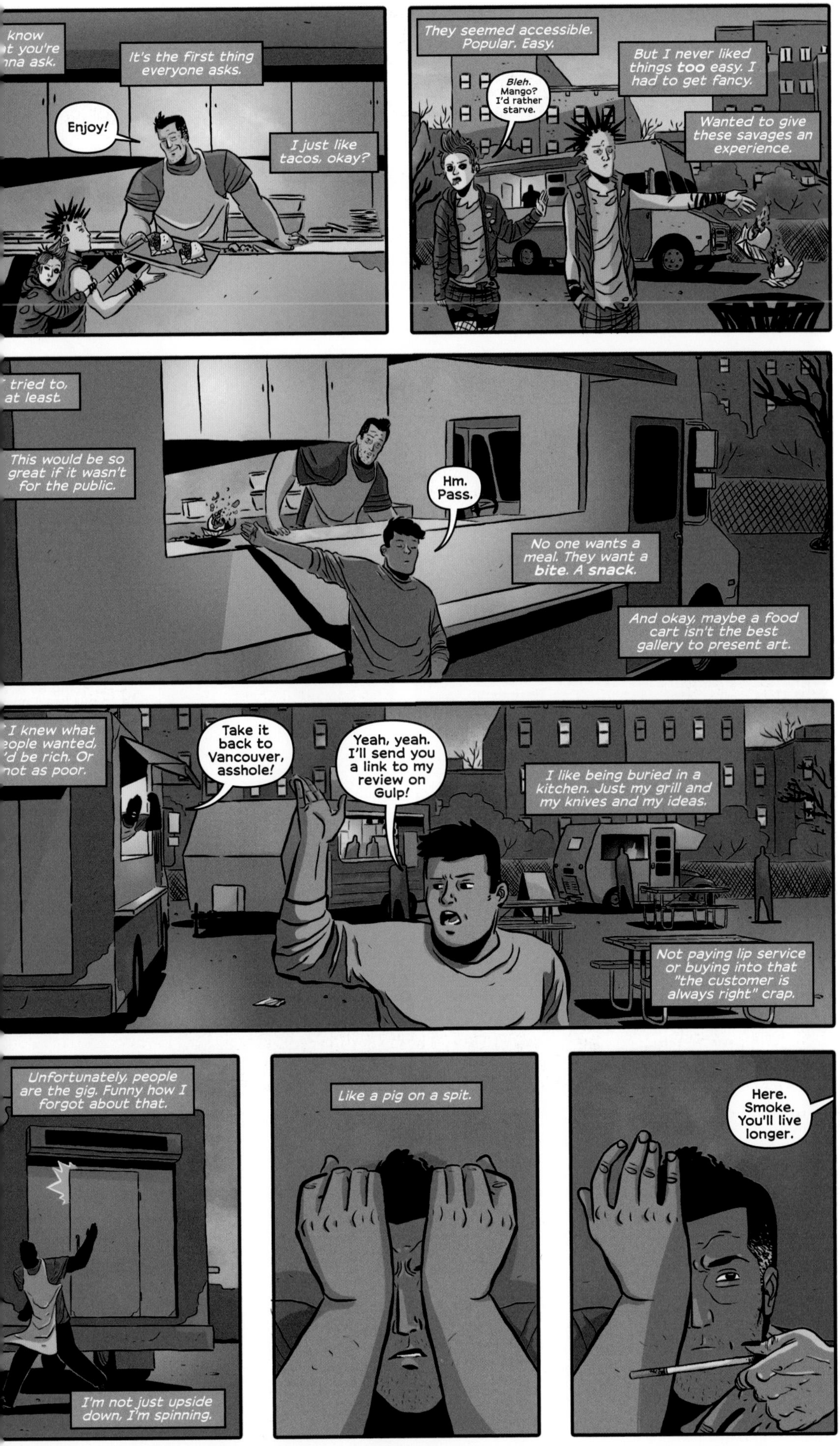
know
t you're
nna ask.
It's the first thing everyone asks.
Enjoy!
I just like tacos, okay?
They seemed accessible. Popular. Easy.
Bleh. Mango? I'd rather starve.
But I never liked things **too** easy. I had to get fancy.
Wanted to give these savages an experience.
tried to, at least.
This would be so great if it wasn't for the public.
Hm. Pass.
No one wants a meal. They want a **bite**. A **snack**.
And okay, maybe a food cart isn't the best gallery to present art.
I knew what
eople wanted,
'd be rich. Or
not as poor.
Take it back to Vancouver, asshole!
Yeah, yeah. I'll send you a link to my review on Gulp!
I like being buried in a kitchen. Just my grill and my knives and my ideas.
Not paying lip service or buying into that "the customer is always right" crap.
Unfortunately, people are the gig. Funny how I forgot about that.
I'm not just upside down, I'm spinning.
Like a pig on a spit.
Here. Smoke. You'll live longer.

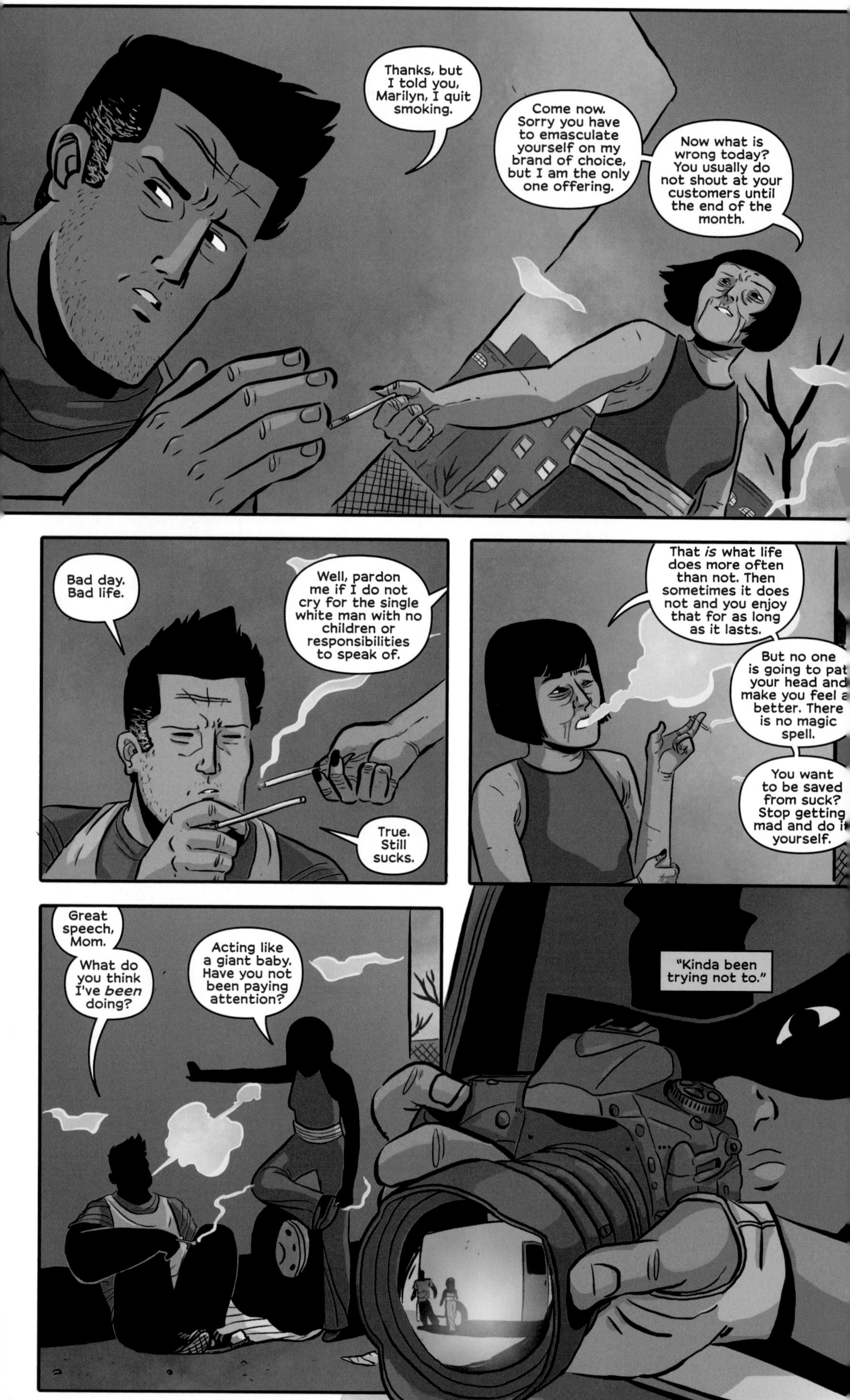
Thanks, but I told you, Marilyn, I quit smoking.
Come now. Sorry you have to emasculate yourself on my brand of choice, but I am the only one offering.
Now what is wrong today? You usually do not shout at your customers until the end of the month.
Bad day. Bad life.
Well, pardon me if I do not cry for the single white man with no children or responsibilities to speak of.
True. Still sucks.
That *is* what life does more often than not. Then sometimes it does not and you enjoy that for as long as it lasts.
But no one is going to pat your head and make you feel a better. There is no magic spell.
You want to be saved from suck? Stop getting mad and do it yourself.
Great speech, Mom.
What do you think I've *been* doing?
Acting like a giant baby. Have you not been paying attention?
"Kinda been trying not to."

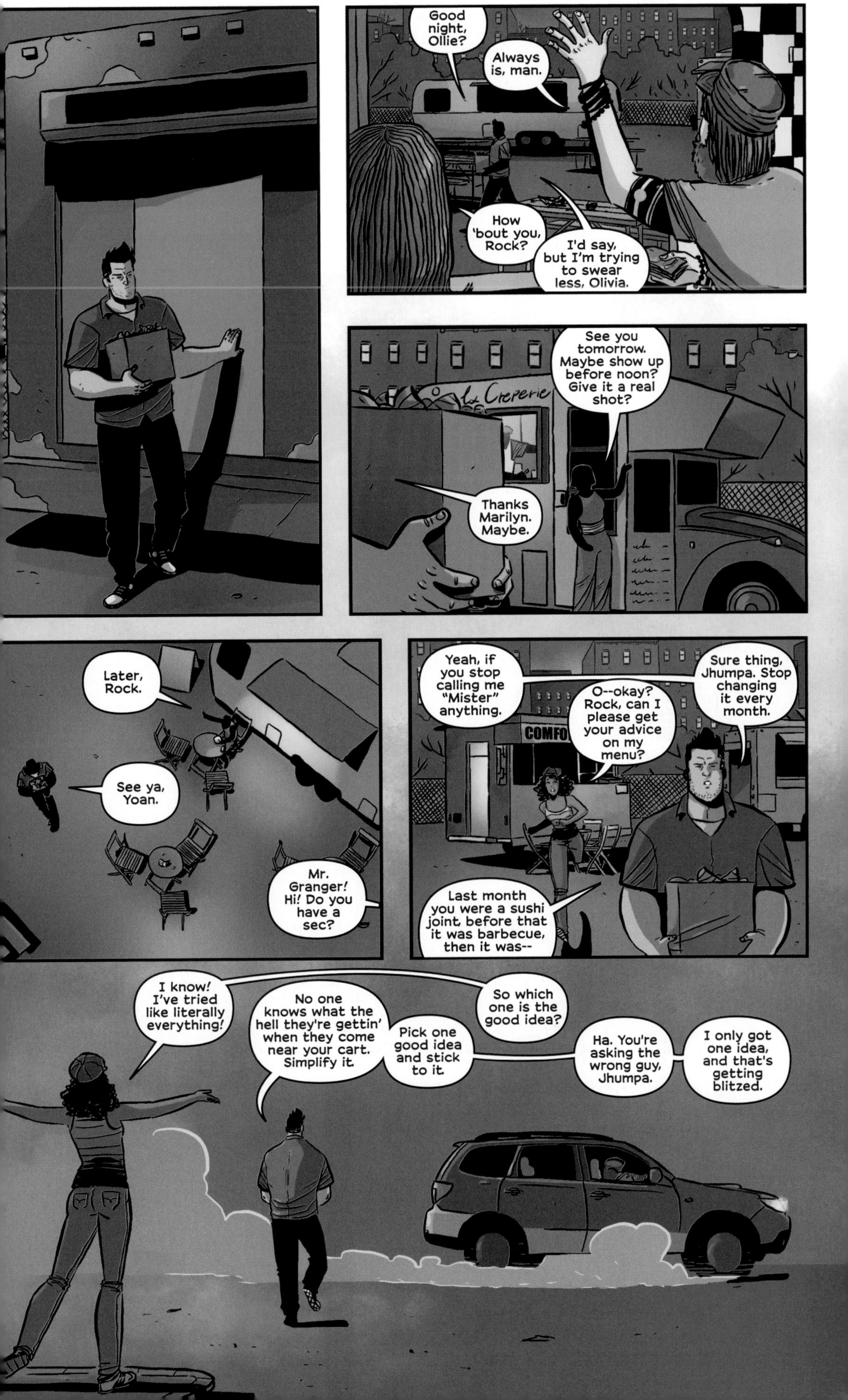

Good night, Ollie?
Always is, man.
How 'bout you, Rock?
I'd say, but I'm trying to swear less, Olivia.
See you tomorrow. Maybe show up before noon? Give it a real shot?
Thanks Marilyn. Maybe.
Later, Rock.
See ya, Yoan.
Mr. Granger! Hi! Do you have a sec?
Yeah, if you stop calling me "Mister" anything.
O--okay? Rock, can I please get your advice on my menu?
Sure thing, Jhumpa. Stop changing it every month.
Last month you were a sushi joint before that it was barbecue, then it was--
I know! I've tried like literally everything!
So which one is the good idea?
No one knows what the hell they're gettin' when they come near your cart. Simplify it.
Pick one good idea and stick to it.
Ha. You're asking the wrong guy, Jhumpa.
I only got one idea, and that's getting blitzed.

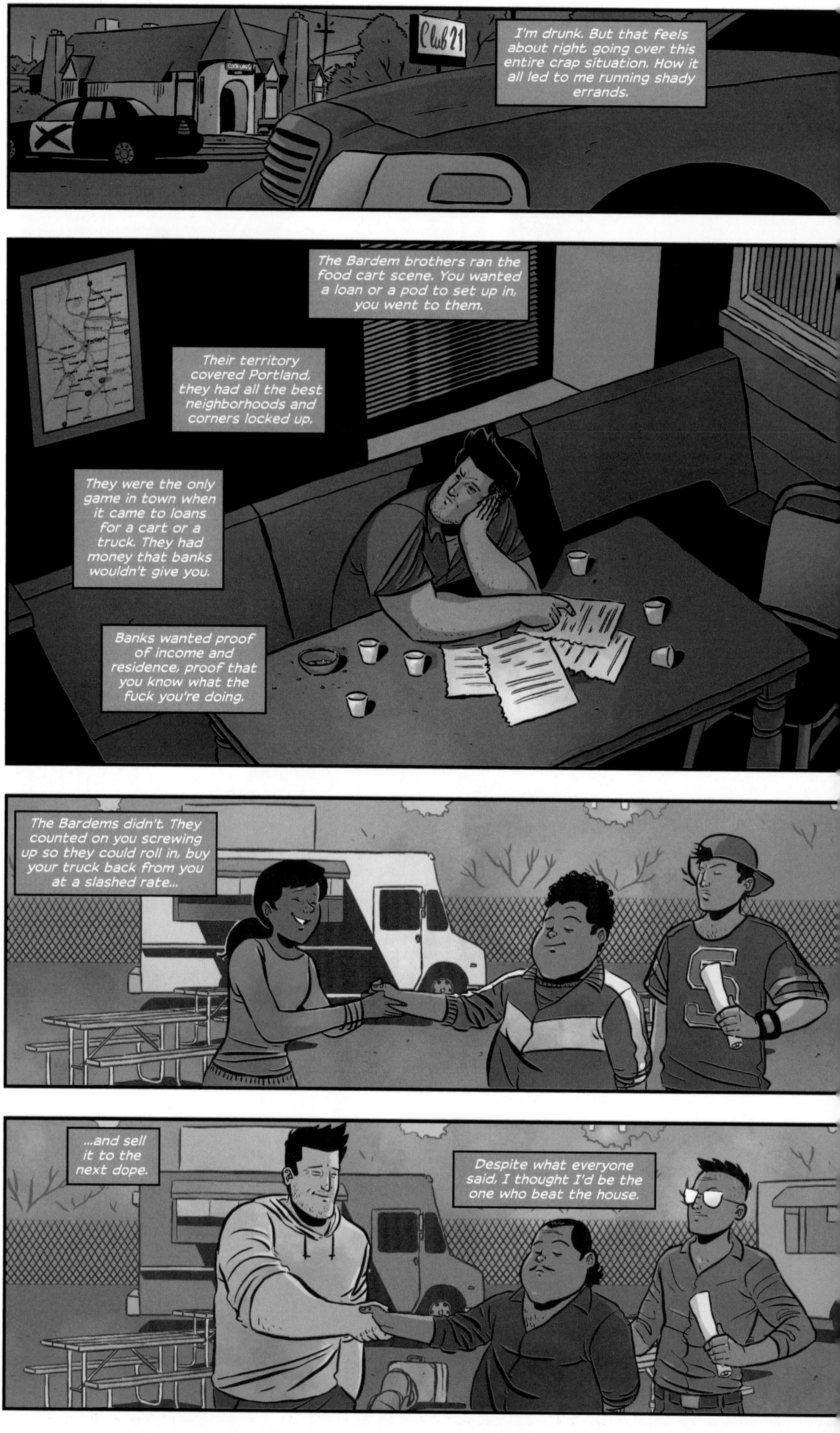
Club 21
I'm drunk. But that feels about right going over this entire crap situation. How it all led to me running shady errands.
The Bardem brothers ran the food cart scene. You wanted a loan or a pod to set up in, you went to them.
Their territory covered Portland, they had all the best neighborhoods and corners locked up.
They were the only game in town when it came to loans for a cart or a truck. They had money that banks wouldn't give you.
Banks wanted proof of income and residence, proof that you know what the fuck you're doing.
The Bardems didn't. They counted on you screwing up so they could roll in, buy your truck back from you at a slashed rate...
...and sell it to the next dope.
Despite what everyone said, I thought I'd be the one who beat the house.

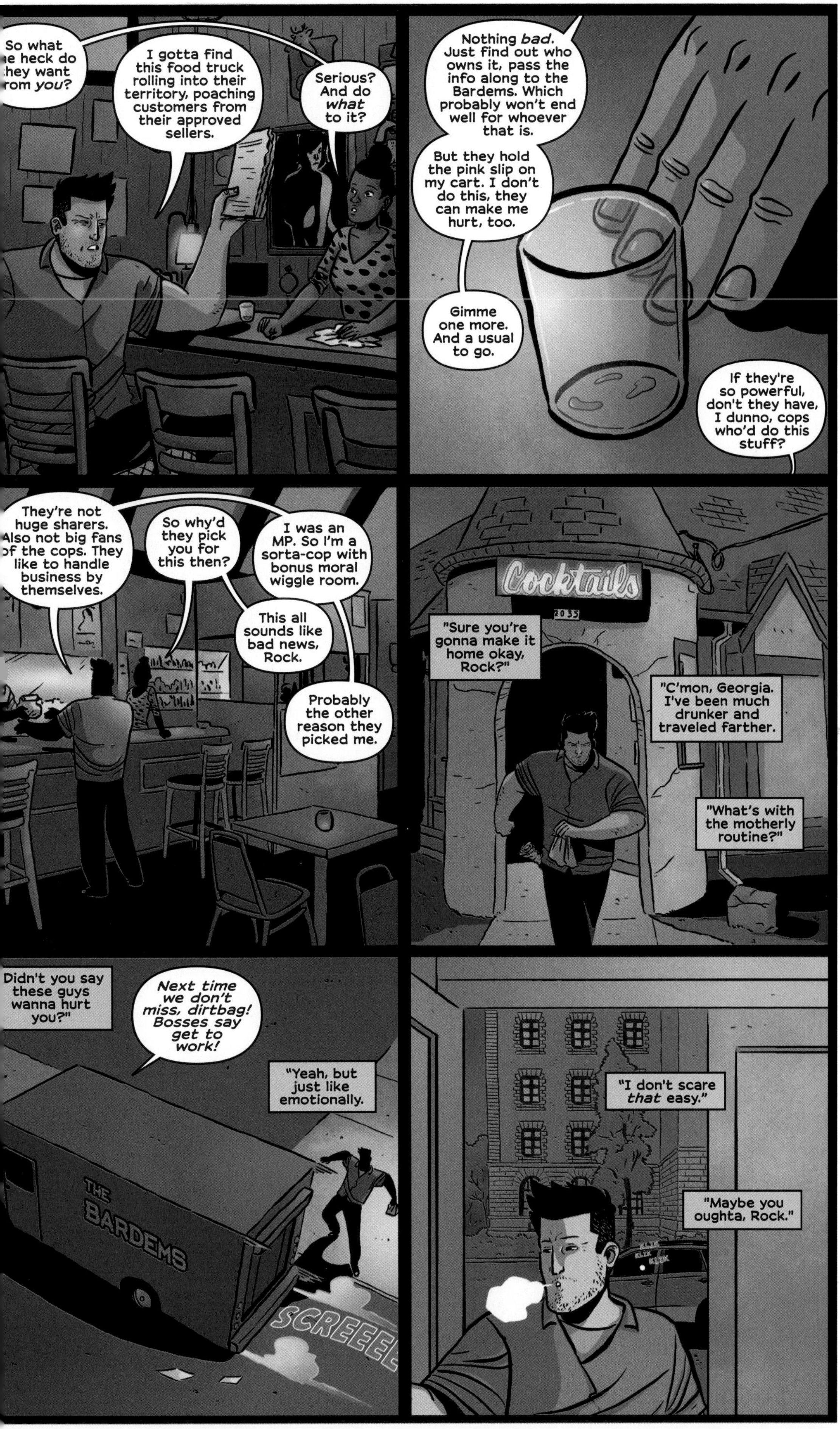

So what
e heck do
hey want
rom *you*?
I gotta find this food truck rolling into their territory, poaching customers from their approved sellers.
Serious? And do *what* to it?
Nothing *bad*. Just find out who owns it, pass the info along to the Bardems. Which probably won't end well for whoever that is.
But they hold the pink slip on my cart. I don't do this, they can make me hurt, too.
Gimme one more. And a usual to go.
If they're so powerful, don't they have, I dunno, cops who'd do this stuff?
They're not huge sharers. Also not big fans of the cops. They like to handle business by themselves.
So why'd they pick you for this then?
I was an MP. So I'm a sorta-cop with bonus moral wiggle room.
This all sounds like bad news, Rock.
Probably the other reason they picked me.
Cocktails
2035
"Sure you're gonna make it home okay, Rock?"
"C'mon, Georgia. I've been much drunker and traveled farther.
"What's with the motherly routine?"
Didn't you say these guys wanna hurt you?"
Next time we don't miss, dirtbag! Bosses say get to work!
"Yeah, but just like emotionally.
THE BARDEMS
SCREEEE
"I don't scare *that* easy."
"Maybe you oughta, Rock."
KLIK KLIK KLIK

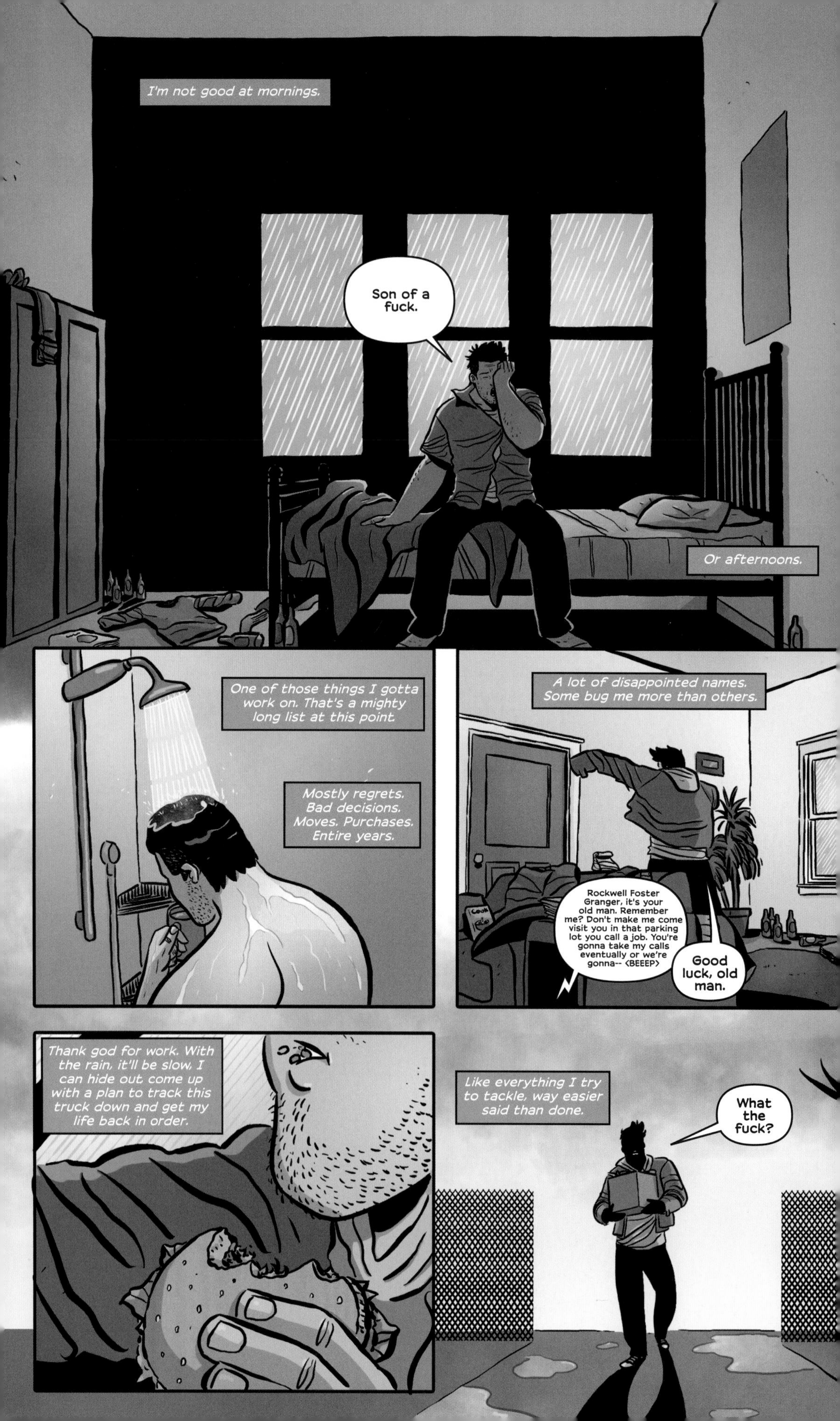
I'm not good at mornings.
Son of a fuck.
Or afternoons.
One of those things I gotta work on. That's a mighty long list at this point.
Mostly regrets. Bad decisions. Moves. Purchases. Entire years.
A lot of disappointed names. Some bug me more than others.
Rockwell Foster Granger, it's your old man. Remember me? Don't make me come visit you in that parking lot you call a job. You're gonna take my calls eventually or we're gonna-- <BEEEP>
Good luck, old man.
Thank god for work. With the rain, it'll be slow. I can hide out come up with a plan to track this truck down and get my life back in order.
Like everything I try to tackle, way easier said than done.
What the fuck?

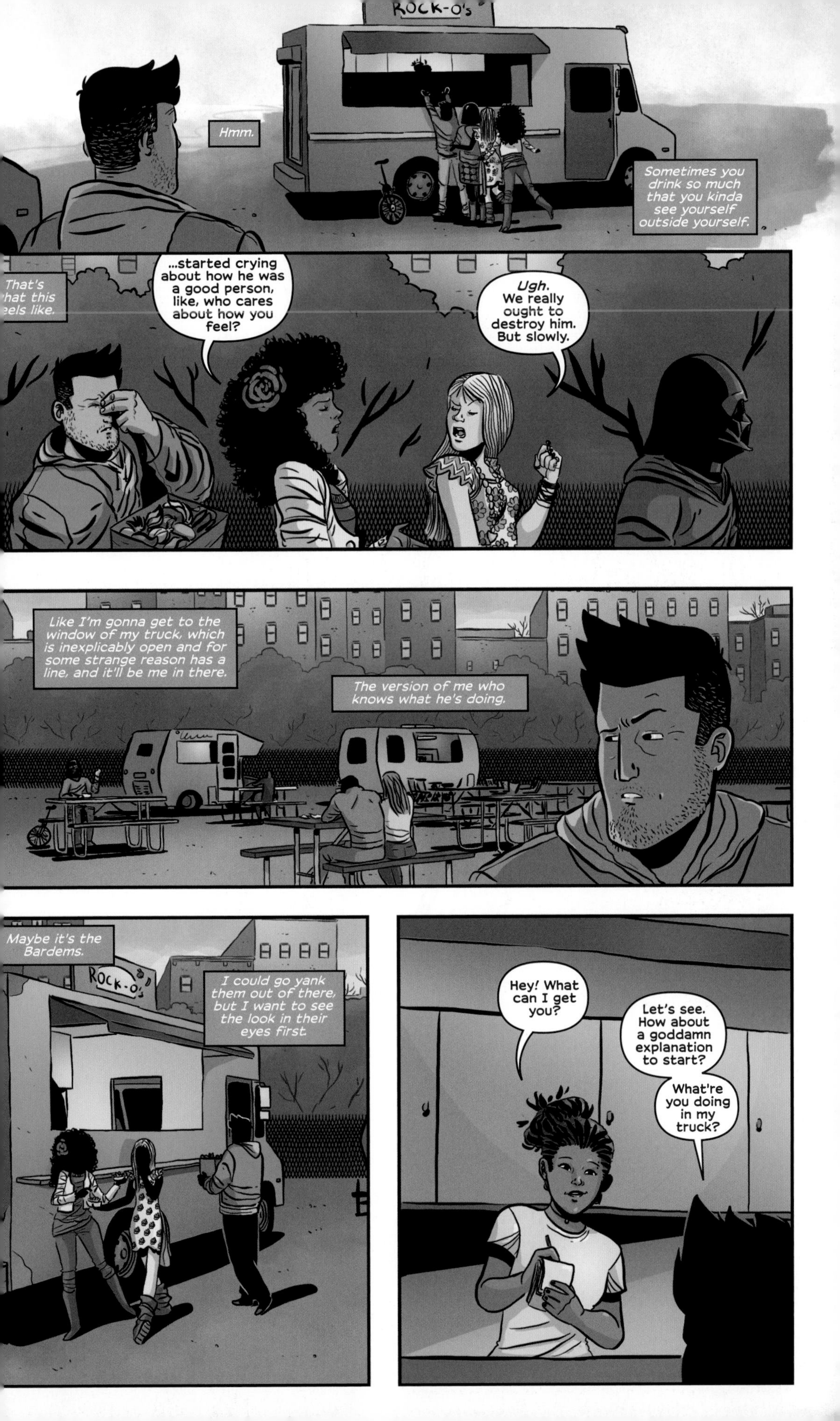
ROCK-O's
Hmm.
Sometimes you drink so much that you kinda see yourself outside yourself.
That's
hat this
eels like.
...started crying about how he was a good person, like, who cares about how you feel?
Ugh. We really ought to destroy him. But slowly.
Like I'm gonna get to the window of my truck, which is inexplicably open and for some strange reason has a line, and it'll be me in there.
The version of me who knows what he's doing.
Maybe it's the Bardems.
ROCK-O's
I could go yank them out of there, but I want to see the look in their eyes first.
Hey! What can I get you?
Let's see. How about a goddamn explanation to start?
What're you doing in my truck?

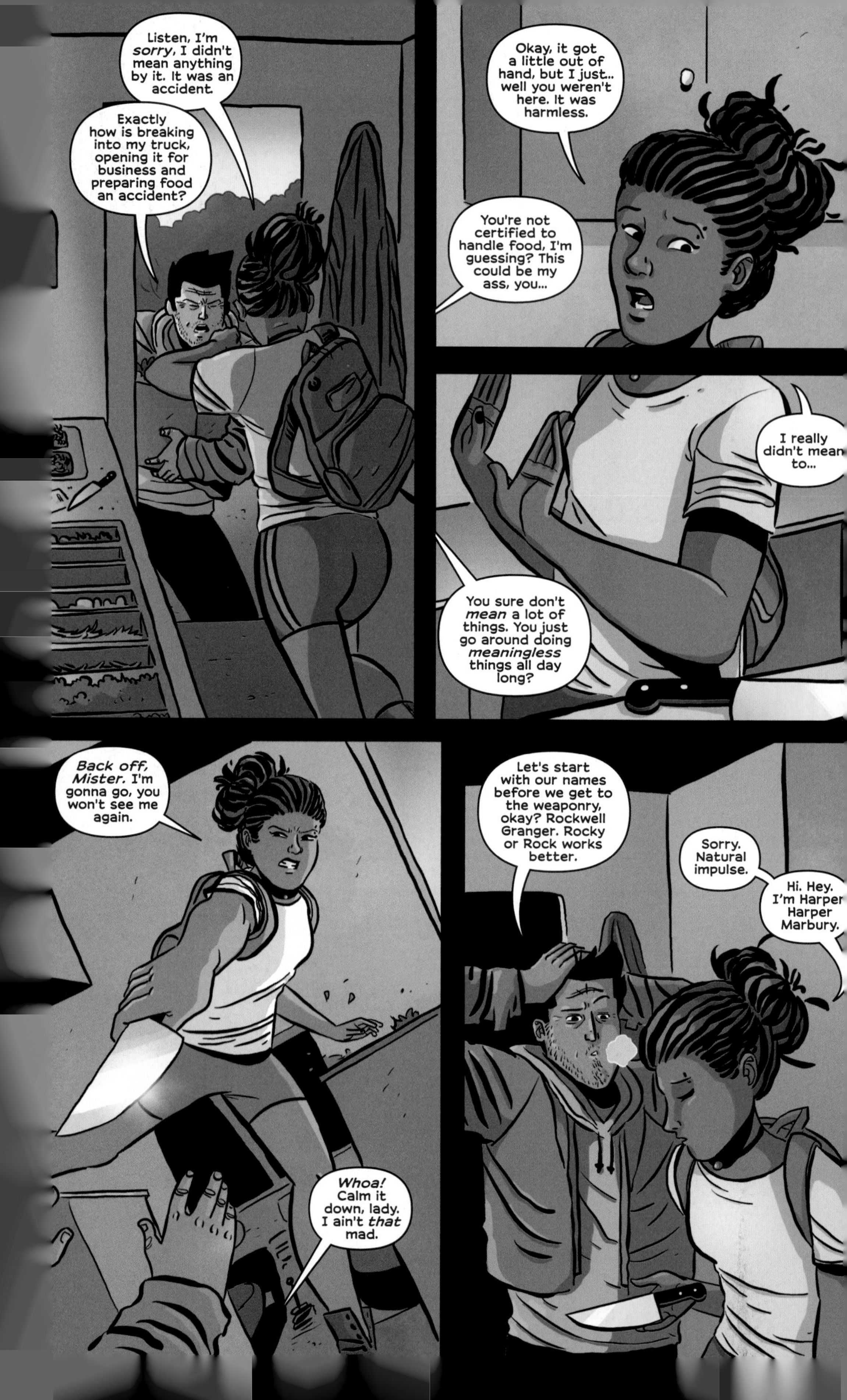
Listen, I'm *sorry*, I didn't mean anything by it. It was an accident.
Exactly how is breaking into my truck, opening it for business and preparing food an accident?
Okay, it got a little out of hand, but I just... well you weren't here. It was harmless.
You're not certified to handle food, I'm guessing? This could be my ass, you...
I really didn't mean to...
You sure don't *mean* a lot of things. You just go around doing *meaningless* things all day long?
Back off, Mister. I'm gonna go, you won't see me again.
Whoa! Calm it down, lady. I ain't *that* mad.
Let's start with our names before we get to the weaponry, okay? Rockwell Granger. Rocky or Rock works better.
Sorry. Natural impulse.
Hi. Hey. I'm Harper Harper Marbury.

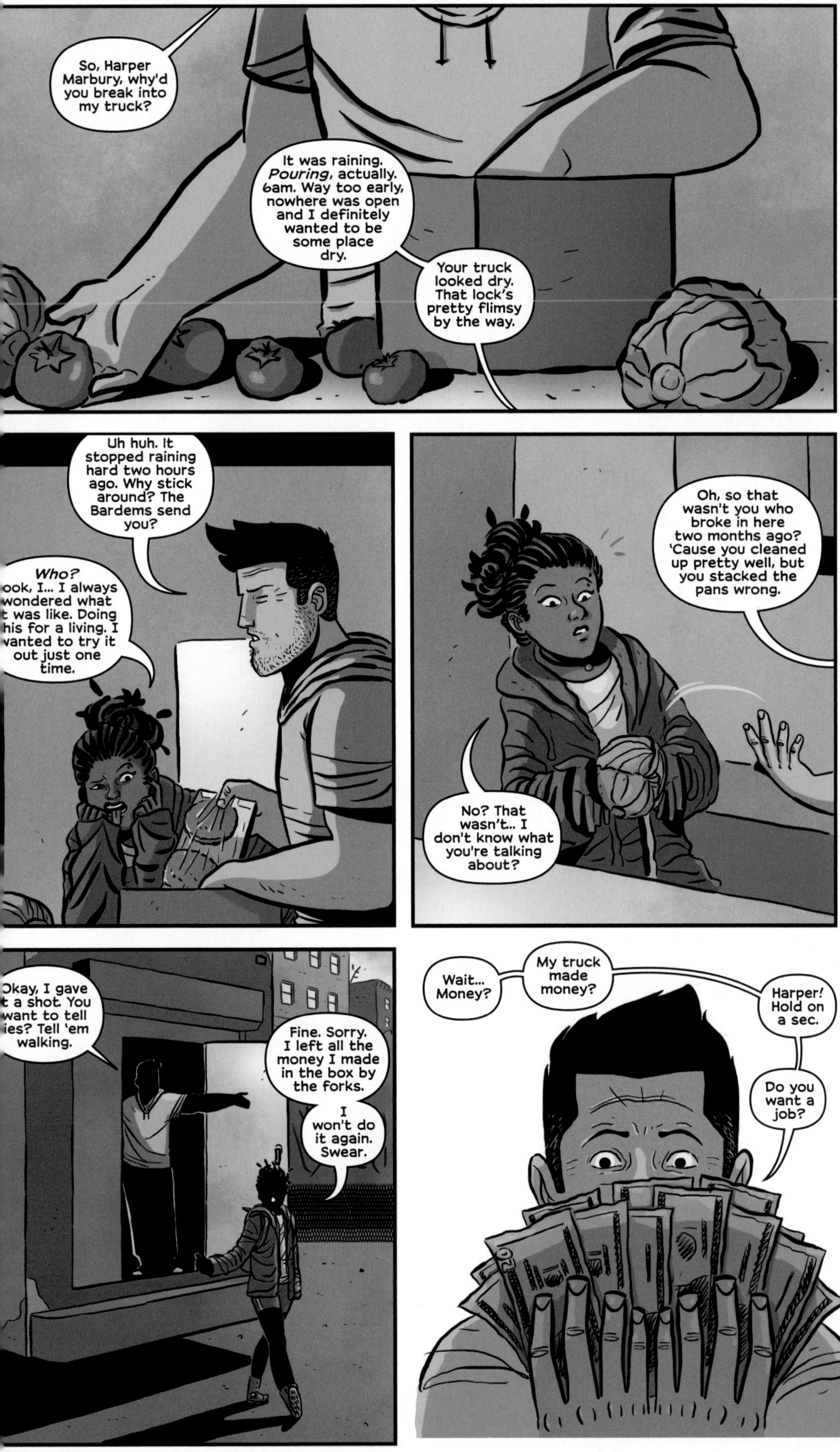
So, Harper Marbury, why'd you break into my truck?
It was raining. *Pouring*, actually. 6am. Way too early, nowhere was open and I definitely wanted to be some place dry.
Your truck looked dry. That lock's pretty flimsy by the way.
Uh huh. It stopped raining hard two hours ago. Why stick around? The Bardems send you?
Who?
ook, I... I always wondered what t was like. Doing his for a living. I vanted to try it out just one time.
Oh, so that wasn't you who broke in here two months ago? 'Cause you cleaned up pretty well, but you stacked the pans wrong.
No? That wasn't.. I don't know what you're talking about?
Okay, I gave t a shot. You want to tell ies? Tell 'em walking.
Fine. Sorry. I left all the money I made in the box by the forks.
I won't do it again. Swear.
Wait... Money?
My truck made money?
Harper! Hold on a sec.
Do you want a job?

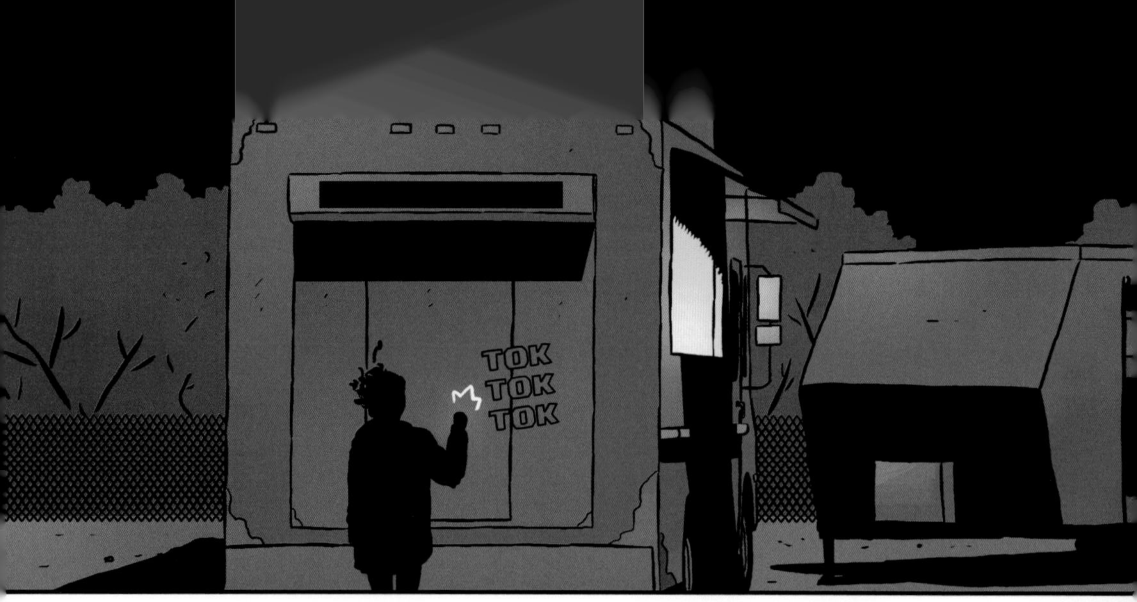
TOK
TOK
TOK

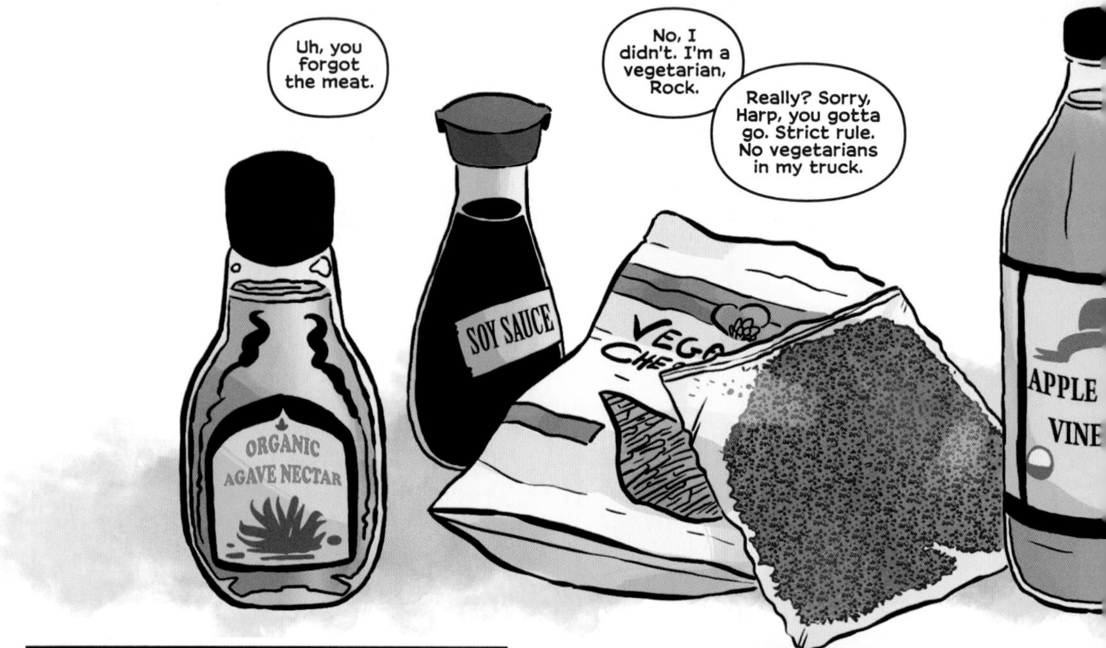
Uh, you forgot the meat.
No, I didn't. I'm a vegetarian, Rock.
Really? Sorry, Harp, you gotta go. Strict rule. No vegetarians in my truck.
ORGANIC AGAVE NECTAR
SOY SAUCE
APPLE
VINE

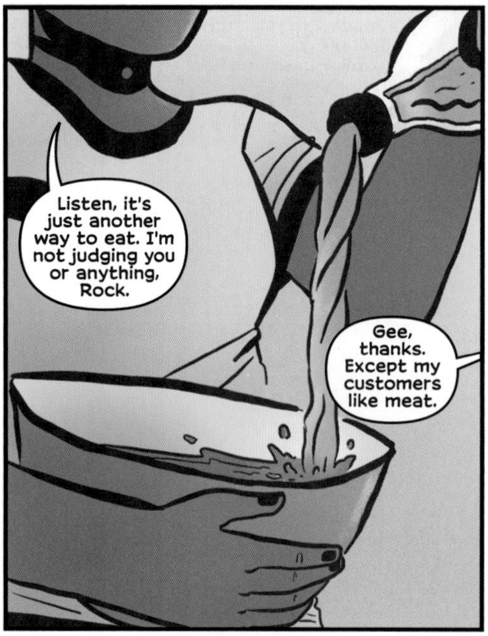
Listen, it's just another way to eat. I'm not judging you or anything, Rock.
Gee, thanks. Except my customers like meat.

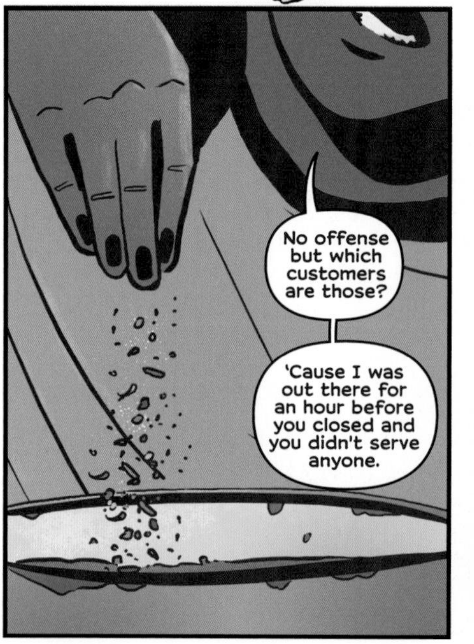
No offense but which customers are those?
'Cause I was out there for an hour before you closed and you didn't serve anyone.

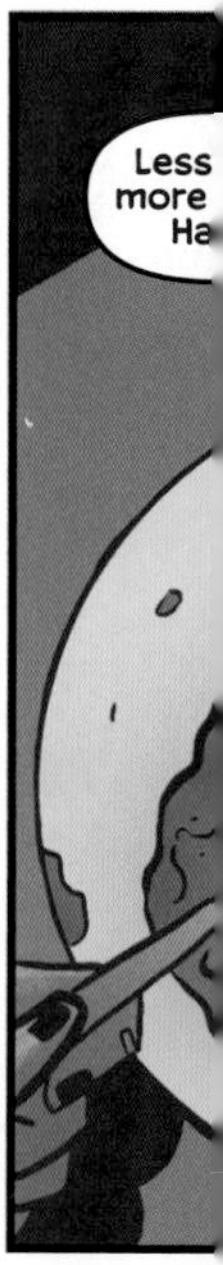
Less
more

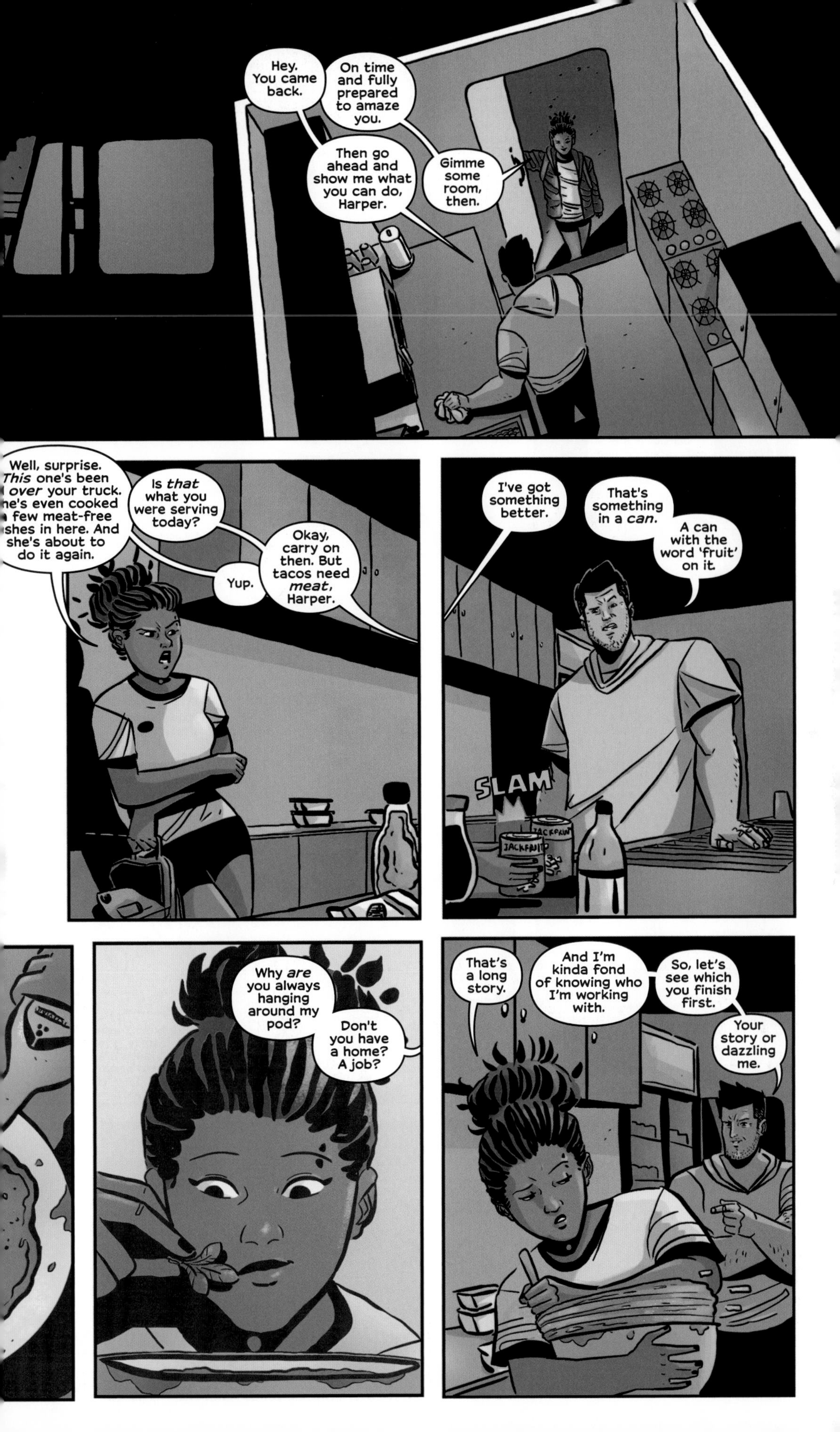
Hey. You came back.
On time and fully prepared to amaze you.
Then go ahead and show me what you can do, Harper.
Gimme some room, then.
Well, surprise. *This* one's been all *over* your truck. She's even cooked a few meat-free dishes in here. And she's about to do it again.
Is *that* what you were serving today?
Yup.
Okay, carry on then. But tacos need *meat*, Harper.
I've got something better.
That's something in a *can*.
A can with the word 'fruit' on it.
SLAM
JACKFRUIT
JACKFRUIT
Why *are* you always hanging around my pod?
Don't you have a home? A job?
That's a long story.
And I'm kinda fond of knowing who I'm working with.
So, let's see which you finish first.
Your story or dazzling me.

I live kinda nearby. It's a roommate situation. Sort of.

What's sort of?

Right now I've got 18 roommates. Not counting the babies, ferrets or dogs.

Do you live in the circus?

No *weirdos* on my truck, either.

Close. The Split Apple Co-op. It's a big... sort of like a commune, I guess?

We're not wearing matching robes or sleeping in one giant bed. It's *'an experiment in living.'*

And in this experiment, I'm the one who cooks for everyone.

Two meals a day, I throw everything we have on hand together.

Usually whatever Ti and Orlando snag from th dumpsters a Freddys.

Harper... Is this dumpster food?

No! Jeez...

I wouldn't bring dumpst-- *found* food to my job interview.

But do I use perfectly good food supermarkets toss just because it's two days old? Hell yes.

I don't know, sure sounds like dumpster food.

Right now we've got a band called Vomit Universe staying at the loft. They're friends with D., the guy who owns Split Apple.

So I've been making myself scarce as much as I can.

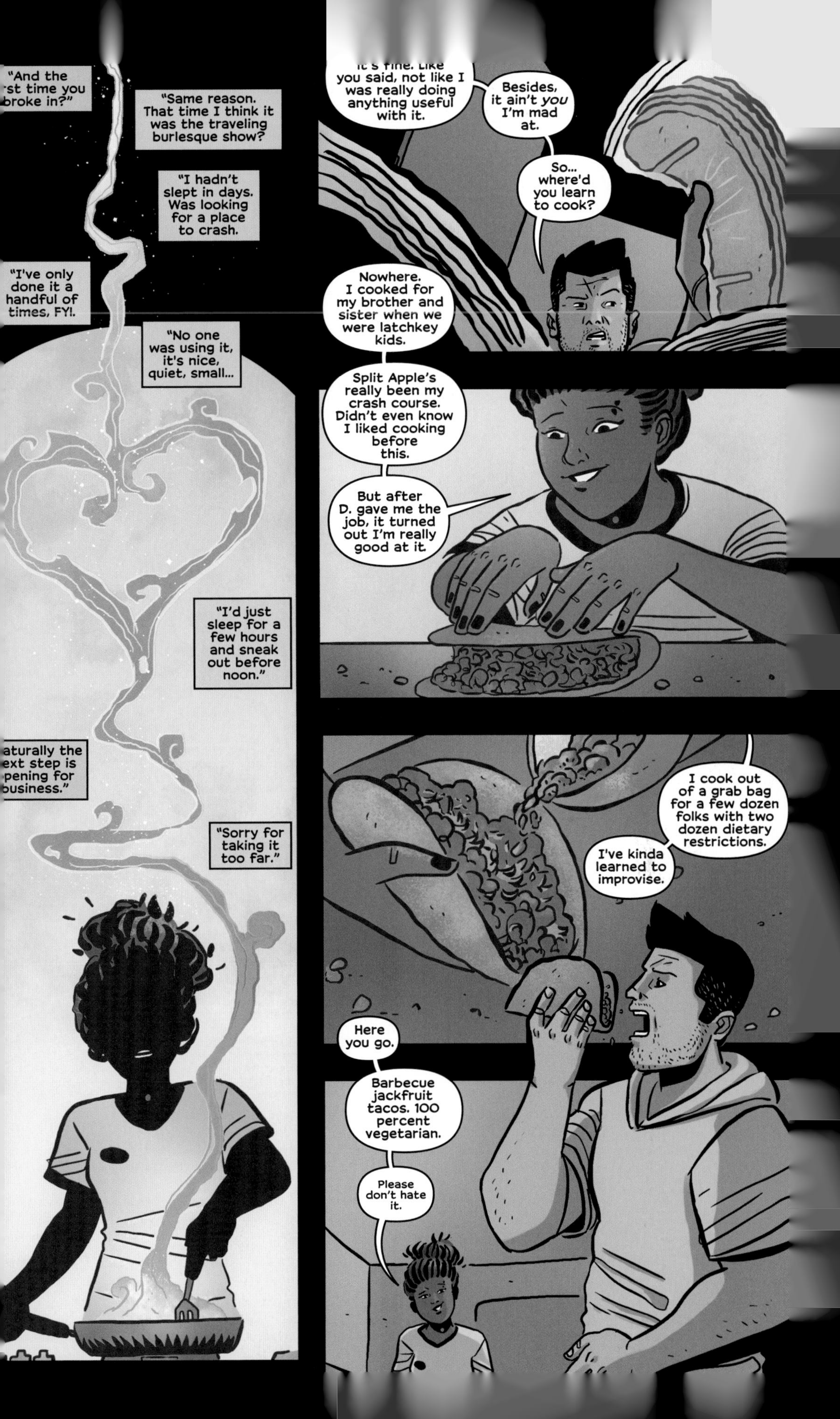
"And the
rst time you
broke in?"
"Same reason. That time I think it was the traveling burlesque show?
"I hadn't slept in days. Was looking for a place to crash.
"I've only done it a handful of times, FYI.
"No one was using it, it's nice, quiet, small...
"I'd just sleep for a few hours and sneak out before noon."
aturally the ext step is pening for business."
"Sorry for taking it too far."
you said, not like I was really doing anything useful with it.
Besides, it ain't *you* I'm mad at.
So... where'd you learn to cook?
Nowhere. I cooked for my brother and sister when we were latchkey kids.
Split Apple's really been my crash course. Didn't even know I liked cooking before this.
But after D. gave me the job, it turned out I'm really good at it.
I cook out of a grab bag for a few dozen folks with two dozen dietary restrictions.
I've kinda learned to improvise.
Here you go.
Barbecue jackfruit tacos. 100 percent vegetarian.
Please don't hate it.

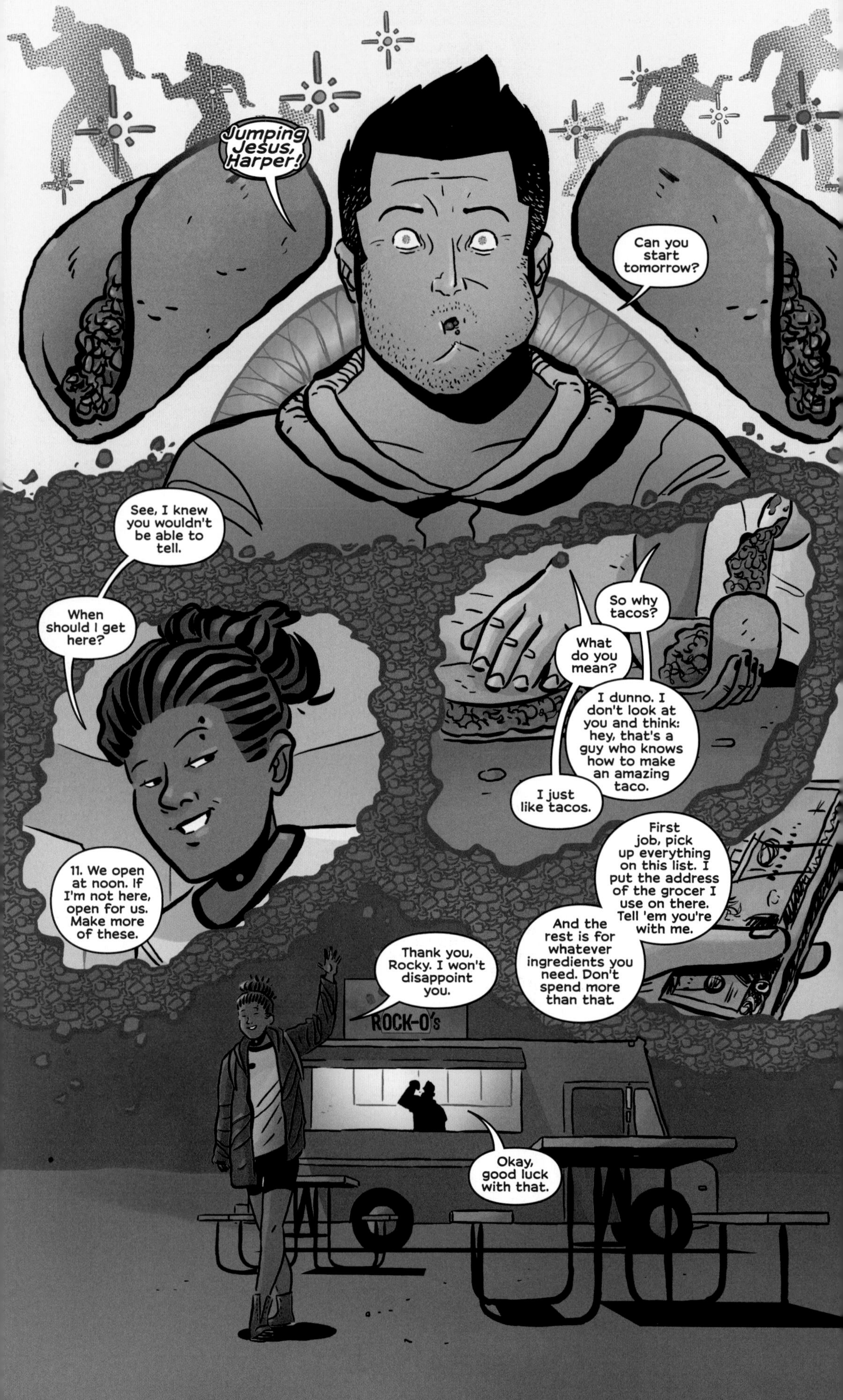
Jumping Jesus, Harper!
Can you start tomorrow?
See, I knew you wouldn't be able to tell.
So why tacos?
What do you mean?
I dunno. I don't look at you and think: hey, that's a guy who knows how to make an amazing taco.
I just like tacos.
When should I get here?
11. We open at noon. If I'm not here, open for us. Make more of these.
First job, pick up everything on this list. I put the address of the grocer I use on there. Tell 'em you're with me.
And the rest is for whatever ingredients you need. Don't spend more than that.
Thank you, Rocky. I won't disappoint you.
ROCK-O's
Okay, good luck with that.

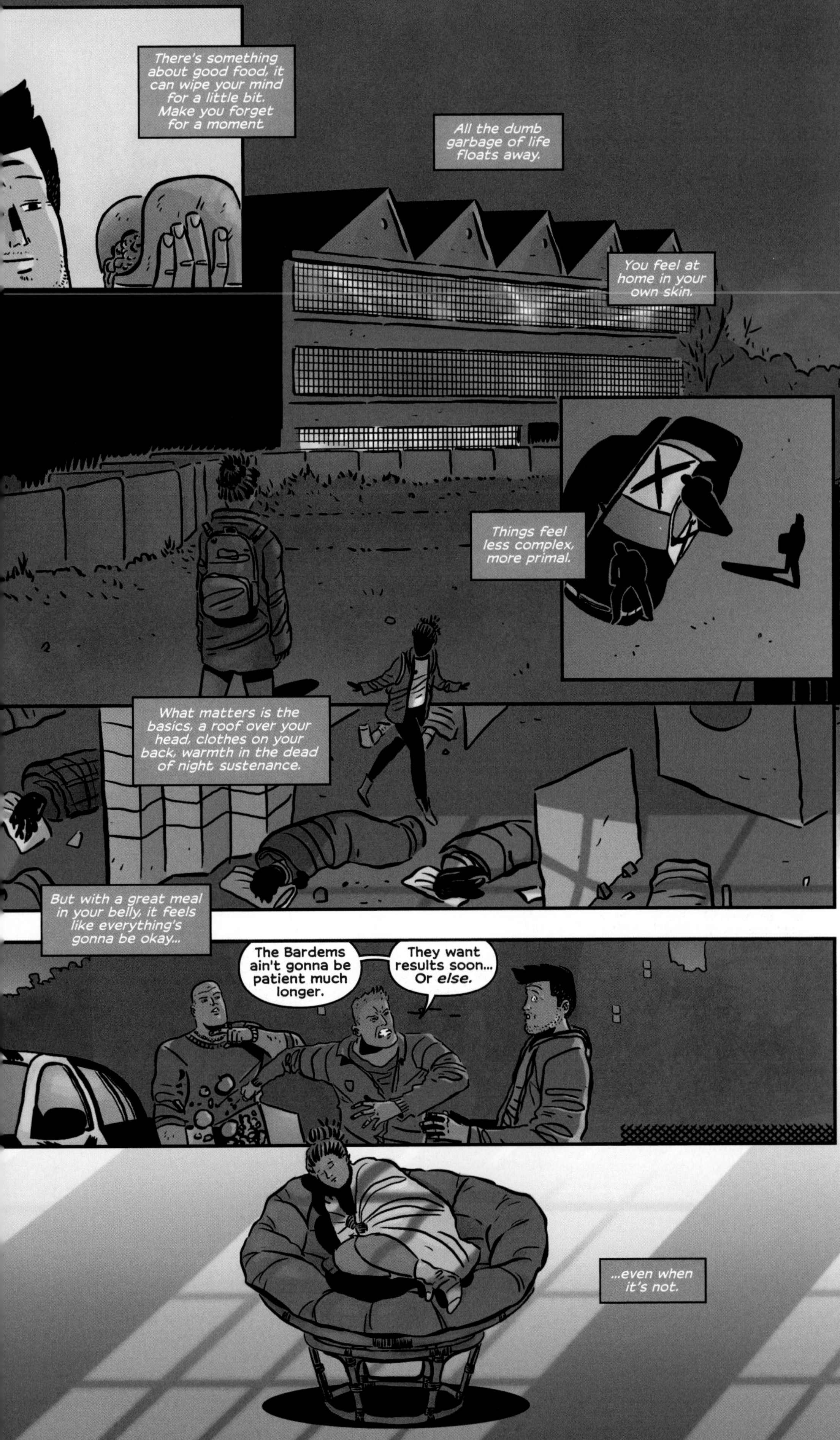
There's something about good food, it can wipe your mind for a little bit. Make you forget for a moment.
All the dumb garbage of life floats away.
You feel at home in your own skin.
Things feel less complex, more primal.
What matters is the basics, a roof over your head, clothes on your back, warmth in the dead of night, sustenance.
But with a great meal in your belly, it feels like everything's gonna be okay...
The Bardems ain't gonna be patient much longer.
They want results soon... Or *else*.
...even when it's not.

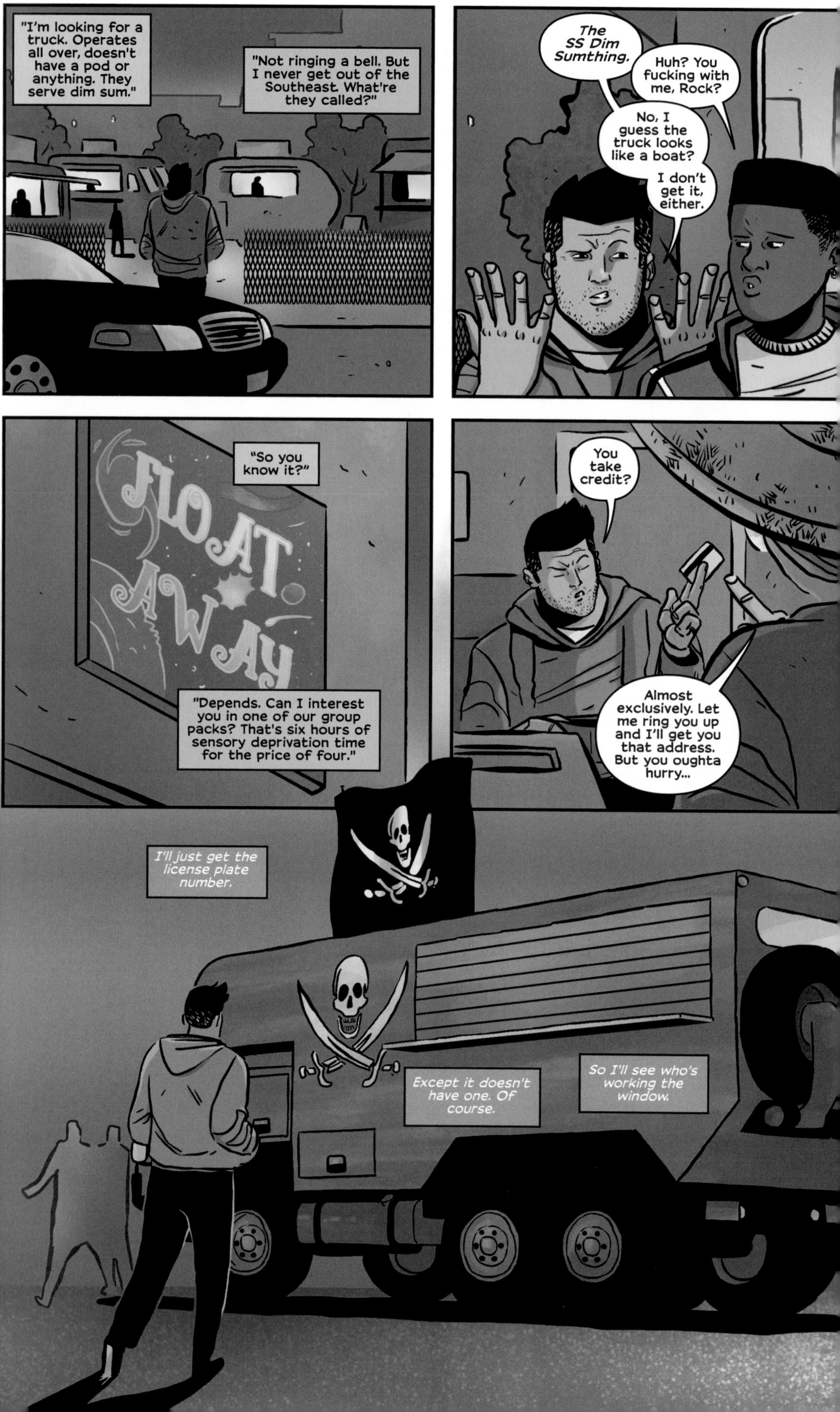
"I'm looking for a truck. Operates all over, doesn't have a pod or anything. They serve dim sum."
"Not ringing a bell. But I never get out of the Southeast. What're they called?"
The SS Dim Sumthing.
Huh? You fucking with me, Rock?
No, I guess the truck looks like a boat?
I don't get it, either.
FLOAT AWAY
"So you know it?"
"Depends. Can I interest you in one of our group packs? That's six hours of sensory deprivation time for the price of four."
You take credit?
Almost exclusively. Let me ring you up and I'll get you that address. But you oughta hurry...
I'll just get the license plate number.
Except it doesn't have one. Of course.
So I'll see who's working the window.

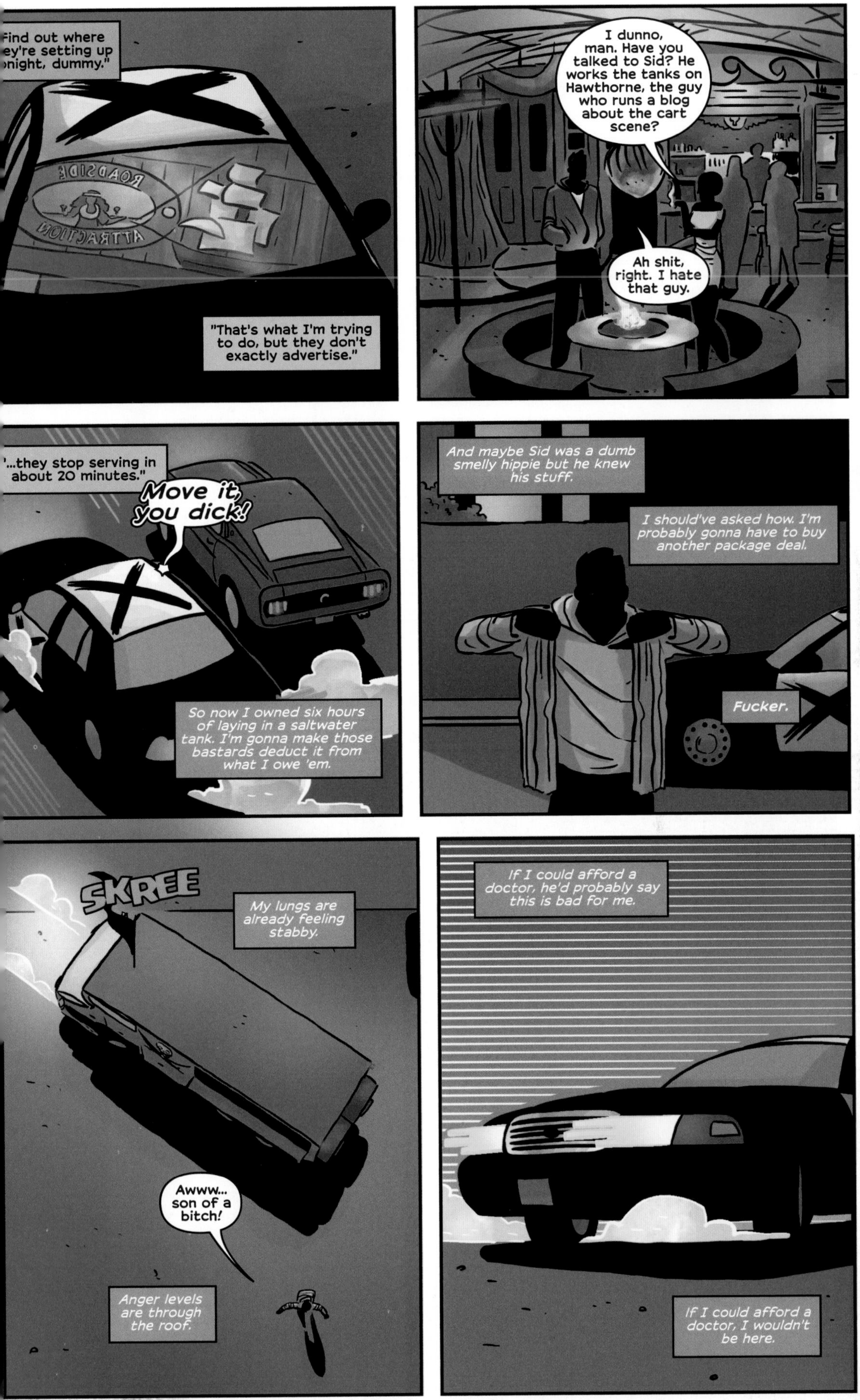

Find out where
ey're setting up
night, dummy."
ROADSIDE ATTRACTION
"That's what I'm trying to do, but they don't exactly advertise."
I dunno, man. Have you talked to Sid? He works the tanks on Hawthorne, the guy who runs a blog about the cart scene?
Ah shit, right. I hate that guy.
"...they stop serving in about 20 minutes."
Move it, you dick!
So now I owned six hours of laying in a saltwater tank. I'm gonna make those bastards deduct it from what I owe 'em.
And maybe Sid was a dumb smelly hippie but he knew his stuff.
I should've asked how. I'm probably gonna have to buy another package deal.
Fucker.
SKREE
My lungs are already feeling stabby.
Awww... son of a bitch!
Anger levels are through the roof.
If I could afford a doctor, he'd probably say this is bad for me.
If I could afford a doctor, I wouldn't be here.

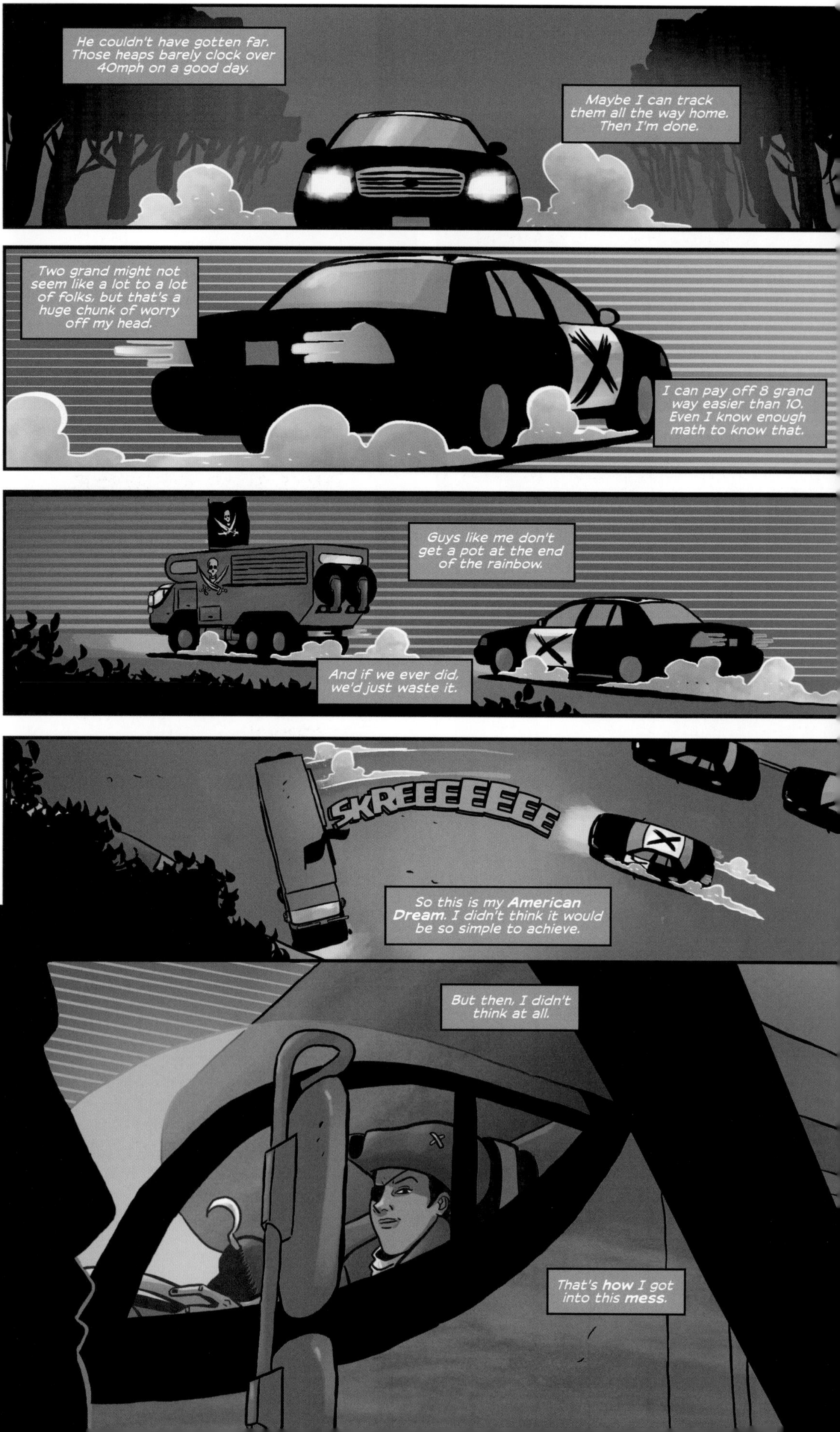
He couldn't have gotten far. Those heaps barely clock over 40mph on a good day.
Maybe I can track them all the way home. Then I'm done.
Two grand might not seem like a lot to a lot of folks, but that's a huge chunk of worry off my head.
I can pay off 8 grand way easier than 10. Even I know enough math to know that.
Guys like me don't get a pot at the end of the rainbow.
And if we ever did, we'd just waste it.
SKREEEEEEE
So this is my **American Dream**. I didn't think it would be so simple to achieve.
But then, I didn't think at all.
That's **how** I got into this **mess**.

TRANSCRIBED
—AND—
TRANSLATED
—BY—
ROCKWELL
GRANGER

HARPER MARBURY'S BBQ JACKFRUIT TACOS

PREP — 10 MINUTES
COOK — 30 MINUTES

. MAKE THE VEGAN BBQ SAUCE

(MAKES ABOUT 2½ CUPS)

5-OUNCE CAN TOMATO SAUCE
3 TBSP AGAVE NECTAR
1 TBSP MOLASSES (OR AN EXTRA TBSP OF AGAVE NECTAR INSTEAD)
2 TBSP APPLE CIDER VINEGAR
2-3 TBSP SOY SAUCE
1 TSP SWEET/SMOKED PAPRIKA
1 TSP CHILI POWDER
1 TSP DRIED OREGANO OR BASIL

COMBINE ALL THESE IN A MIXING BOWL AND WHISK IT TOGETHER UNTIL SMOOTH

PERSONAL INTERJECTION

IF YOU CAN WAIT, LET THE SAUCE STAND FOR AN HOUR OR SO TO LET THE FLAVORS MESH A BIT MORE, BUT IT'S STILL GOOD RIGHT AWAY.

2. MAKE THE JACKFRUIT

(TECHNICALLY THIS CAN SERVE 4 PEOPLE, OR 2 ACTUAL PEOPLE, OR JUST EAT IT ALL YOURSELF IF NO ONE IS AROUND TO JUDGE YOU.)

- 2 CANS OF YOUNG GREEN JACKFRUIT IN WATER (NO SYRUP, NO BRINE)
- ¼ CUP BBQ SEASONING
  - 2 TBSP BROWN SUGAR
  - 1 TSP PAPRIKA
  - 1 TSP GARLIC POWDER
  - ½ TSP SALT
  - ½ TSP PEPPER
  - ½ TSP CHILI POWDER
- COOKING OIL OF YOUR CHOICE (OLIVE IS MY GO-TO. ADVOCADO IS GOOD, BUT IT'S SPENDY.)

1. RINSE, DRAIN + DRY THE JACKFRUIT
2. TOSS JACKFRUIT WITH BBQ SEASONING TIL COATED
3. ADD 1-2 TSP COOKING OIL TO SKILLET, HEAT ON MEDIUM
4. ADD SEASONED JACKFRUIT AND MIX/COOK 2-3 MINUTES FOR COLOR
5. ADD BBQ SAUCE + ENOUGH WATER TO THIN IT OUT, STIR
6. REDUCE HEAT DOWN TO LOW-MEDIUM, COVER FOR 20 MINUTES
7. TURN HEAT TO MED.-HIGH + COOK ANOTHER 2-3 MINUTES
8. REMOVE FROM HEAT
9. SHRED JACKFRUIT WITH FORKS
10. MAKE TACOS WITH IT

[redacted]

3. MAKE SOME TACOS

- USE WITH YOUR STANDARD TACO INGREDIENTS
- ALSO GOOD IN SANDWICHES OR ON ITS OWN WITH FRIED POLENTA
- LEFTOVERS KEEP IN THE FRIDGE FOR A FEW DAYS (OR LONGER, IF YOU'RE NOT RISK AVERSE)

2: RECIPE FOR DISASTER

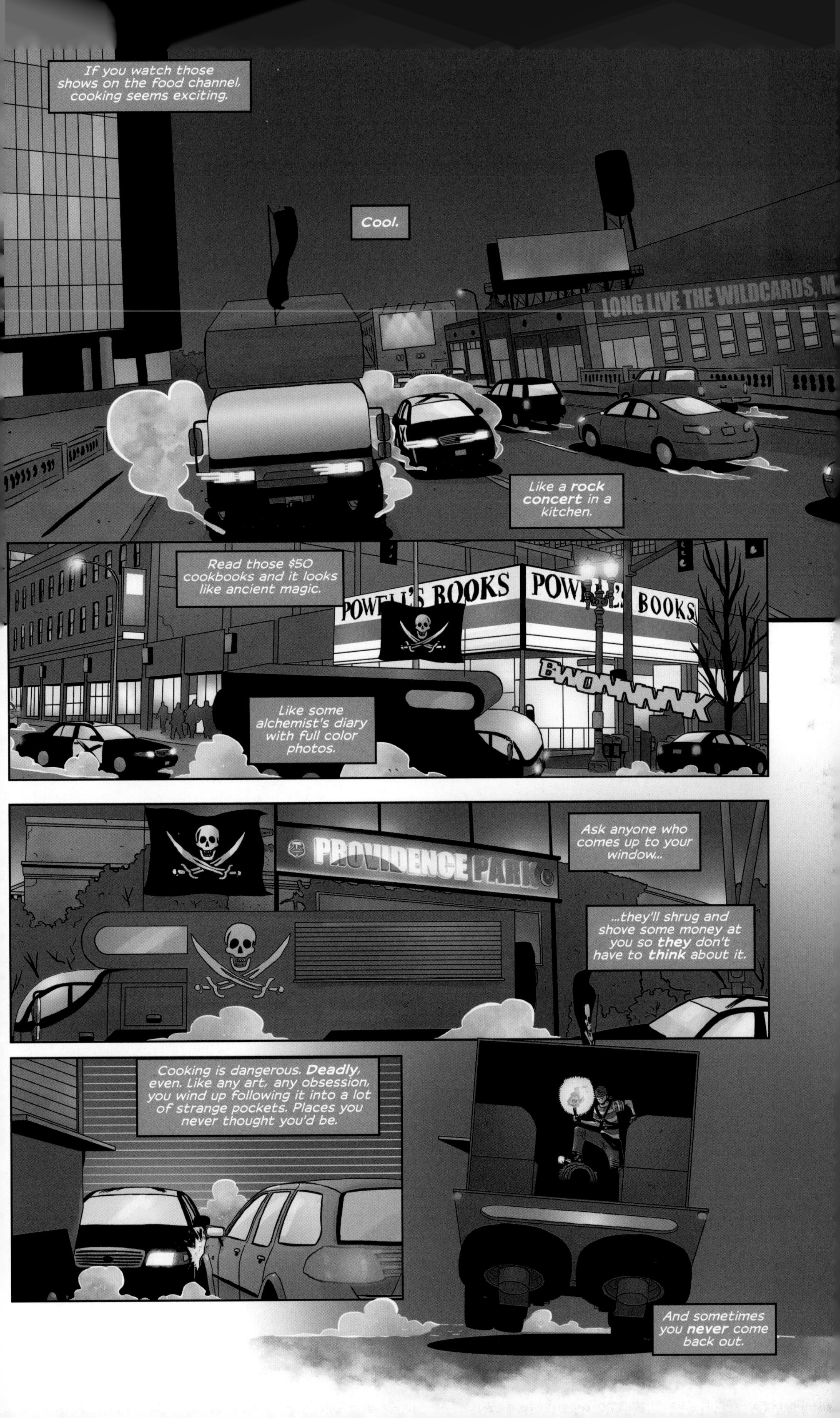
If you watch those shows on the food channel, cooking seems exciting.
Cool.
LONG LIVE THE WILDCARDS, M
Like a **rock concert** in a kitchen.
Read those $50 cookbooks and it looks like ancient magic.
POWELL'S BOOKS
BWONNNNK
Like some alchemist's diary with full color photos.
PROVIDENCE PARK
Ask anyone who comes up to your window...
...they'll shrug and shove some money at you so **they** don't have to **think** about it.
Cooking is dangerous. **Deadly**, even. Like any art, any obsession, you wind up following it into a lot of strange pockets. Places you never thought you'd be.
And sometimes you **never** come back out.

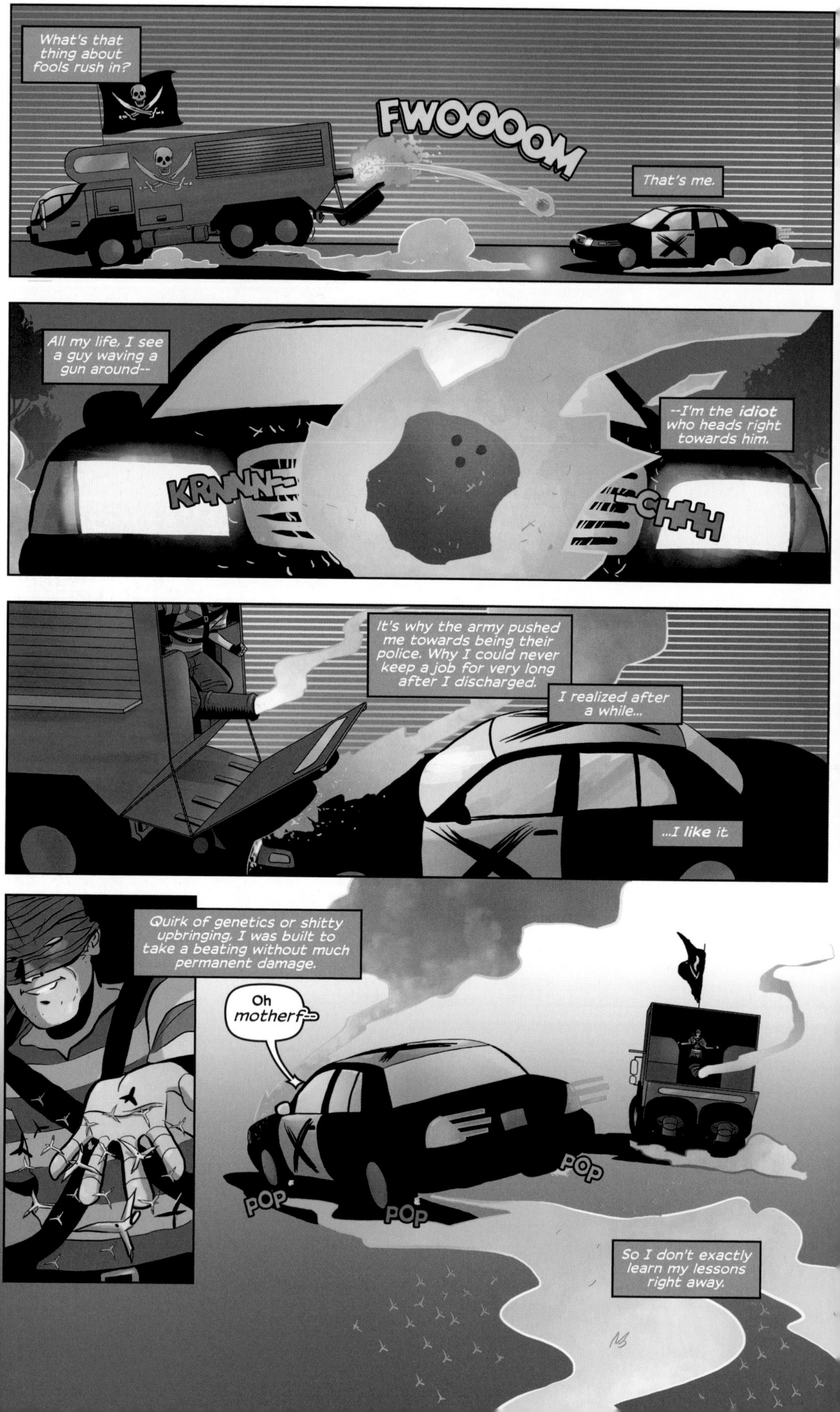
What's that thing about fools rush in?
FWOOOOOM
That's me.
All my life, I see a guy waving a gun around--
--I'm the idiot who heads right towards him.
KRNNN--CHHH
It's why the army pushed me towards being their police. Why I could never keep a job for very long after I discharged.
I realized after a while...
...I like it
Quirk of genetics or shitty upbringing, I was built to take a beating without much permanent damage.
Oh motherf--
POP
POP
POP
So I don't exactly learn my lessons right away.

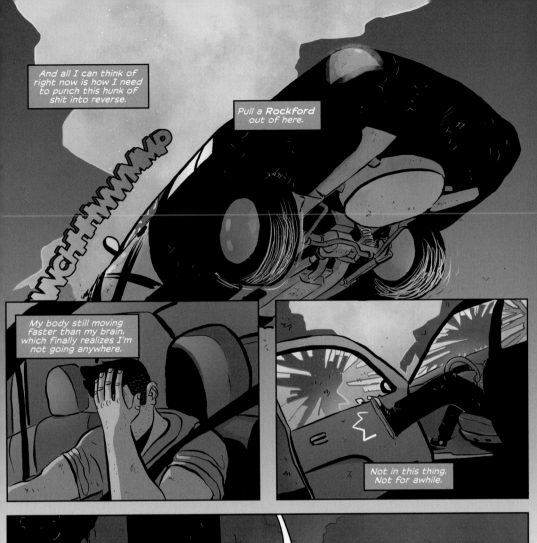

And all I can think of right now is how I need to punch this hunk of shit into reverse.

Pull a *Rockford* out of here.

My body still moving faster than my brain, which finally realizes I'm not going anywhere.

Not in this thing. Not for awhile.

What? Are you gonna *shoot* me?

All this. Just 'cause I wanted to make tacos.

The look... ♫ ♫of love... Is in... ♫Your eyes...♪

FLICK

Go on. Do it then.

♫so much more than ♫ words could ♪ ever say... ♫

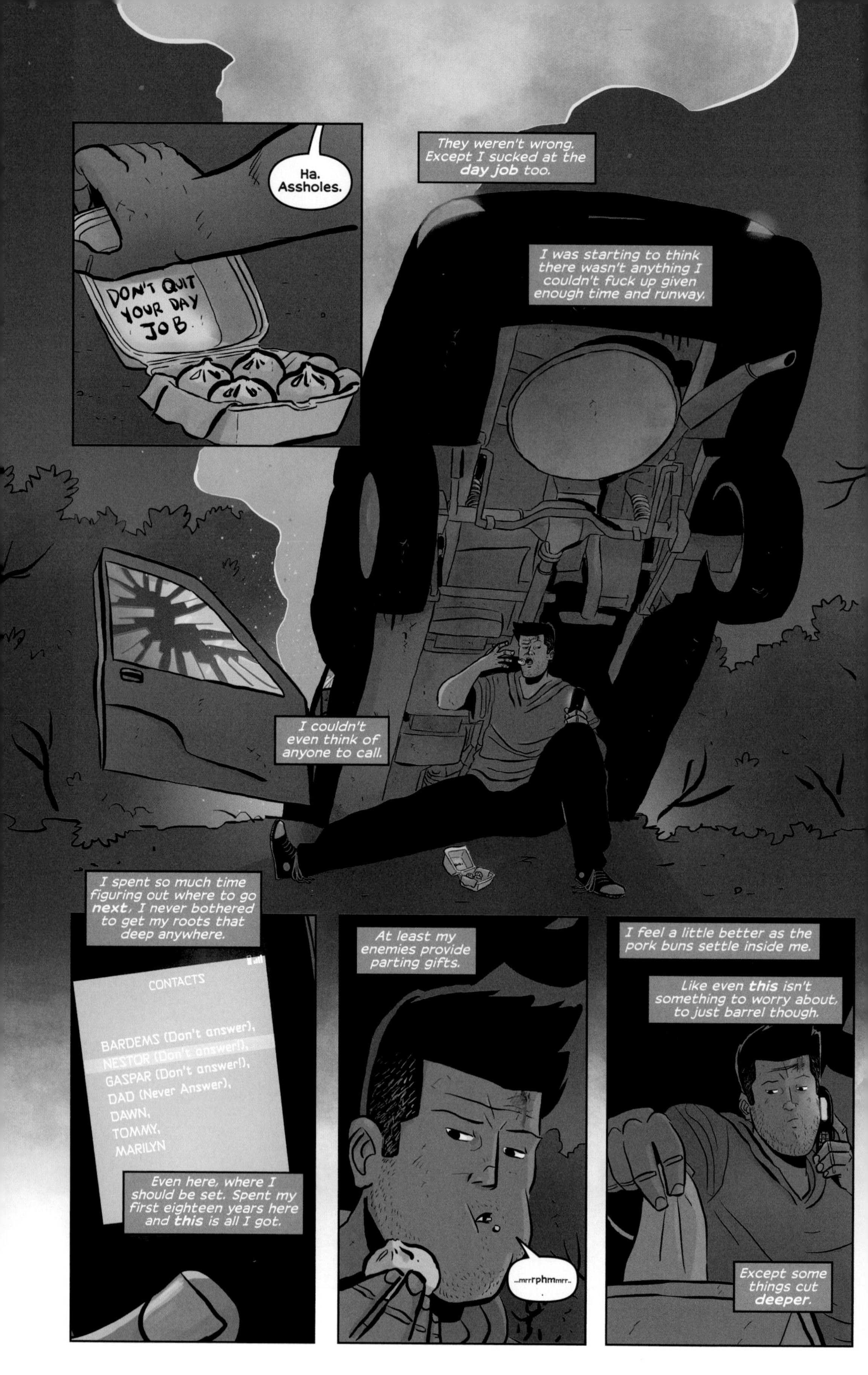
DON'T QUIT YOUR DAY JOB
Ha. Assholes.
They weren't wrong. Except I sucked at the day job too.
I was starting to think there wasn't anything I couldn't fuck up given enough time and runway.
I couldn't even think of anyone to call.
I spent so much time figuring out where to go next, I never bothered to get my roots that deep anywhere.
CONTACTS
BARDEMS (Don't answer),
NESTOR (Don't answer!),
GASPAR (Don't answer!),
DAD (Never Answer),
DAWN,
TOMMY,
MARILYN
Even here, where I should be set. Spent my first eighteen years here and this is all I got.
At least my enemies provide parting gifts.
...mrrrphmmrr...
I feel a little better as the pork buns settle inside me.
Like even this isn't something to worry about, to just barrel though.
Except some things cut deeper.

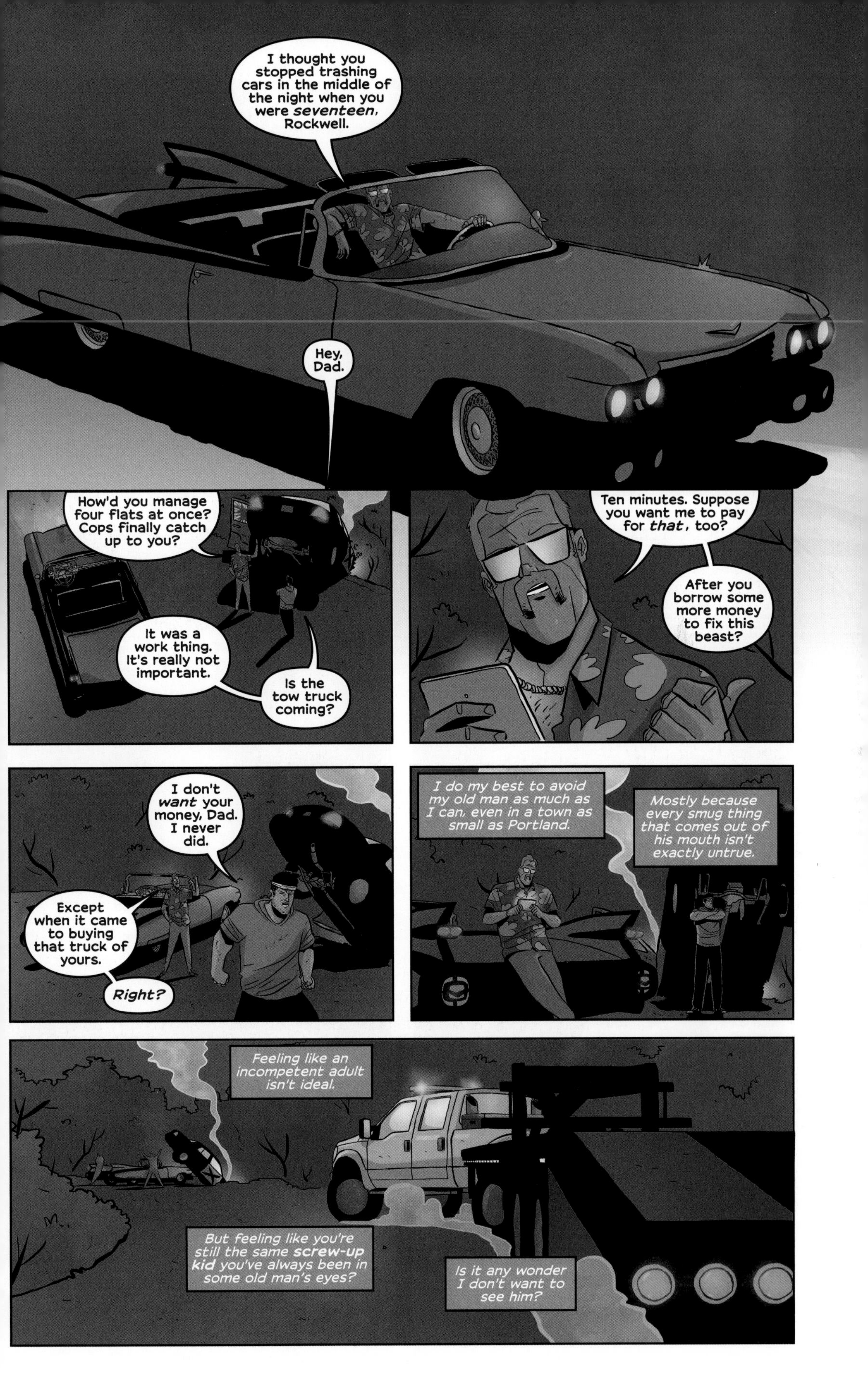
I thought you stopped trashing cars in the middle of the night when you were *seventeen*, Rockwell.
Hey, Dad.
How'd you manage four flats at once? Cops finally catch up to you?
It was a work thing. It's really not important.
Is the tow truck coming?
Ten minutes. Suppose you want me to pay for *that*, too?
After you borrow some more money to fix this beast?
I don't *want* your money, Dad. I never did.
Except when it came to buying that truck of yours.
Right?
I do my best to avoid my old man as much as I can, even in a town as small as Portland.
Mostly because every smug thing that comes out of his mouth isn't exactly untrue.
Feeling like an incompetent adult isn't ideal.
But feeling like you're still the same ***screw-up kid*** *you've always been in some old man's eyes?*
Is it any wonder I don't want to see him?

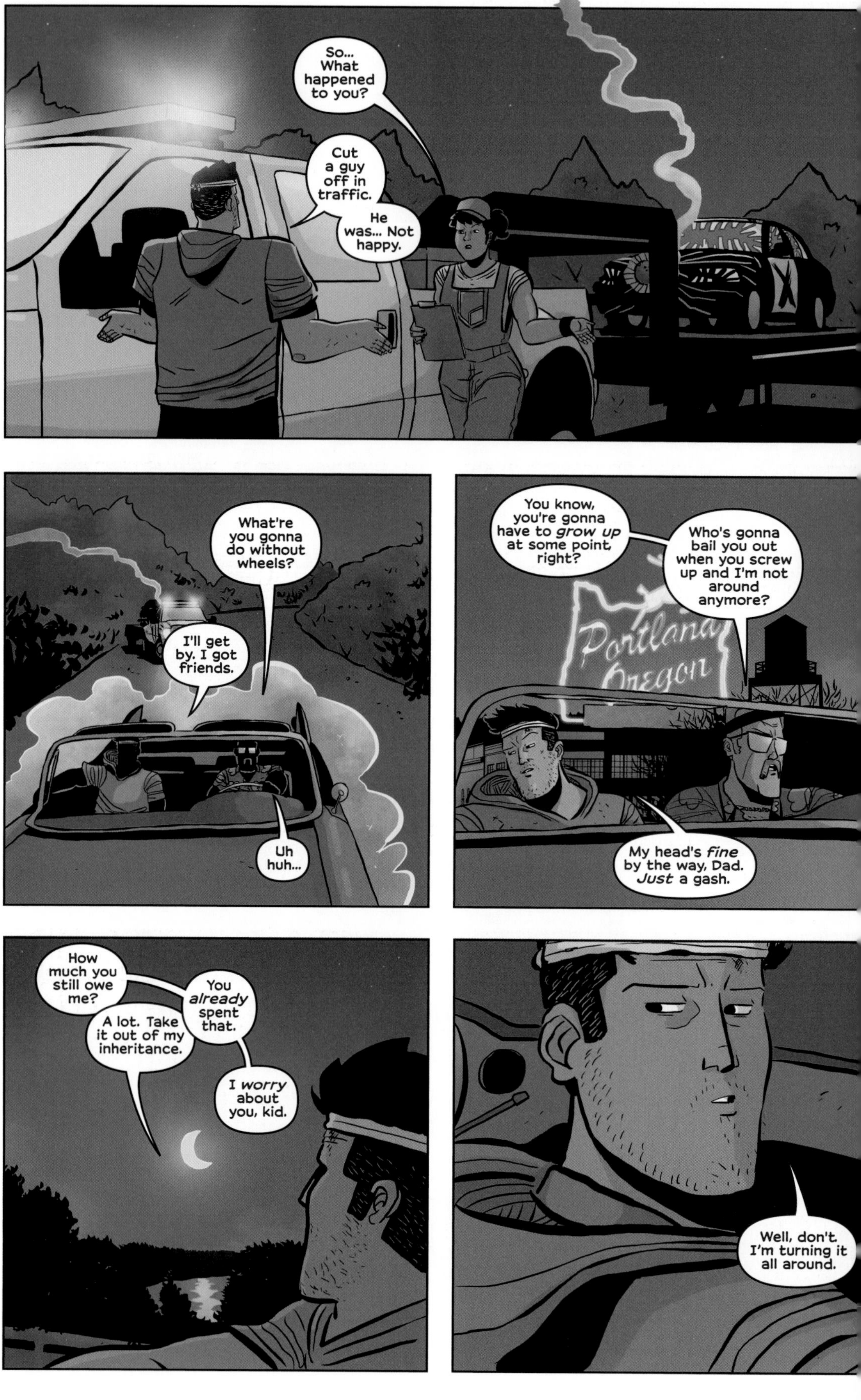
So... What happened to you?
Cut a guy off in traffic.
He was... Not happy.
What're you gonna do without wheels?
I'll get by. I got friends.
Uh huh...
You know, you're gonna have to *grow up* at some point, right?
Who's gonna bail you out when you screw up and I'm not around anymore?
Portland Oregon
My head's *fine* by the way, Dad. *Just* a gash.
How much you still owe me?
A lot. Take it out of my inheritance.
You *already* spent that.
I *worry* about you, kid.
Well, don't. I'm turning it all around.

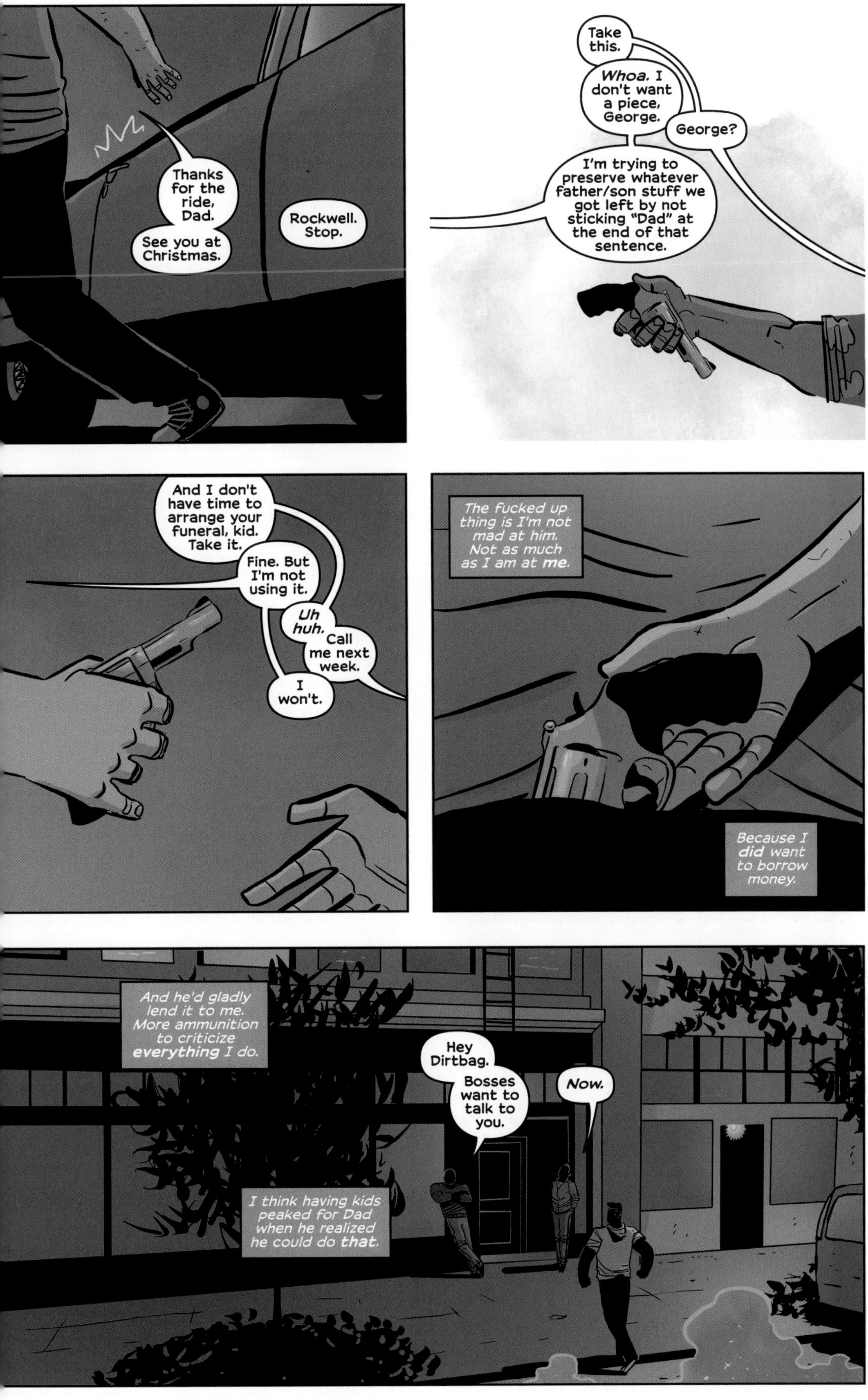
Thanks for the ride, Dad.
See you at Christmas.
Rockwell. Stop.
Take this.
Whoa. I don't want a piece, George.
George?
I'm trying to preserve whatever father/son stuff we got left by not sticking "Dad" at the end of that sentence.
And I don't have time to arrange your funeral, kid. Take it.
Fine. But I'm not using it.
Uh huh.
Call me next week.
I won't.
*The fucked up thing is I'm not mad at him. Not as much as I am at **me**.*
*Because I **did** want to borrow money.*
*And he'd gladly lend it to me. More ammunition to criticize **everything** I do.*
Hey Dirtbag.
Bosses want to talk to you.
Now.
*I think having kids peaked for Dad when he realized he could do **that**.*

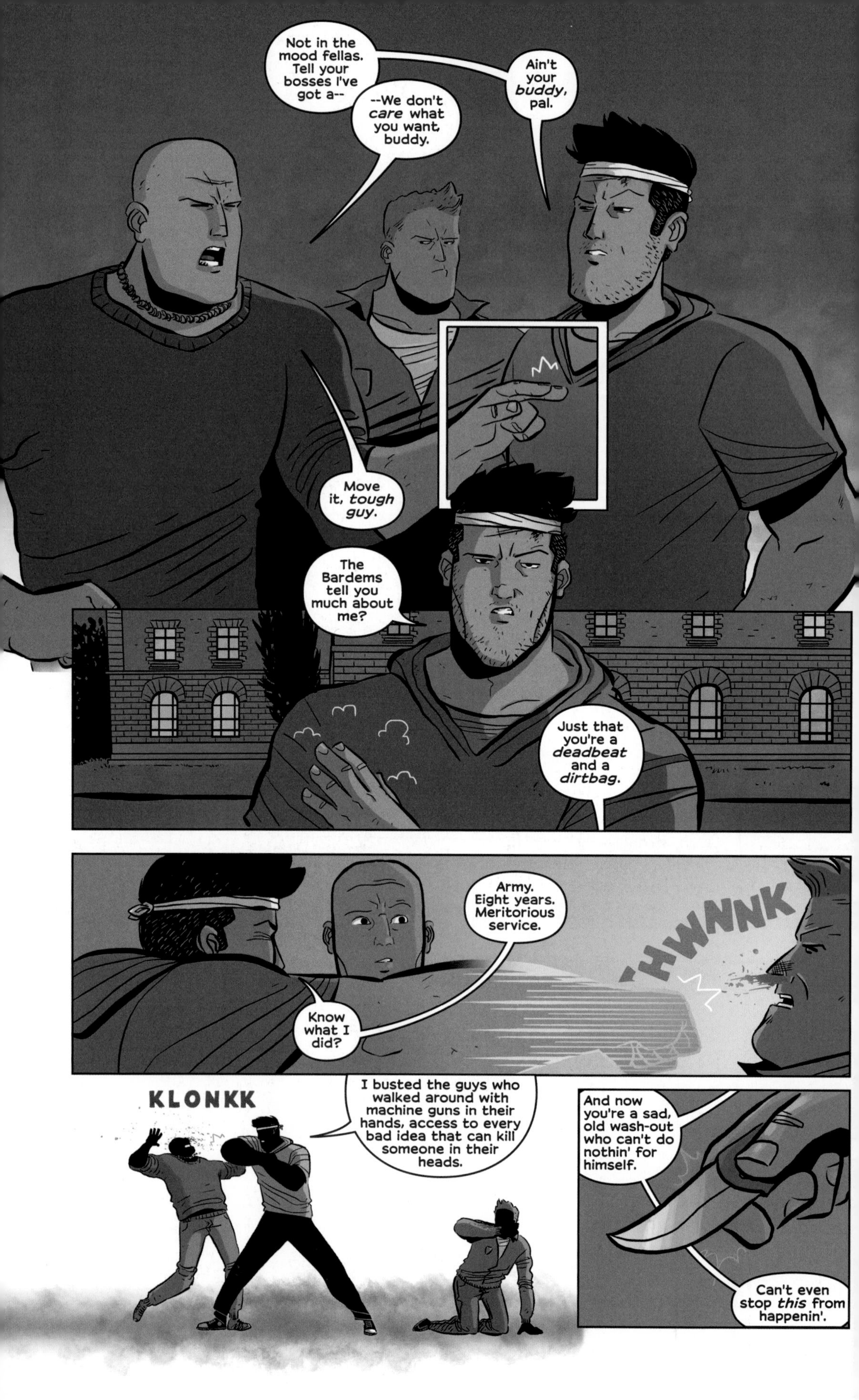
Not in the mood fellas. Tell your bosses I've got a--
--We don't *care* what you want, buddy.
Ain't your *buddy*, pal.
Move it, *tough guy*.
The Bardems tell you much about me?
Just that you're a *deadbeat* and a *dirtbag*.
Army. Eight years. Meritorious service.
Know what I did?
HWNNK
KLONKK
I busted the guys who walked around with machine guns in their hands, access to every bad idea that can kill someone in their heads.
And now you're a sad, old wash-out who can't do nothin' for himself.
Can't even stop *this* from happenin'.

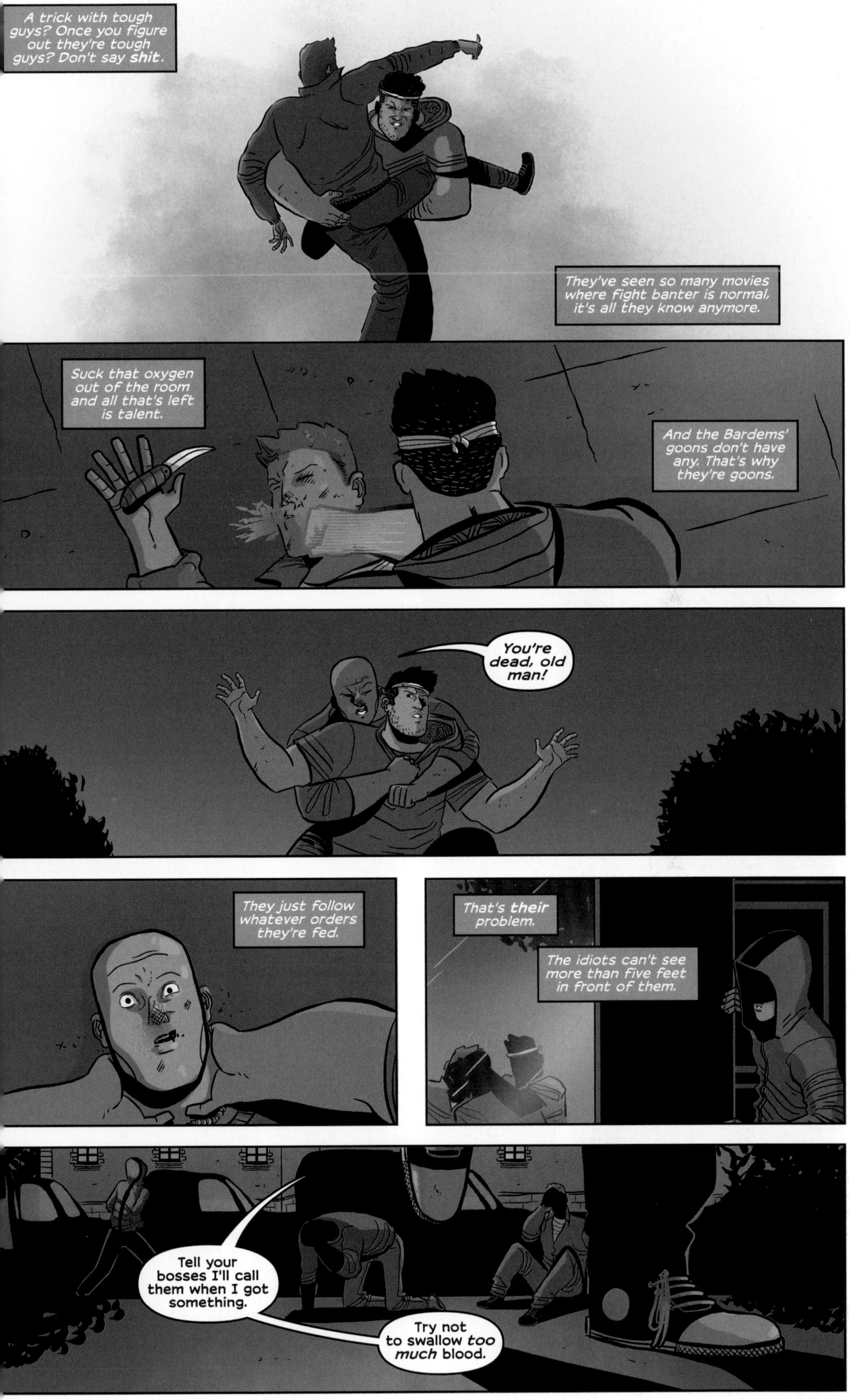
A trick with tough guys? Once you figure out they're tough guys? Don't say **shit**.
They've seen so many movies where fight banter is normal, it's all they know anymore.
Suck that oxygen out of the room and all that's left is talent.
And the Bardems' goons don't have any. That's why they're goons.
You're dead, old man!
They just follow whatever orders they're fed.
That's **their** problem.
The idiots can't see more than five feet in front of them.
Tell your bosses I'll call them when I got something.
Try not to swallow *too much* blood.

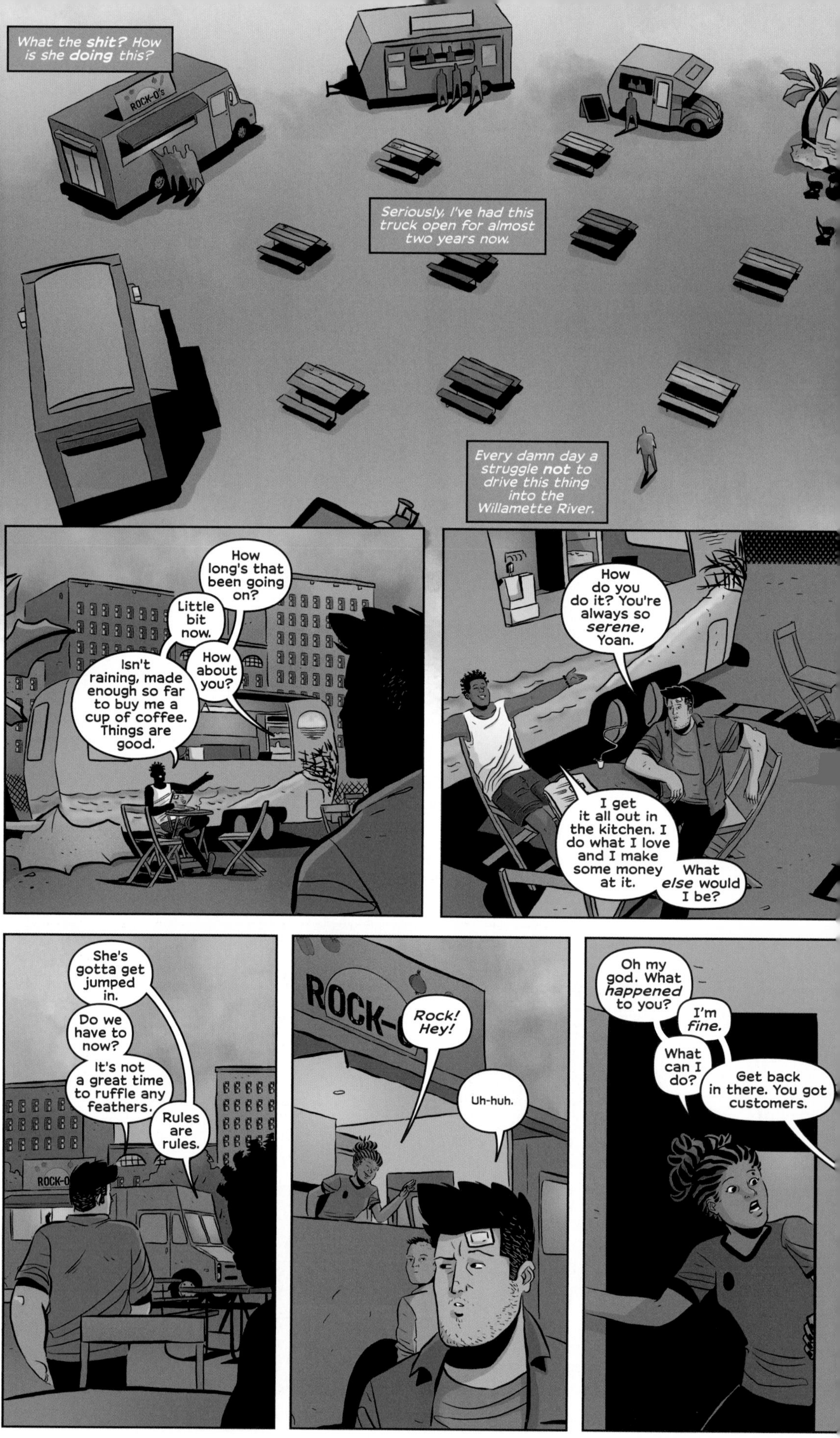
What the *shit?* How is she *doing* this?
ROCK-O's
Seriously, I've had this truck open for almost two years now.
Every damn day a struggle *not* to drive this thing into the Willamette River.
How long's that been going on?
Little bit now.
How about you?
Isn't raining, made enough so far to buy me a cup of coffee. Things are good.
How do you do it? You're always so *serene,* Yoan.
I get it all out in the kitchen. I do what I love and I make some money at it.
What *else* would I be?
She's gotta get jumped in.
Do we have to now?
It's not a great time to ruffle any feathers.
Rules are rules.
ROCK-O
ROCK-O
Rock! Hey!
Uh-huh.
Oh my god. What *happened* to you?
I'm *fine.*
What can I do?
Get back in there. You got customers.

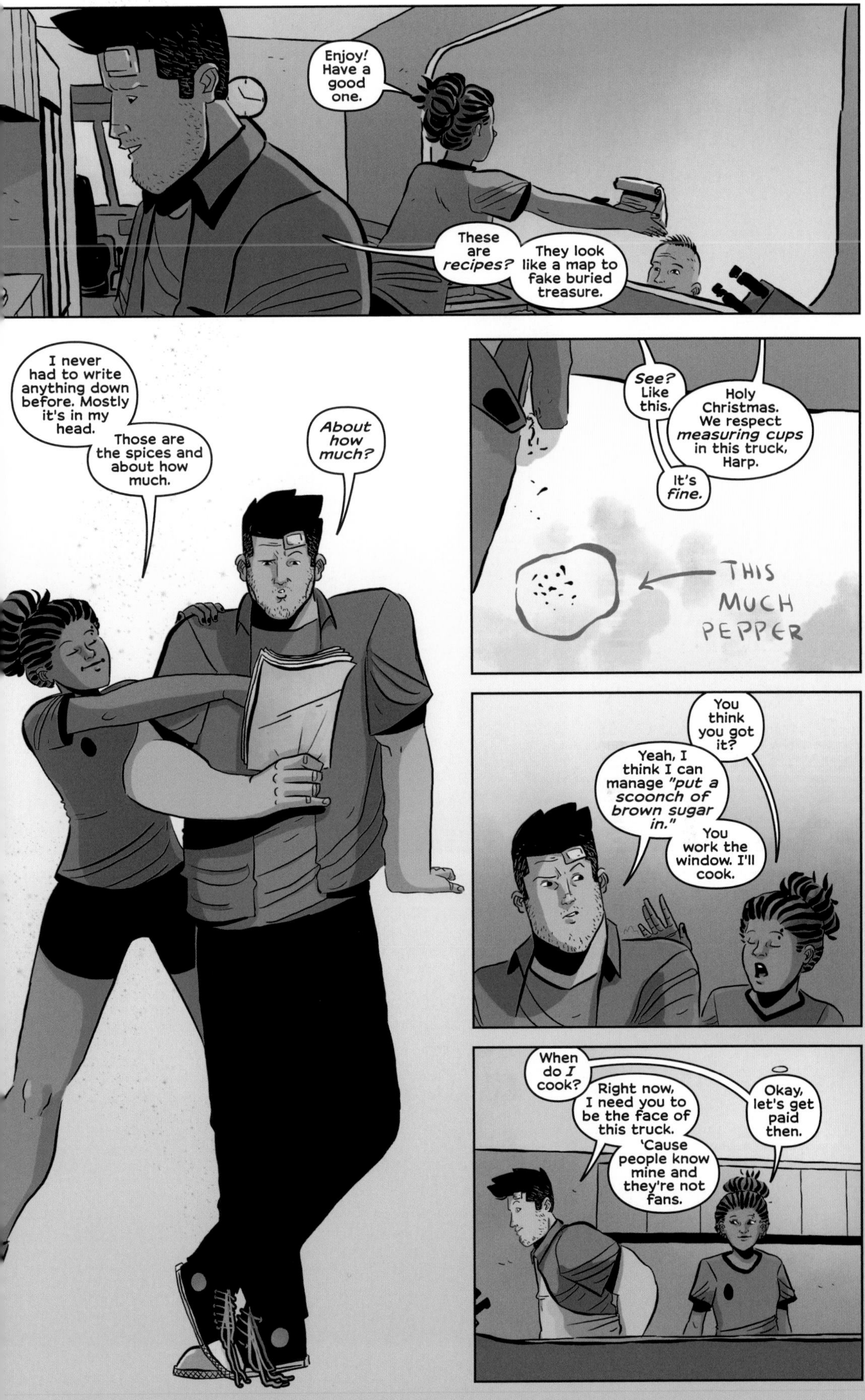
Enjoy! Have a good one.
These are *recipes?*
They look like a map to fake buried treasure.
I never had to write anything down before. Mostly it's in my head.
Those are the spices and about how much.
About how much?
See? Like this.
Holy Christmas. We respect *measuring cups* in this truck, Harp.
It's *fine.*
THIS MUCH PEPPER
You think you got it?
Yeah, I think I can manage *"put a scoonch of brown sugar in."*
You work the window. I'll cook.
When do *I* cook?
Right now, I need you to be the face of this truck.
'Cause people know mine and they're not fans.
Okay, let's get paid then.

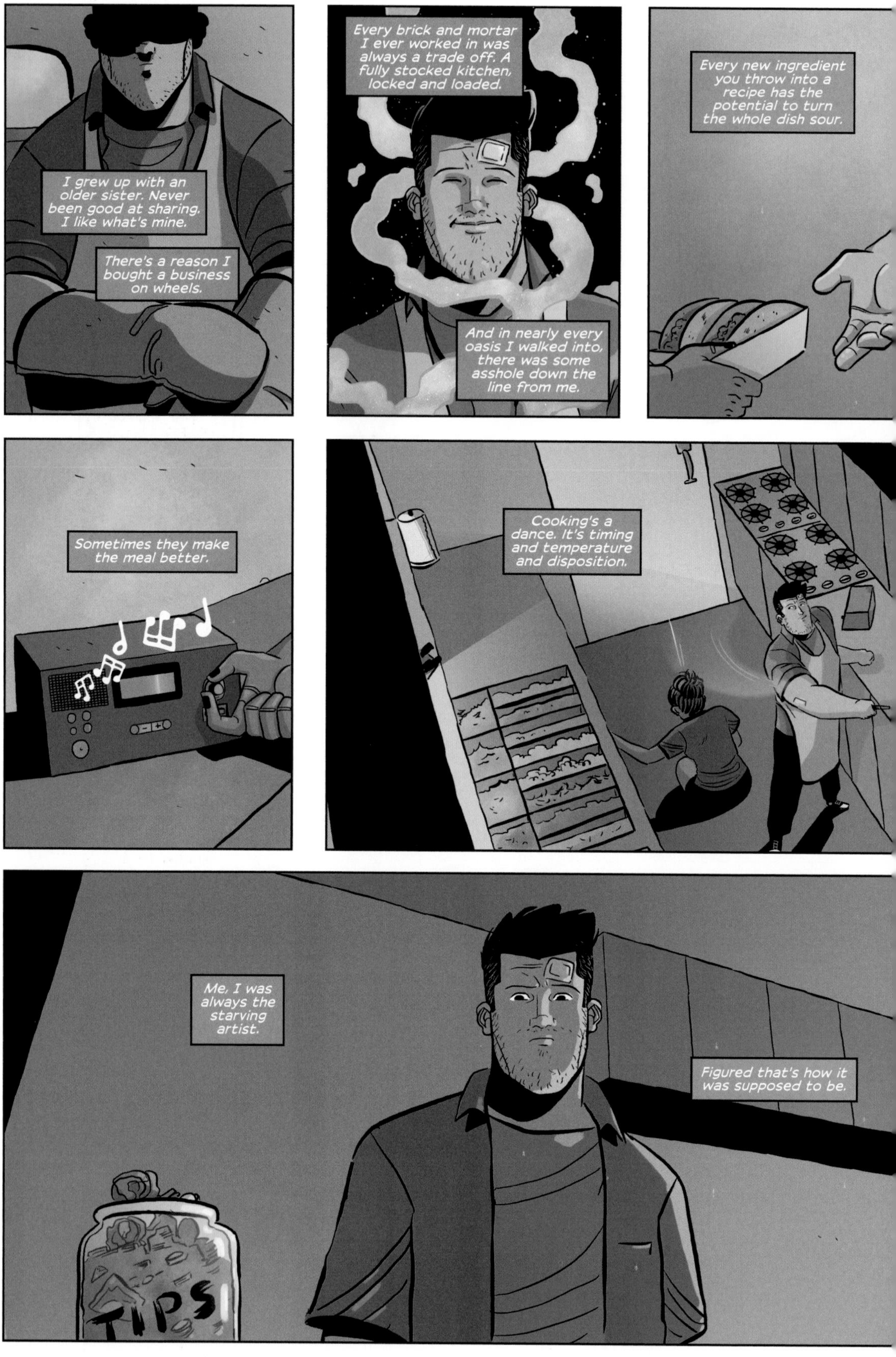
I grew up with an older sister. Never been good at sharing. I like what's mine.
There's a reason I bought a business on wheels.
Every brick and mortar I ever worked in was always a trade off. A fully stocked kitchen, locked and loaded.
And in nearly every oasis I walked into, there was some asshole down the line from me.
Every new ingredient you throw into a recipe has the potential to turn the whole dish sour.
Sometimes they make the meal better.
Cooking's a dance. It's timing and temperature and disposition.
Me, I was always the starving artist.
Figured that's how it was supposed to be.
TIPS

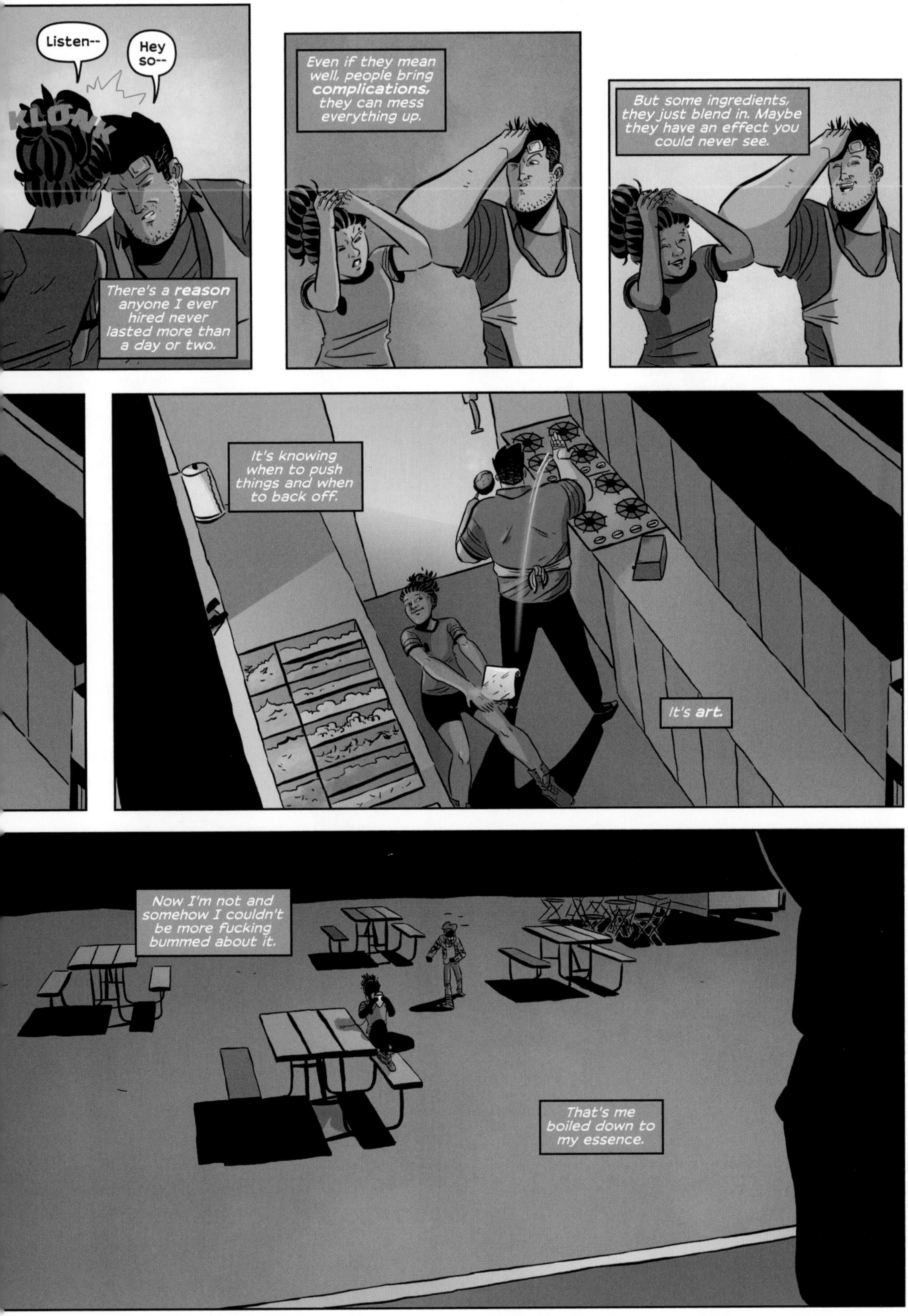
Listen--
Hey so--
KLONK
There's a reason anyone I ever hired never lasted more than a day or two.
Even if they mean well, people bring complications, they can mess everything up.
But some ingredients, they just blend in. Maybe they have an effect you could never see.
It's knowing when to push things and when to back off.
It's art.
Now I'm not and somehow I couldn't be more fucking bummed about it.
That's me boiled down to my essence.

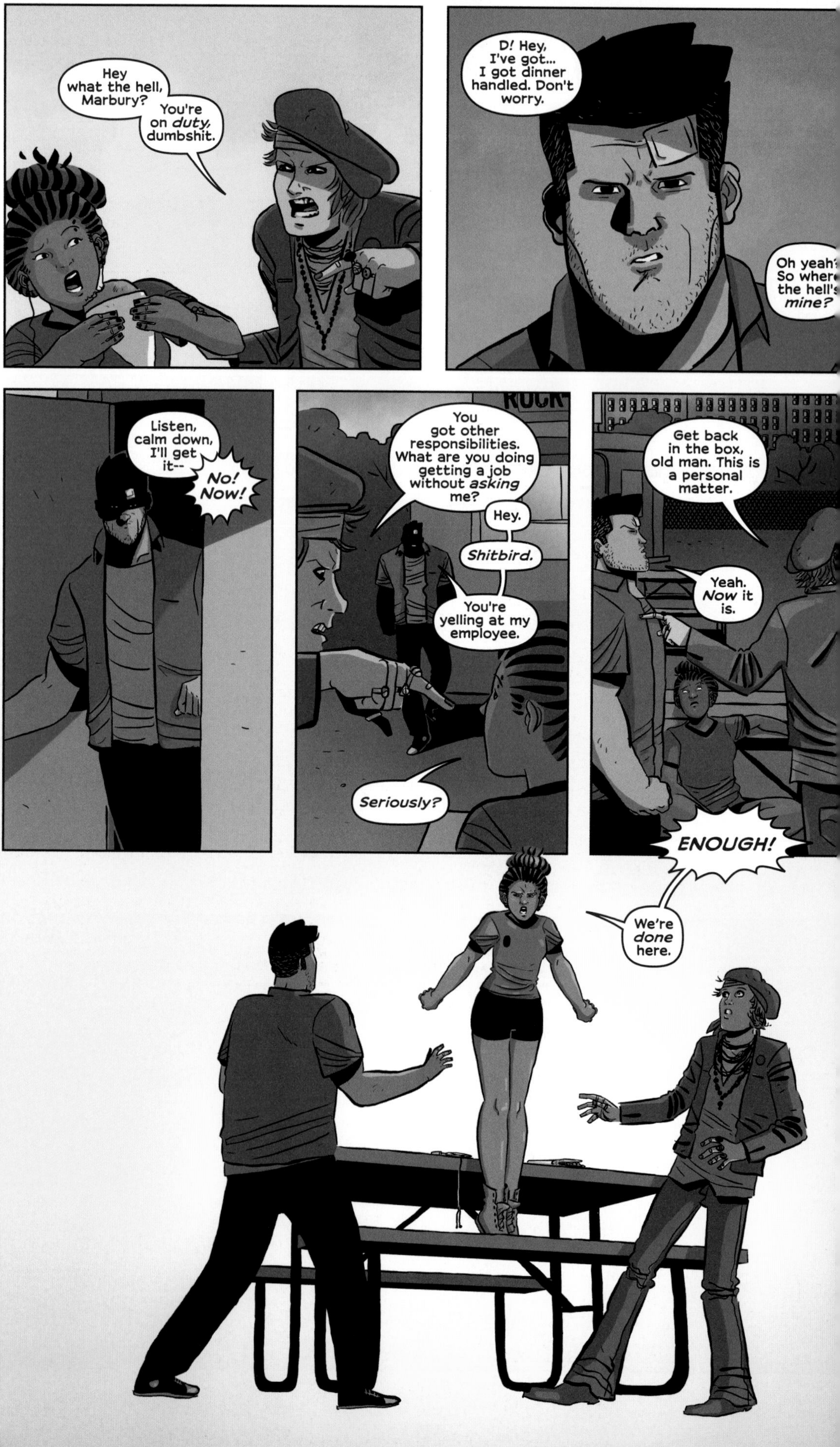

Hey what the hell, Marbury?
You're on *duty*, dumbshit.
D! Hey, I've got... I got dinner handled. Don't worry.
Oh yeah? So where the hell's *mine?*
Listen, calm down, I'll get it--
No! Now!
You got other responsibilities. What are you doing getting a job without *asking* me?
Hey.
Shitbird.
You're yelling at my employee.
Seriously?
Get back in the box, old man. This is a personal matter.
Yeah. *Now* it is.
ENOUGH!
We're *done* here.

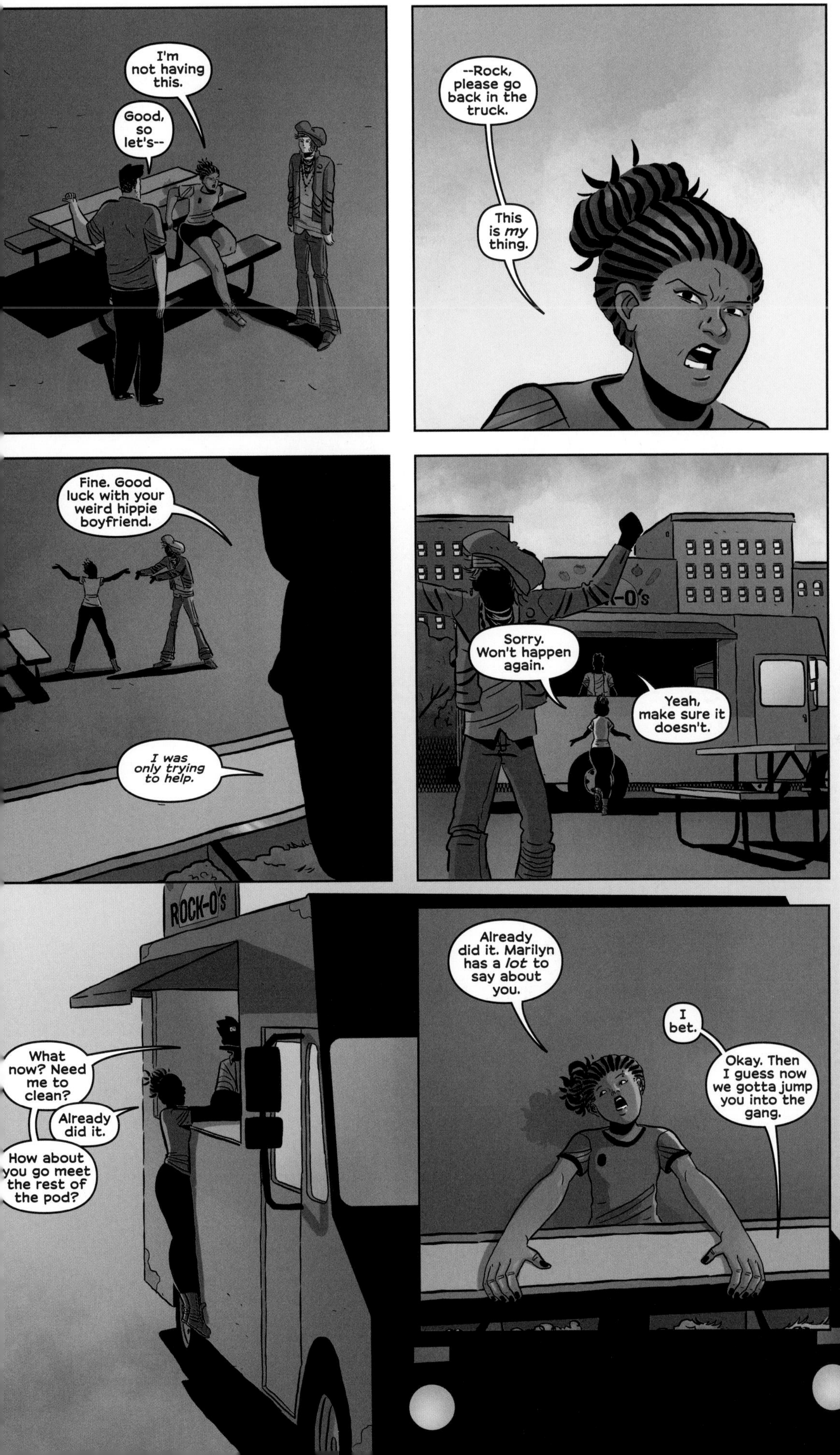
I'm not having this.
Good, so let's--
--Rock, please go back in the truck.
This is *my* thing.
Fine. Good luck with your weird hippie boyfriend.
I was only trying to help.
Sorry. Won't happen again.
Yeah, make sure it doesn't.
ROCK-O's
What now? Need me to clean?
Already did it.
How about you go meet the rest of the pod?
Already did it. Marilyn has a *lot* to say about you.
I bet.
Okay. Then I guess now we gotta jump you into the gang.

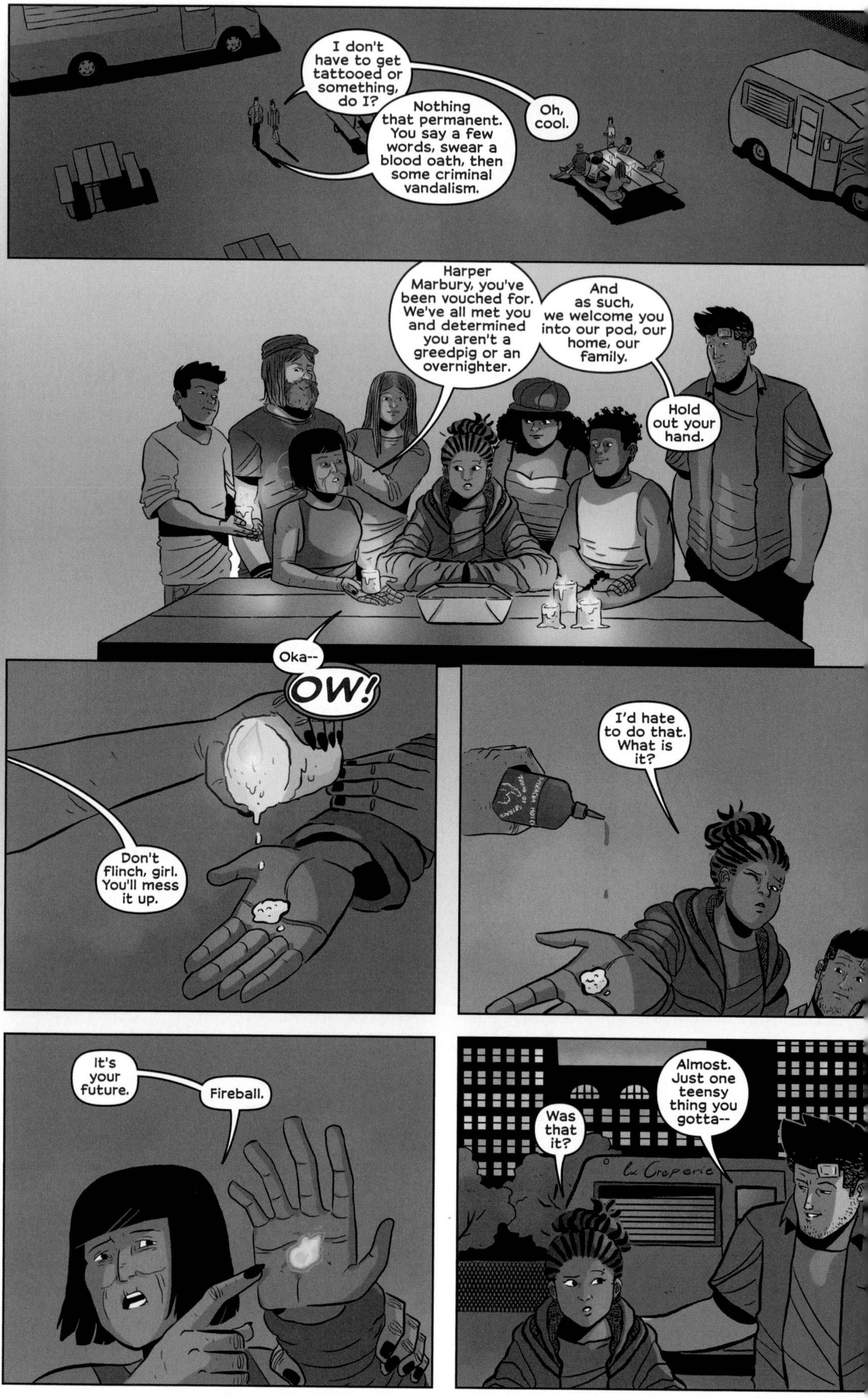

I don't have to get tattooed or something, do I?
Oh, cool.
Nothing that permanent. You say a few words, swear a blood oath, then some criminal vandalism.
Harper Marbury, you've been vouched for. We've all met you and determined you aren't a greedpig or an overnighter.
And as such, we welcome you into our pod, our home, our family.
Hold out your hand.
Oka--
OW!
Don't flinch, girl. You'll mess it up.
I'd hate to do that. What is it?
It's your future.
Fireball.
Was that it?
Almost. Just one teensy thing you gotta--
La Creperie

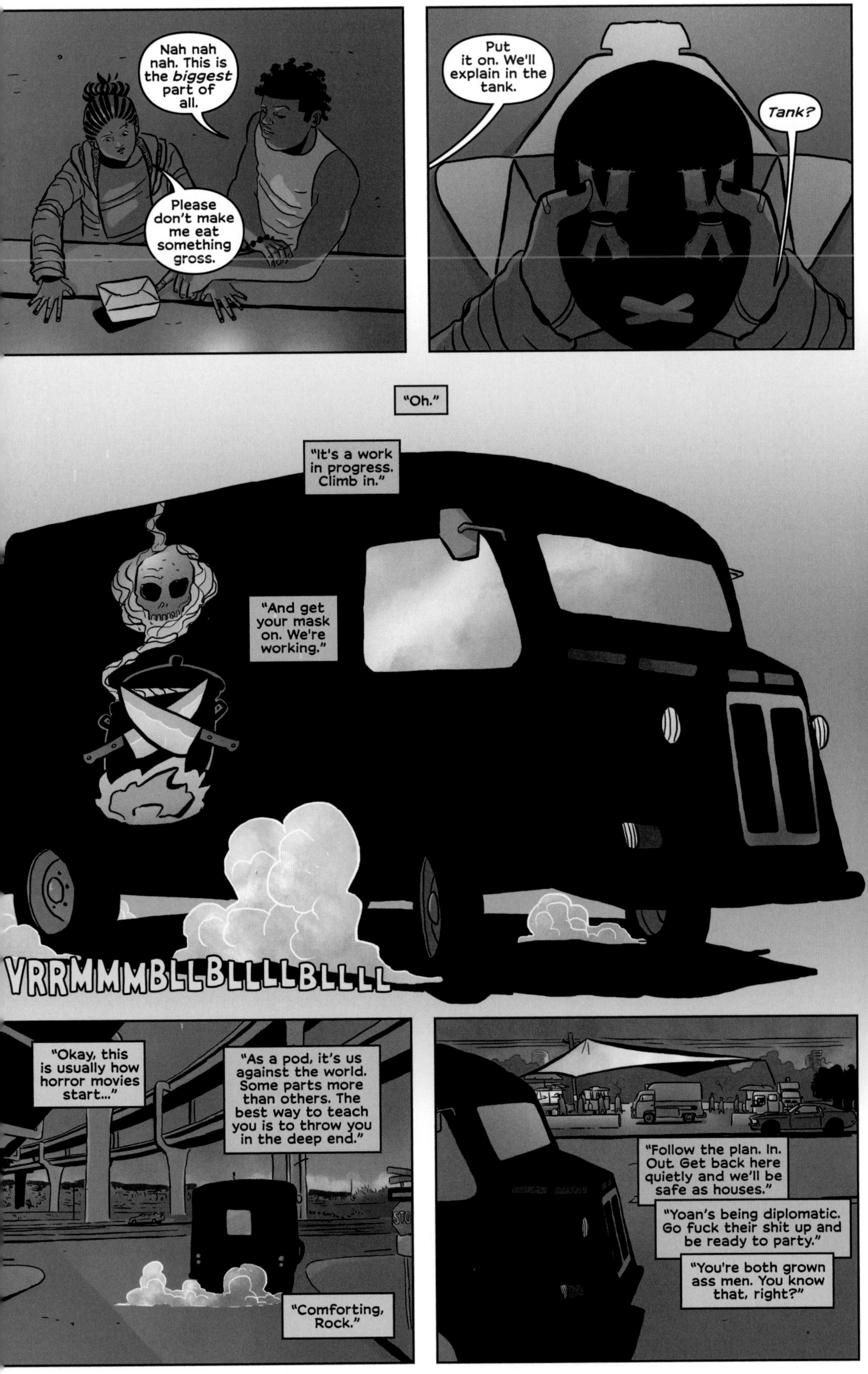
Nah nah nah. This is the *biggest* part of all.
Please don't make me eat something gross.
Put it on. We'll explain in the tank.
Tank?
"Oh."
"It's a work in progress. Climb in."
"And get your mask on. We're working."
VRRMMMMBLLBLLLLBLLLL
"Okay, this is usually how horror movies start..."
"As a pod, it's us against the world. Some parts more than others. The best way to teach you is to throw you in the deep end."
"Comforting, Rock."
"Follow the plan. In. Out. Get back here quietly and we'll be safe as houses."
"Yoan's being diplomatic. Go fuck their shit up and be ready to party."
"You're both grown ass men. You know that, right?"

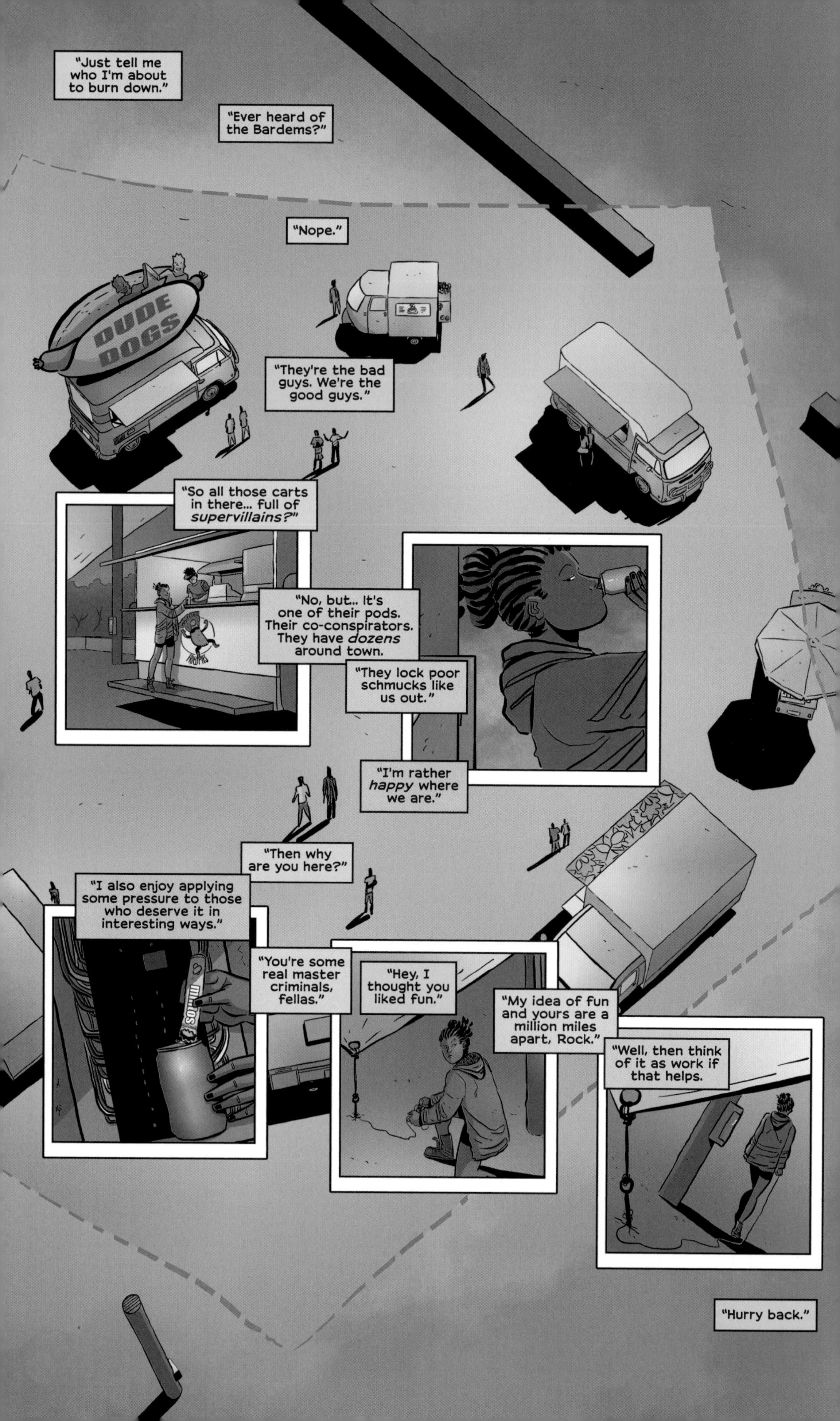
"Just tell me who I'm about to burn down."
"Ever heard of the Bardems?"
"Nope."
DUDE DOGS
"They're the bad guys. We're the good guys."
"So all those carts in there... full of *supervillains?*"
"No, but... It's one of their pods. Their co-conspirators. They have *dozens* around town.
"They lock poor schmucks like us out."
"I'm rather *happy* where we are."
"Then why are you here?"
"I also enjoy applying some pressure to those who deserve it in interesting ways."
"You're some real master criminals, fellas."
"Hey, I thought you liked fun."
"My idea of fun and yours are a million miles apart, Rock."
"Well, then think of it as work if that helps.
"Hurry back."

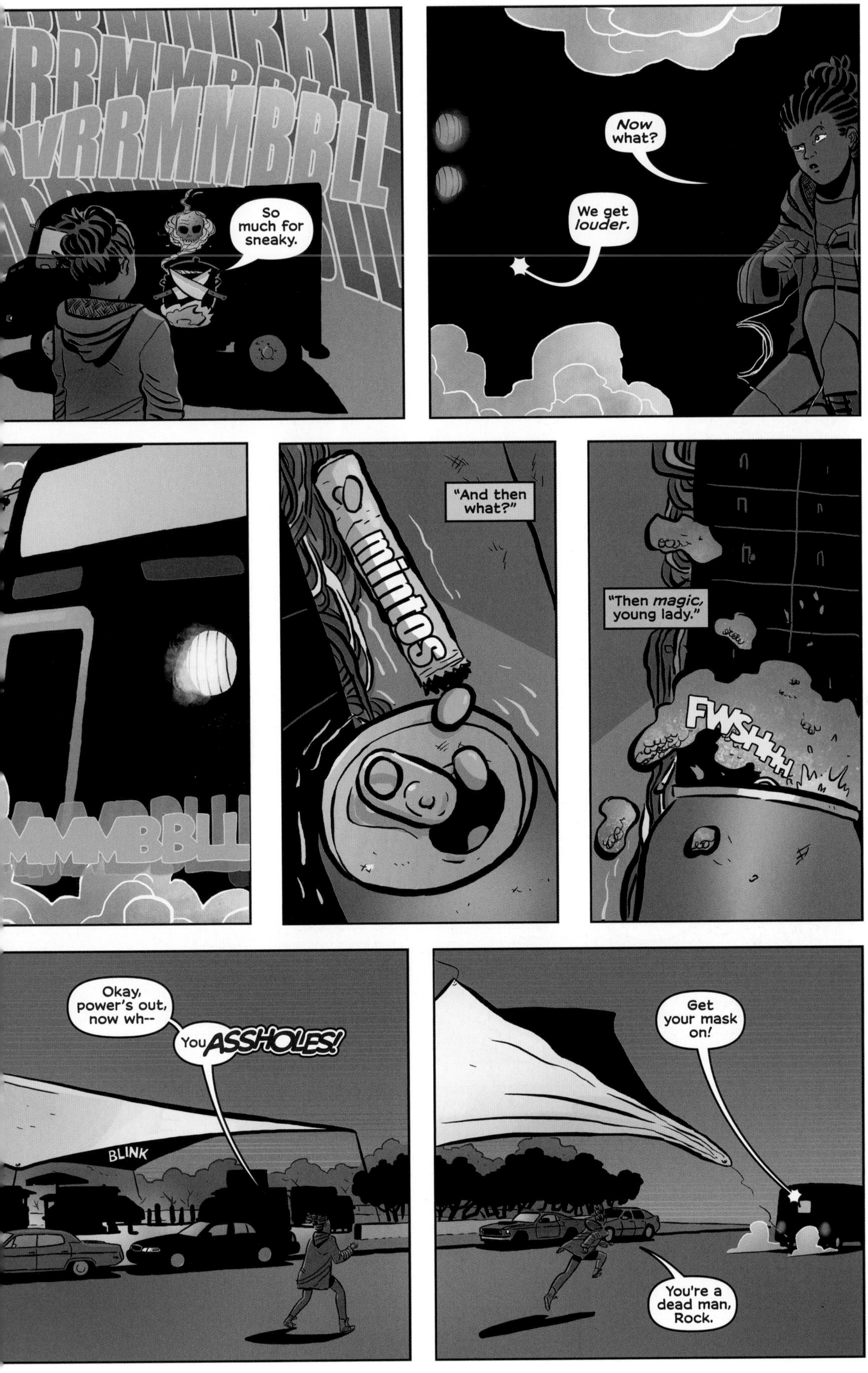
VRRMMMBBLL
So much for sneaky.
Now what?
We get louder.
MMMBBLL
"And then what?"
mintos
"Then magic, young lady."
FWSHHH
Okay, power's out, now wh--
You ASSHOLES!
BLINK
Get your mask on!
You're a dead man, Rock.

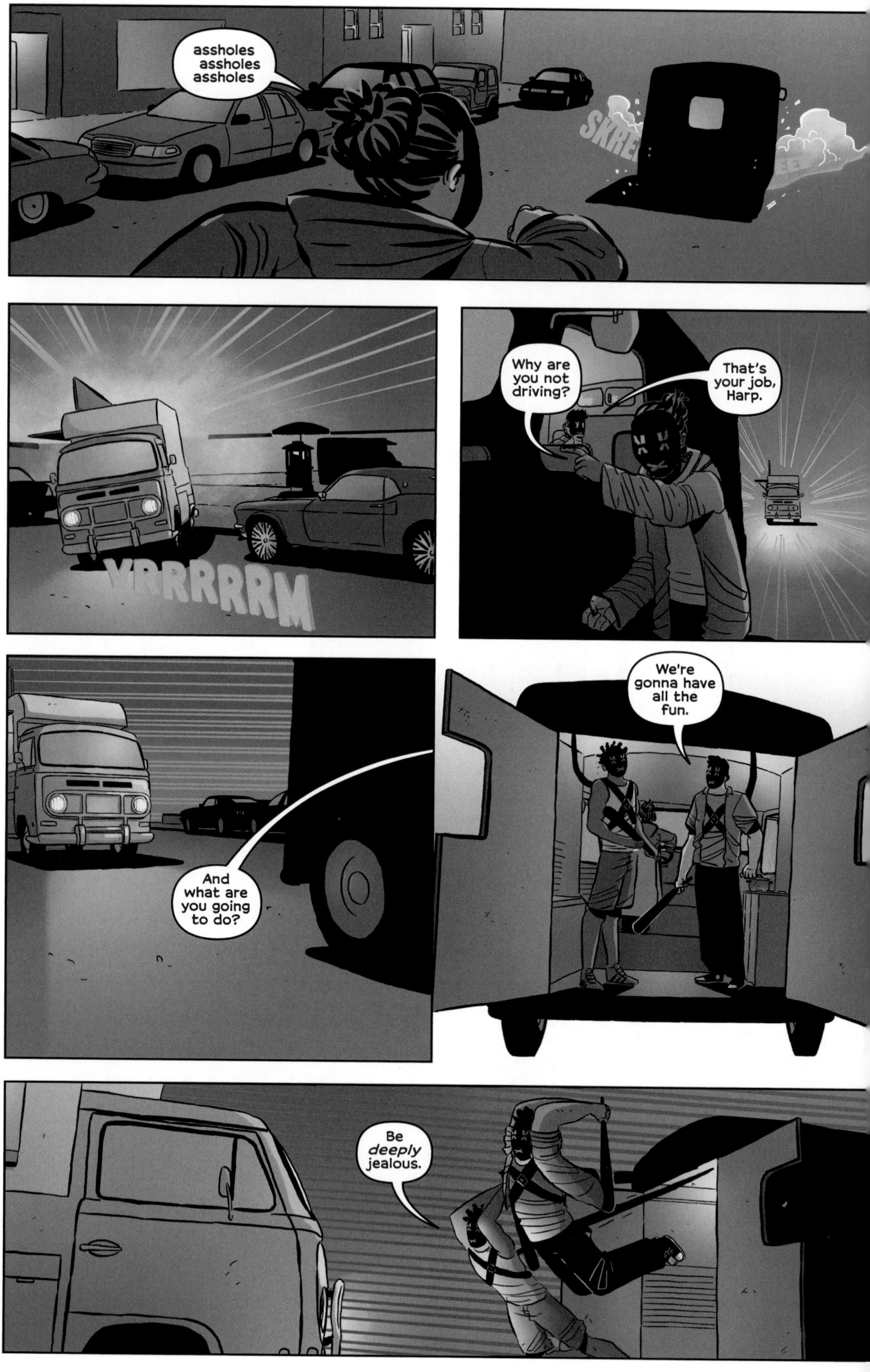
assholes assholes assholes
SKRE
EEE
VRRRRRM
Why are you not driving?
That's your job, Harp.
And what are you going to do?
We're gonna have all the fun.
Be *deeply* jealous.

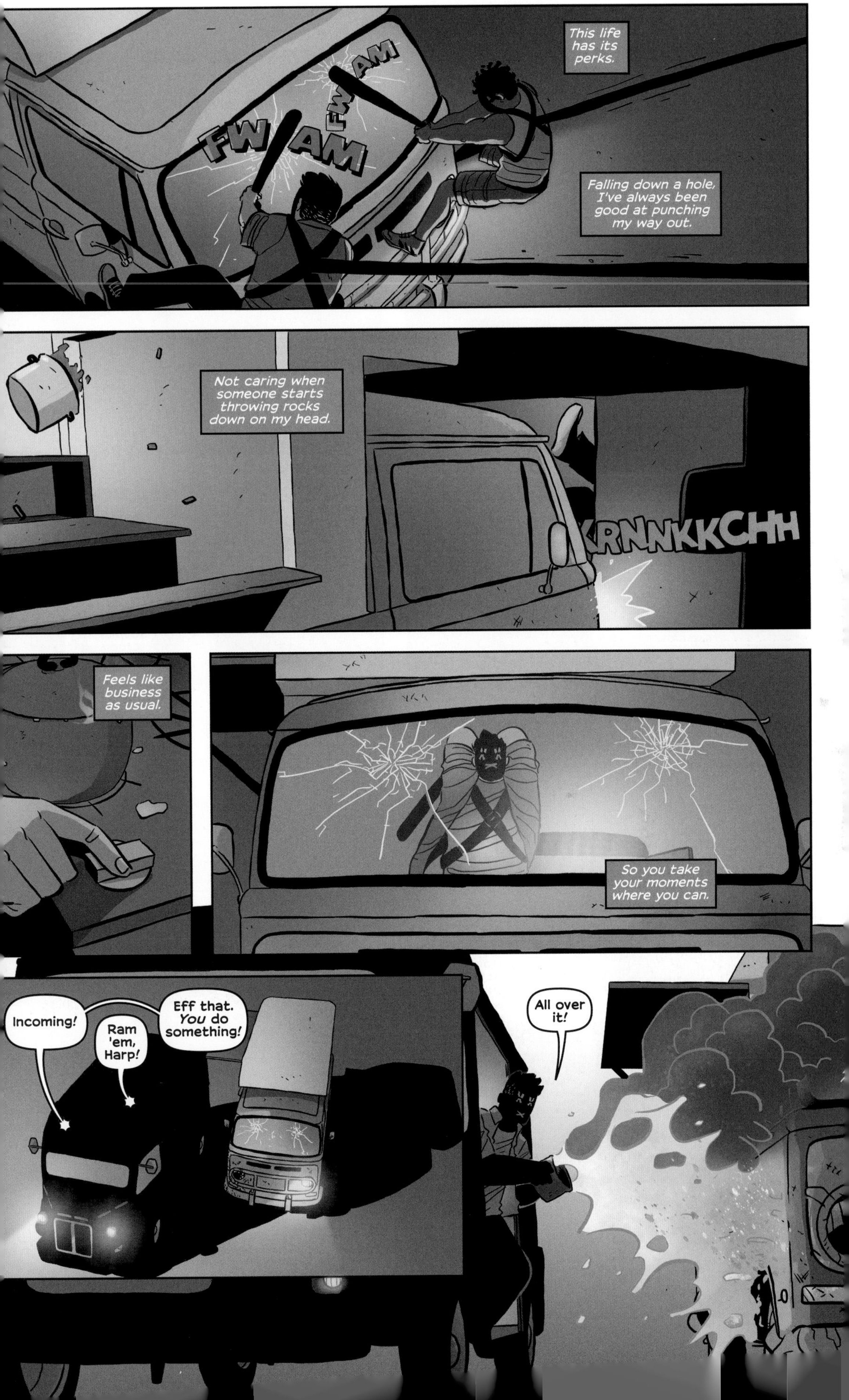
This life has its perks.
FWAM
FWAM
Falling down a hole, I've always been good at punching my way out.
Not caring when someone starts throwing rocks down on my head.
KRNNKKCHH
Feels like business as usual.
So you take your moments where you can.
Incoming!
Ram 'em, Harp!
Eff that. *You* do something!
All over it!

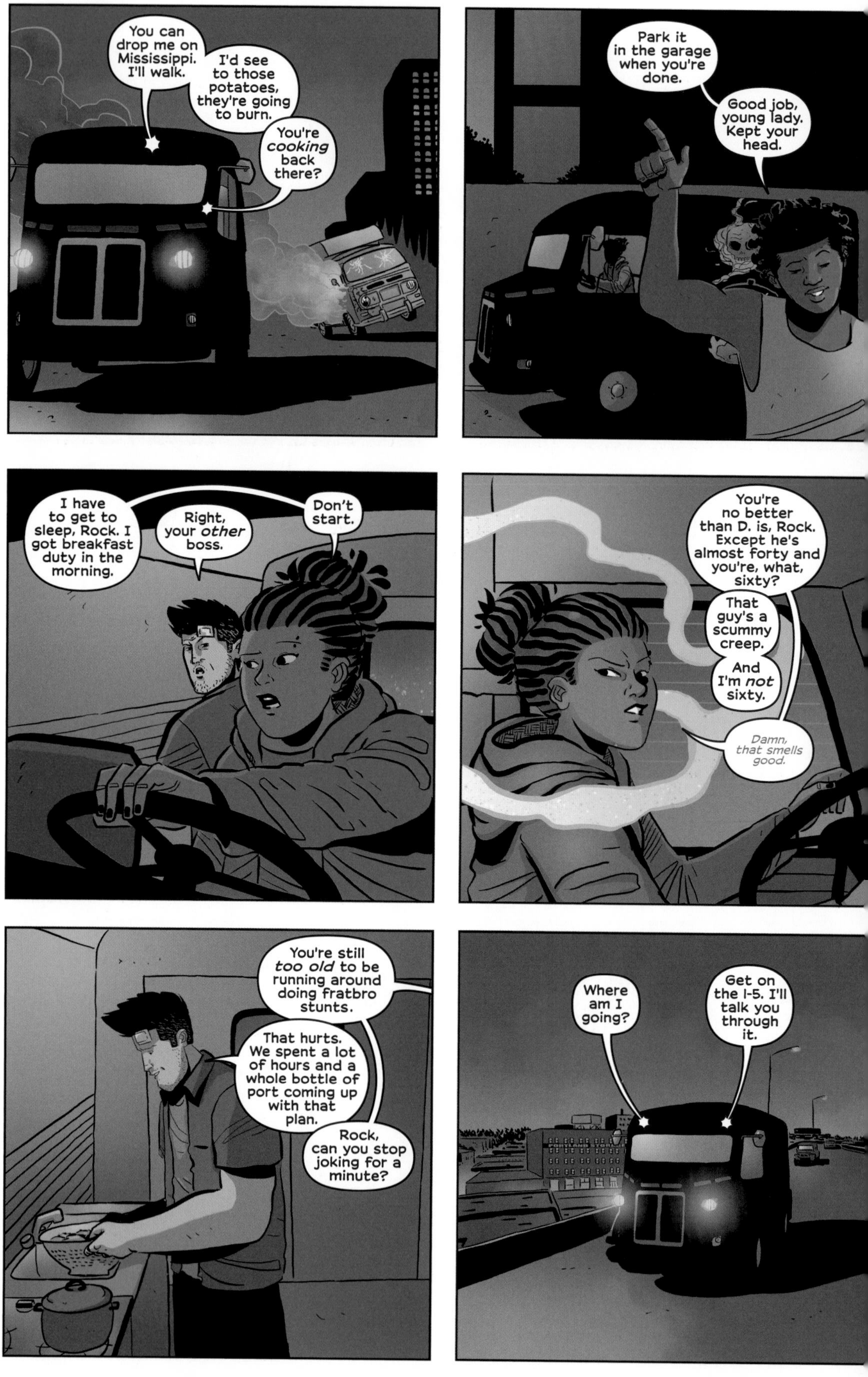
You can drop me on Mississippi. I'll walk.
I'd see to those potatoes, they're going to burn.
You're *cooking* back there?
Park it in the garage when you're done.
Good job, young lady. Kept your head.
I have to get to sleep, Rock. I got breakfast duty in the morning.
Right, your *other* boss.
Don't start.
You're no better than D. is, Rock. Except he's almost forty and you're, what, sixty?
That guy's a scummy creep.
And I'm *not* sixty.
Damn, that smells good.
You're still *too old* to be running around doing fratbro stunts.
That hurts. We spent a lot of hours and a whole bottle of port coming up with that plan.
Rock, can you stop joking for a minute?
Where am I going?
Get on the I-5. I'll talk you through it.

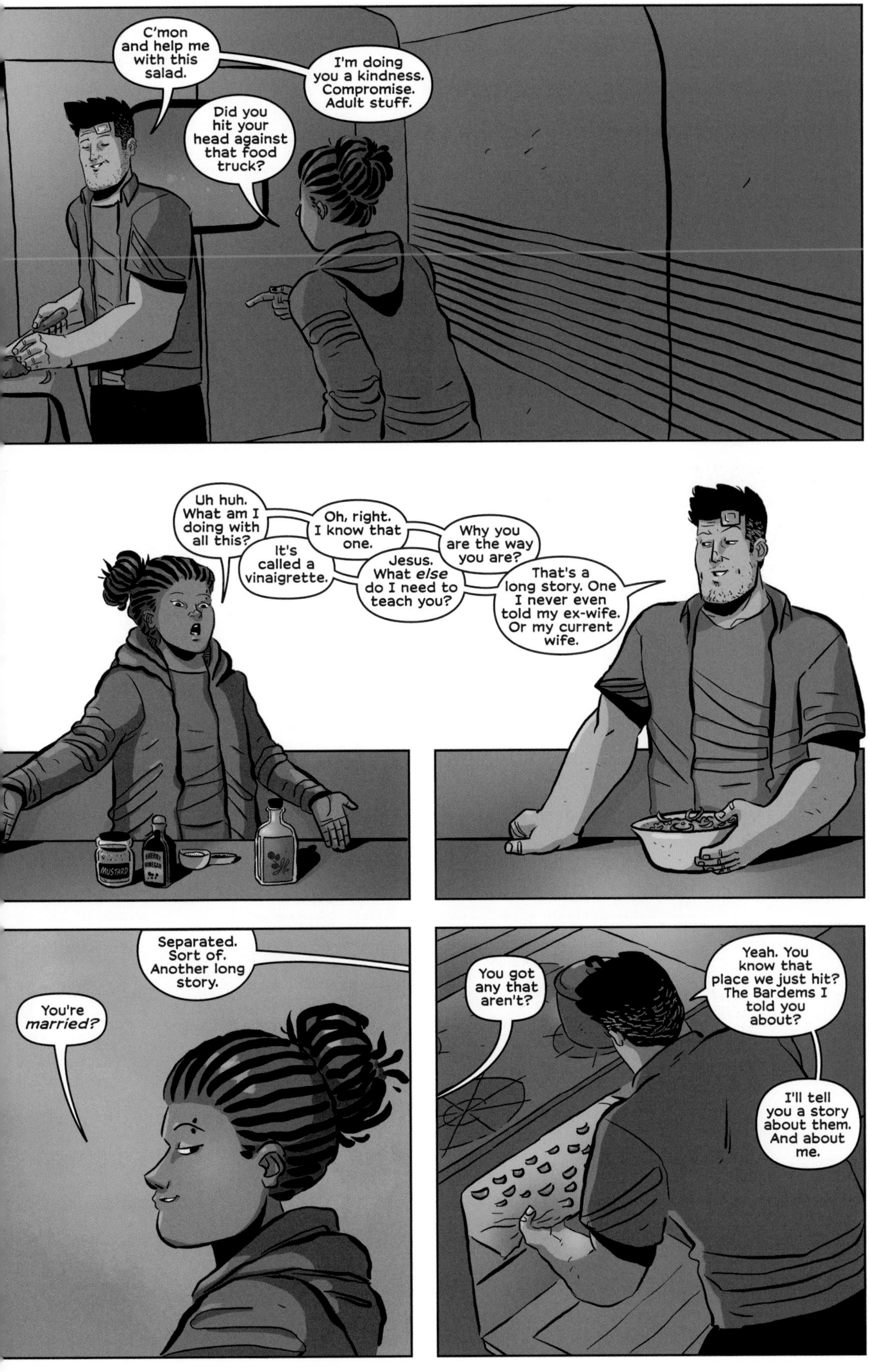
C'mon and help me with this salad.
I'm doing you a kindness. Compromise. Adult stuff.
Did you hit your head against that food truck?
Uh huh. What am I doing with all this?
It's called a vinaigrette.
Oh, right. I know that one.
Jesus. What *else* do I need to teach you?
Why you are the way you are?
That's a long story. One I never even told my ex-wife. Or my current wife.
MUSTARD
SHERRY VINEGAR
You're *married?*
Separated. Sort of. Another long story.
You got any that aren't?
Yeah. You know that place we just hit? The Bardems I told you about?
I'll tell you a story about them. And about me.

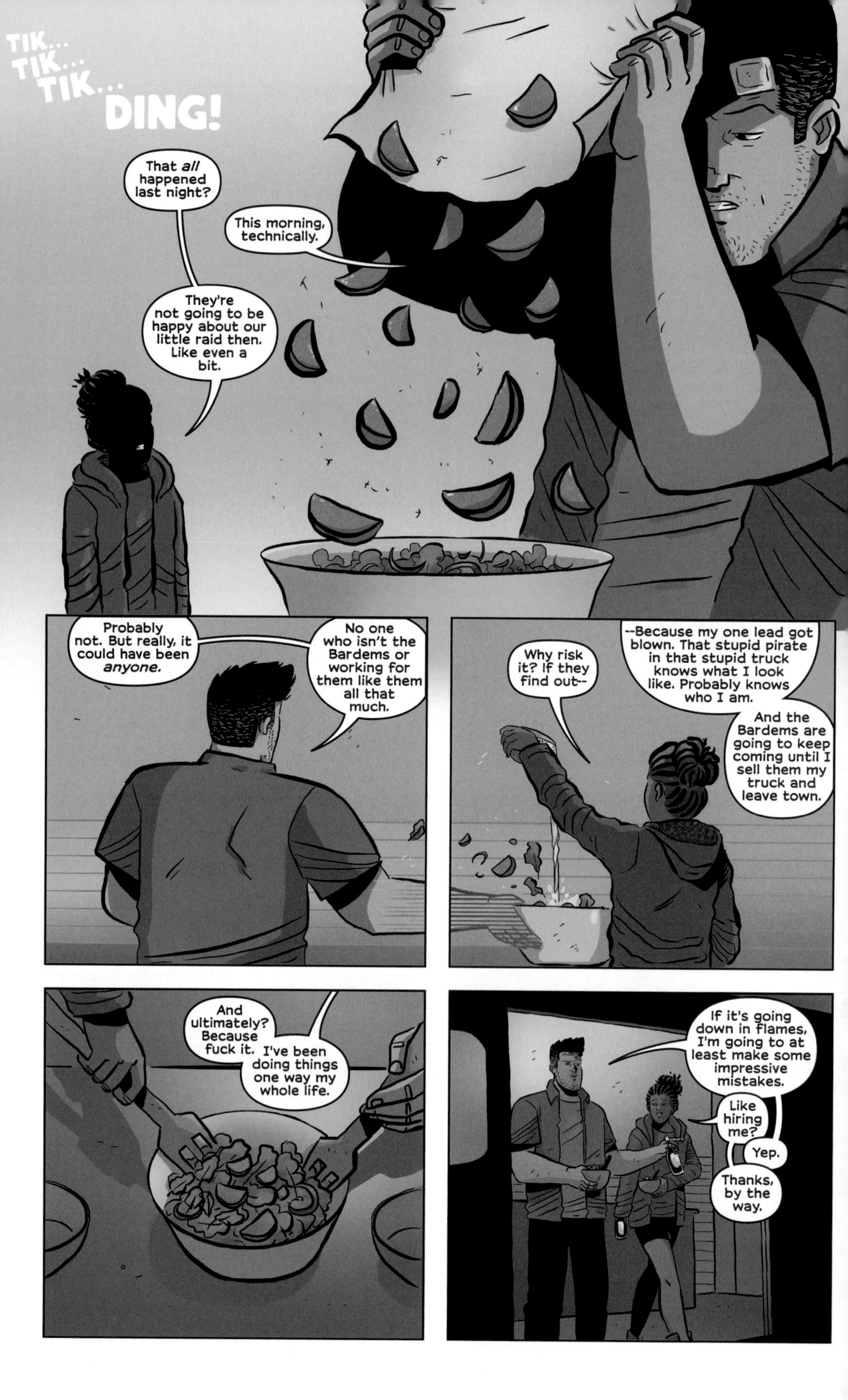
TIK... TIK... TIK...
DING!
That *all* happened last night?
This morning, technically.
They're not going to be happy about our little raid then. Like even a bit.
Probably not. But really, it could have been *anyone.*
No one who isn't the Bardems or working for them like them all that much.
Why risk it? If they find out--
--Because my one lead got blown. That stupid pirate in that stupid truck knows what I look like. Probably knows who I am.
And the Bardems are going to keep coming until I sell them my truck and leave town.
And ultimately? Because fuck it.
I've been doing things one way my whole life.
If it's going down in flames, I'm going to at least make some impressive mistakes.
Like hiring me?
Yep.
Thanks, by the way.

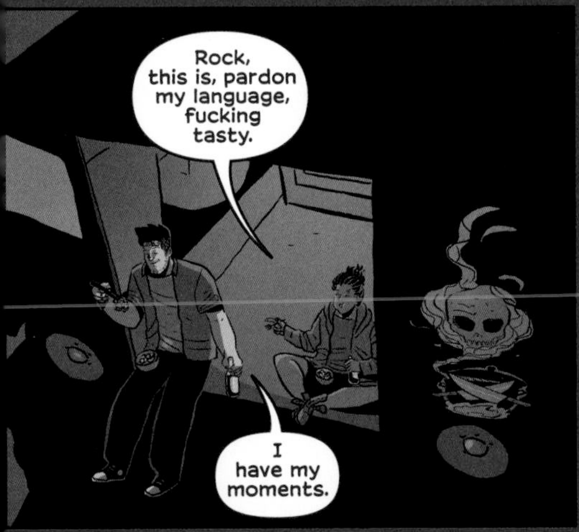
Rock, this is, pardon my language, fucking tasty.
I have my moments.

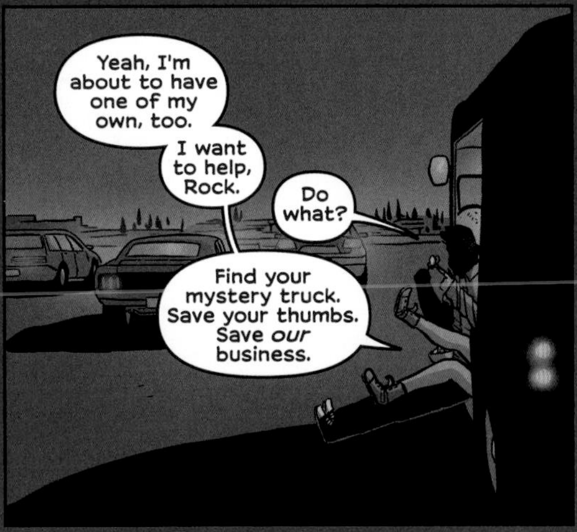
Yeah, I'm about to have one of my own, too.
I want to help, Rock.
Do what?
Find your mystery truck. Save your thumbs. Save *our* business.

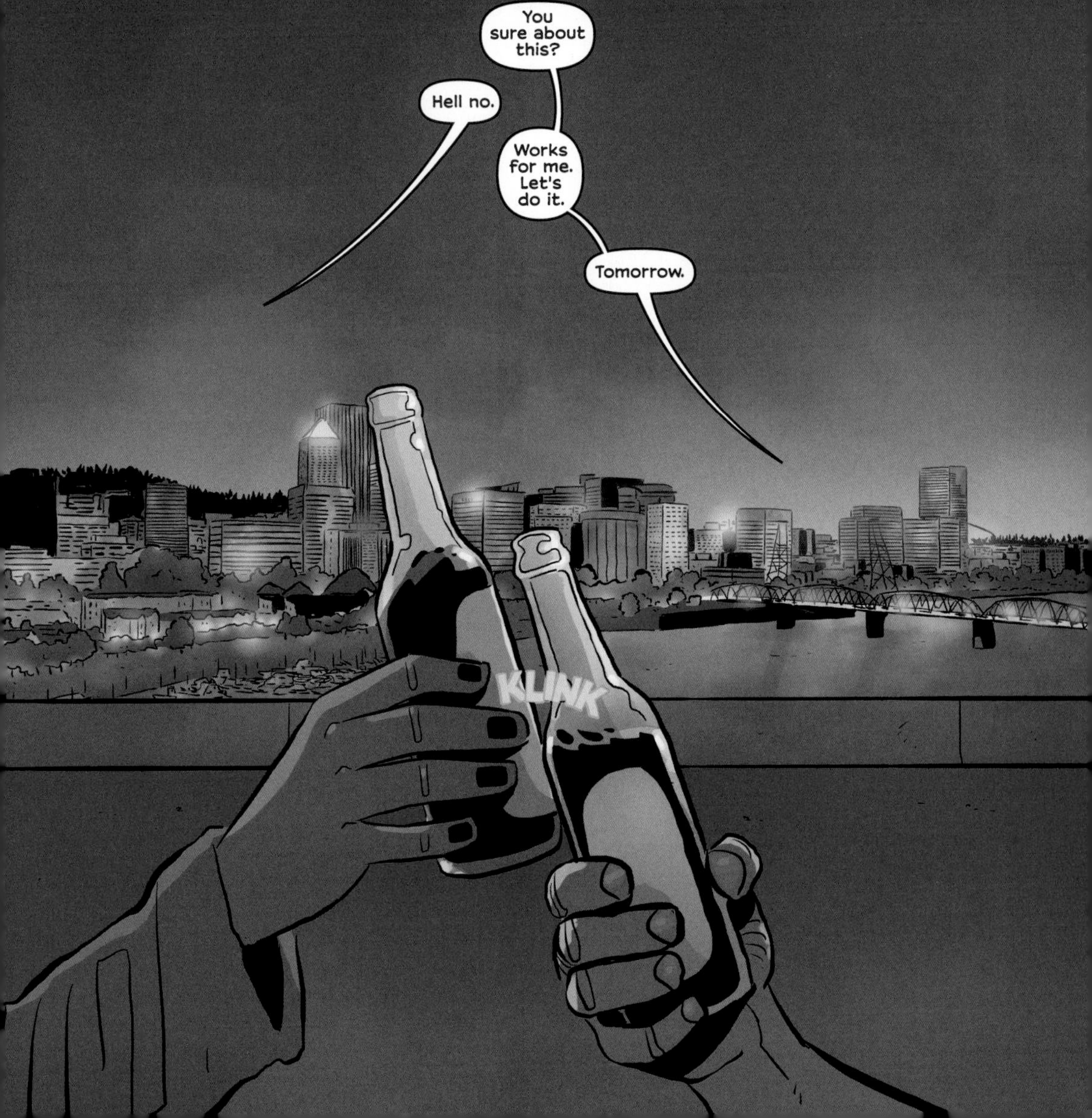
You sure about this?
Hell no.
Works for me. Let's do it.
Tomorrow.
KLINK

ROCKWELL GRANGER'S CAR COMBAT SALAD

IF YOU HAVE TO EAT A SALAD, MIGHT AS WELL EAT THIS ONE

INGREDIENTS

PREP TIME – 10 MINUTES
COOK TIME – 25 MINUTES

<u>NOT</u> FROM THE DUMPSTER!)

- 1 LB OF FINGERLING POTATOES, HALVED
- 2 TBSP OLIVE OIL
- 1 TBSP CHOPPED FRESH PARSLEY
- 1 TBSP CHOPPED FRESH DILL
- 1 TSP. CHOPPED FRESH ROSEMARY
- 1 TSP CHOPPED FRESH THYME
- 2 GARLIC CLOVES MINCED
  (NO ONE LIKES MINCING GARLIC, BUT DO IT ANYWAY)
- ½ TSP SALT
- PEPPER TO TASTE (A SCOONCH, ACCORDING TO SOME)
- 3 CUPS ARUGULA
- JUICE OF ONE LEMON

> SURE, YOU <u>COULD</u> SKIMP AND NOT GET FRESH INGREDIENTS. MAYBE NO ONE WILL KNOW. BUT <u>YOU'LL</u> KNOW AND HAVE TO LIVE WITH THAT SHAME <u>FOREVER</u>.

IT'S <u>A</u> DAMN SALAD. <u>IT'S</u> <u>NOT</u> THAT HARD.

1. PREHEAT OVEN TO 400° F. IDEALLY NOT WHILE IN A RUNNING BATTLE WITH ANOTHER FOOD CART POD, BUT SOMETIMES SHIT HAPPENS.

2. HALVE THOSE POTATOES (OR PRE-HALVE THEM IF YOU'RE GOOD AT PLANNING YOUR LIFE.)

3. MIX THE OLIVE OIL, SALT... PARSLEY, DILL, ROSEMARY AND THYME

4. TOSS THOSE HALVED POTATOES WITH THE MIXTURE, PICTURE THE FACE OF AN ENEMY FOR TRUE TOSSING POWER.

5. SPREAD THE POTATOES ON A PAN OR A BAKING SHEET IN ONE LAYER. BAKE FOR 15 MINUTES. SMOKE 'EM IF YOU GOT 'EM.

6. TAKE THE POTATOES OUT, SPRINKLE THEM WITH THE GARLIC & TOSS, SOMEHOW MAKING SURE TO DO THIS WITHOUT GETTING POTATOES ALL OVER THE FUCKING FLOOR. IF YOU CAN DO THIS, CONGRATS, YOU'RE AN HONEST TO GOD CHEF. I'M STILL WORKING ON THIS PART OF THE JOB.

7. PUT POTATOES BACK IN THE OVEN FOR ANOTHER 10 MINUTES UNTIL THEY'RE ALL BROWN AND CRISPY ON THE EDGES. OR MAYBE NOT, MAYBE YOU'RE ONE OF THOSE WEIRDOS WHO LIKES THEM MUSHY. NO ACCOUNTING FOR TASTE.

8. WHEN THE POTATOES ARE DONE, PLACE THEM IN A BOWL WITH THE ARUGULA AND TOSS TO COMBINE. SQUEEZE THE LEMON JUICE OVER EVERYTHING, TOSS ONE LAST TIME AND SERVE WITH A BEER. BEER'S NOT NECESSARY BUT IT TASTES AMAZING AFTER POSSIBLY ALMOST DYING .

9. DREAM ABOUT EATING A BURGER INSTEAD UNTIL YOUR BOWL IS EMPTY.

3: SECRET SAUCE

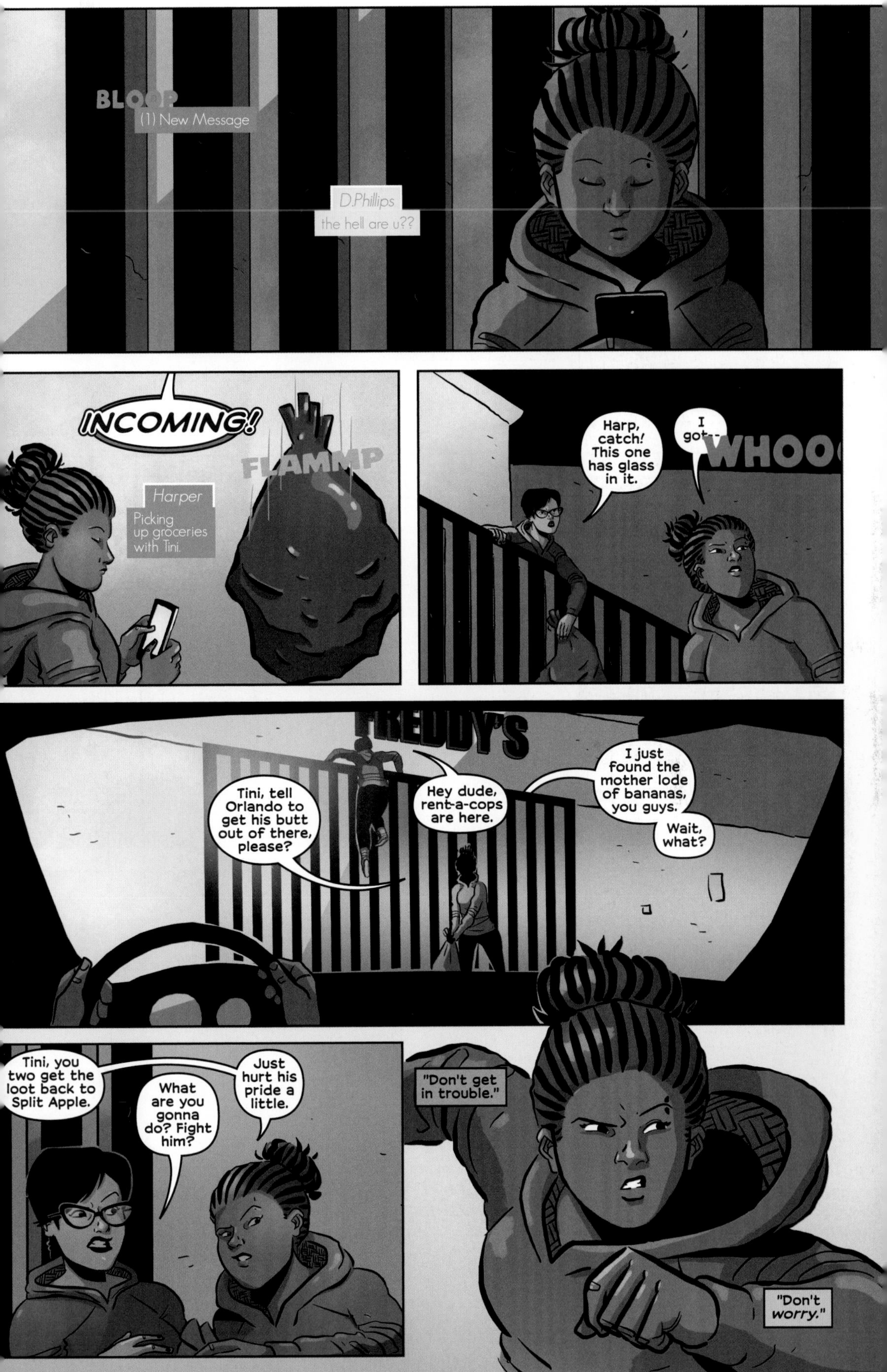
BLOOP
(1) New Message
D.Phillips
the hell are u??
INCOMING!
FLAMMP
Harper
Picking up groceries with Tini.
Harp, catch! This one has glass in it.
I got--
WHOO
FREDDY'S
Tini, tell Orlando to get his butt out of there, please?
Hey dude, rent-a-cops are here.
I just found the mother lode of bananas, you guys.
Wait, what?
Tini, you two get the loot back to Split Apple.
What are you gonna do? Fight him?
Just hurt his pride a little.
"Don't get in trouble."
"Don't worry."

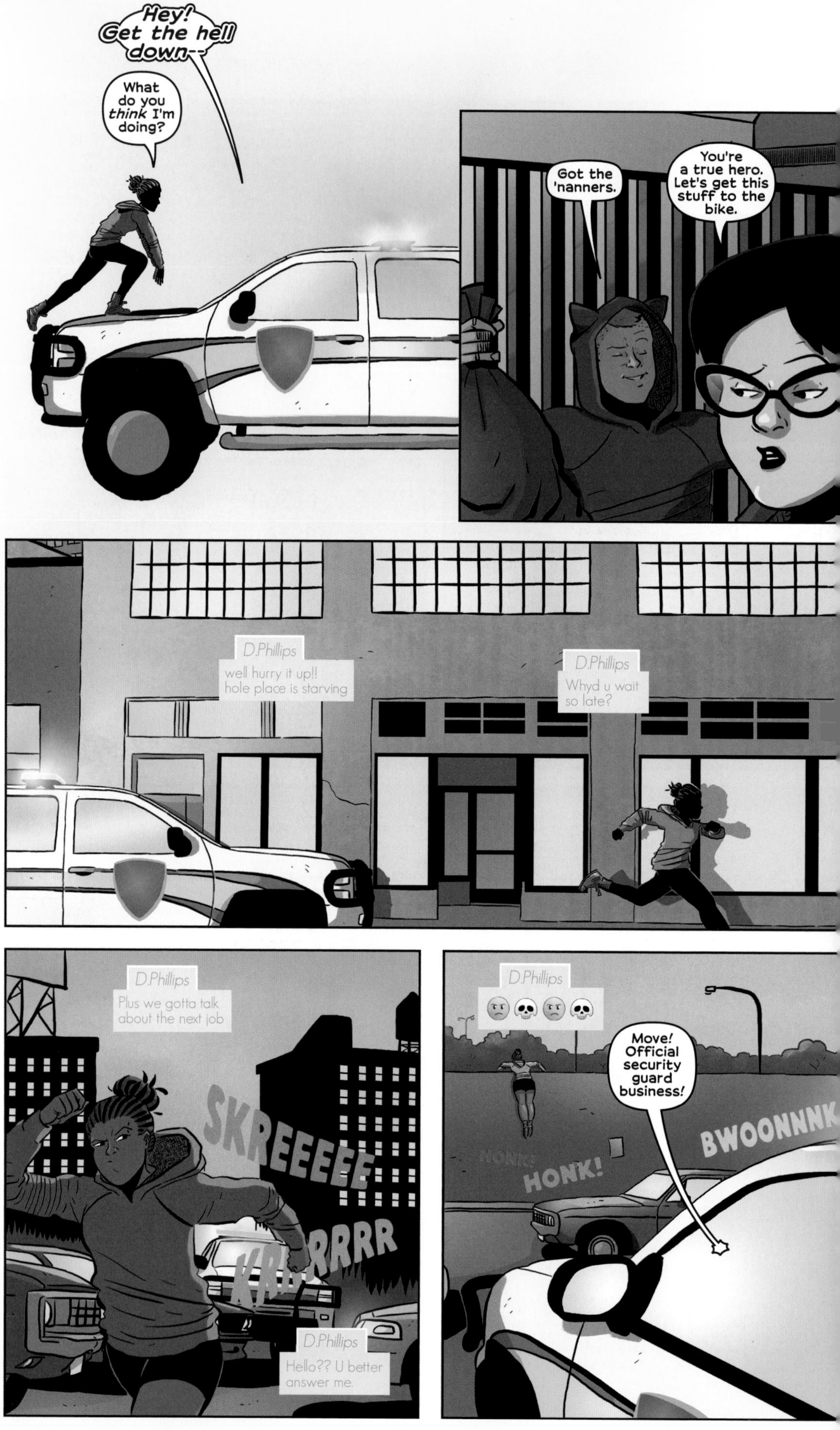
Hey! Get the hell down--
What do you think I'm doing?
Got the 'nanners.
You're a true hero. Let's get this stuff to the bike.
D.Phillips
well hurry it up!! hole place is starving
D.Phillips
Whyd u wait so late?
D.Phillips
Plus we gotta talk about the next job
SKREEEEEE
KR…RRRR
D.Phillips
Hello?? U better answer me.
D.Phillips
Move! Official security guard business!
HONK!
HONK!
BWOONNNK

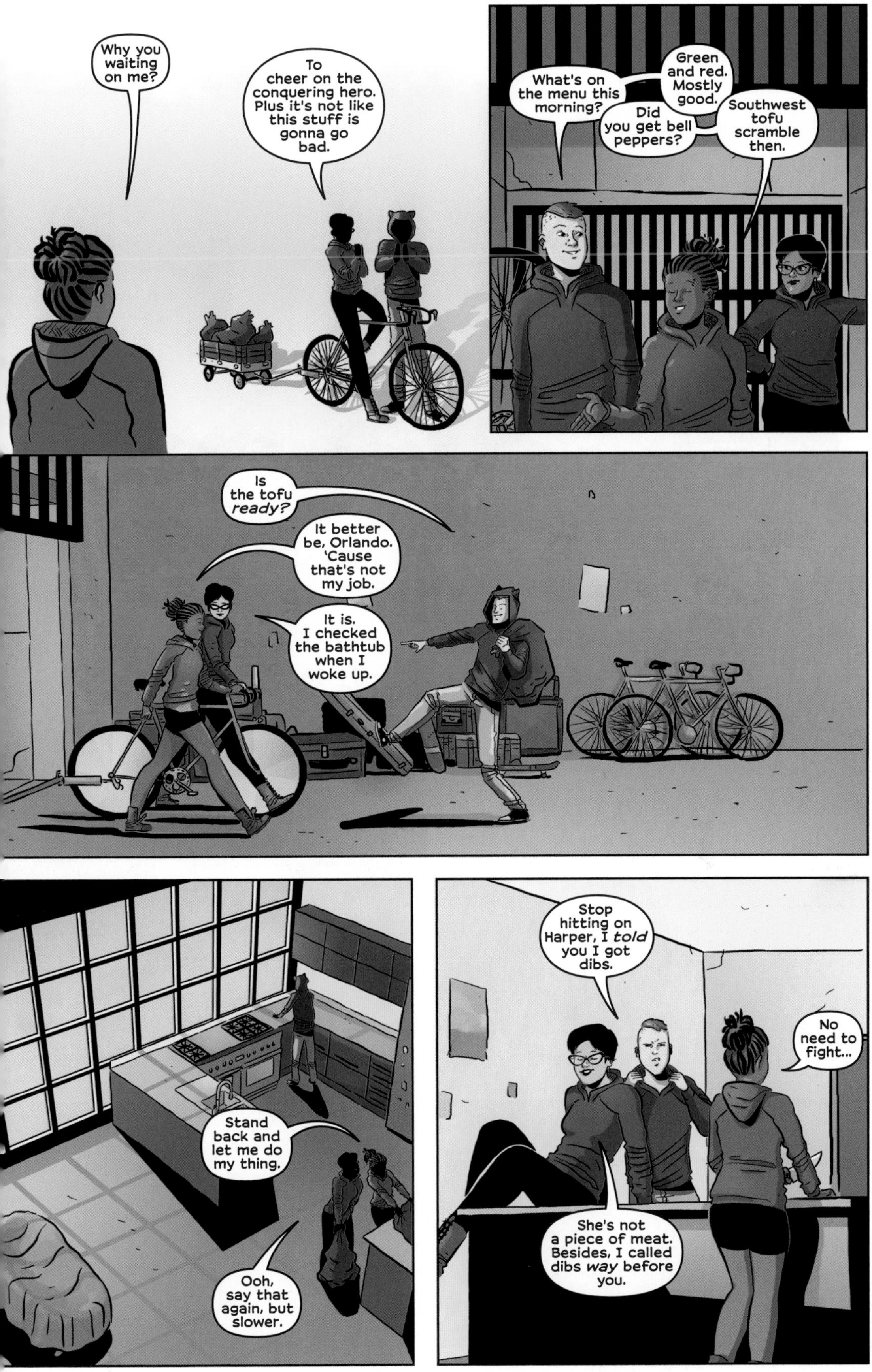
Why you waiting on me?
To cheer on the conquering hero. Plus it's not like this stuff is gonna go bad.
What's on the menu this morning?
Green and red. Mostly good.
Did you get bell peppers?
Southwest tofu scramble then.
Is the tofu *ready?*
It better be, Orlando. 'Cause that's not my job.
It is. I checked the bathtub when I woke up.
Stand back and let me do my thing.
Ooh, say that again, but slower.
Stop hitting on Harper, I *told* you I got dibs.
No need to fight...
She's not a piece of meat. Besides, I called dibs *way* before you.

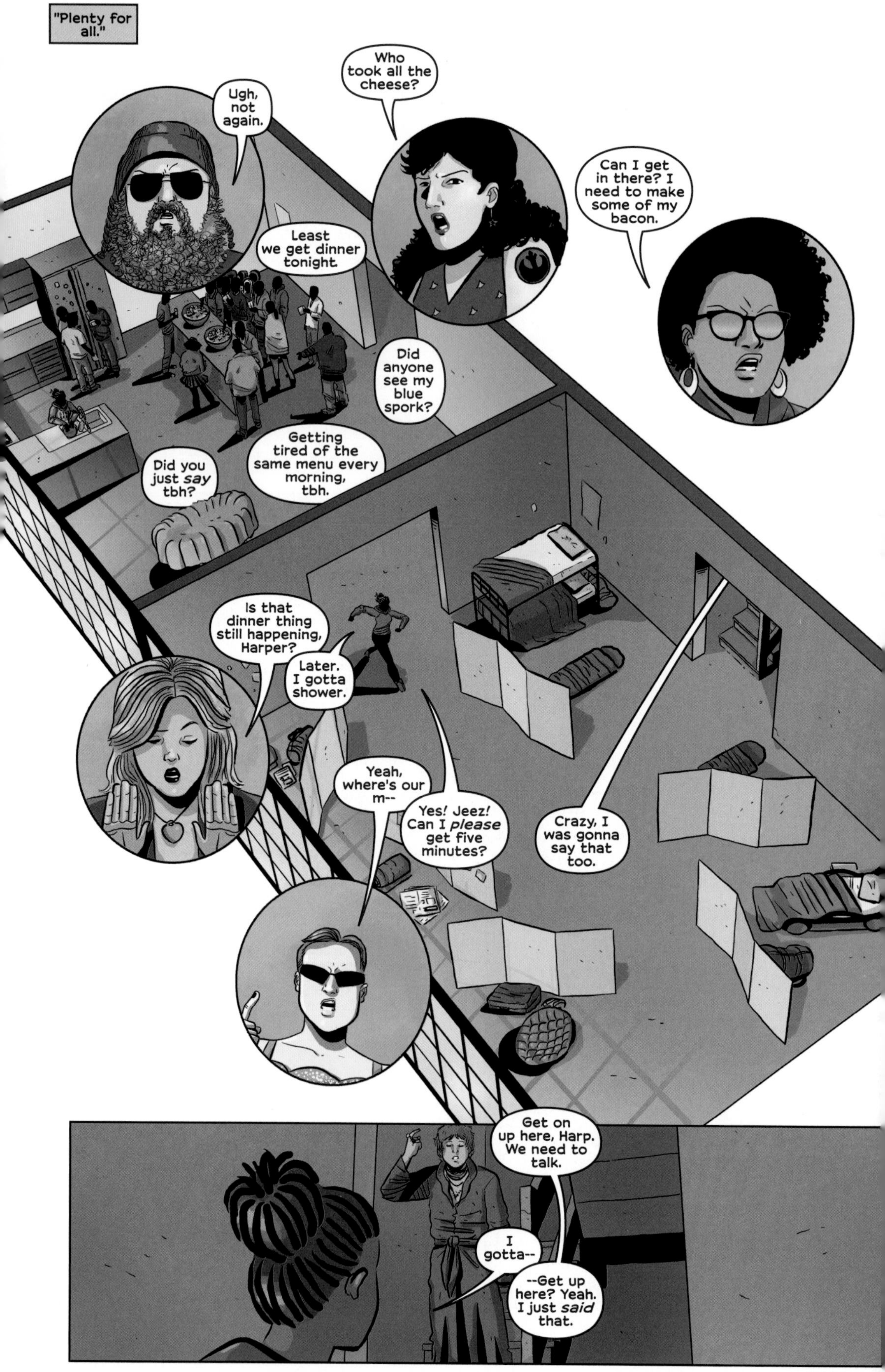
"Plenty for all."
Ugh, not again.
Least we get dinner tonight.
Who took all the cheese?
Can I get in there? I need to make some of my bacon.
Did anyone see my blue spork?
Getting tired of the same menu every morning, tbh.
Did you just *say* tbh?
Is that dinner thing still happening, Harper?
Later. I gotta shower.
Yeah, where's our m--
Yes! Jeez! Can I *please* get five minutes?
Crazy, I was gonna say that too.
Get on up here, Harp. We need to talk.
I gotta--
--Get up here? Yeah. I just *said* that.

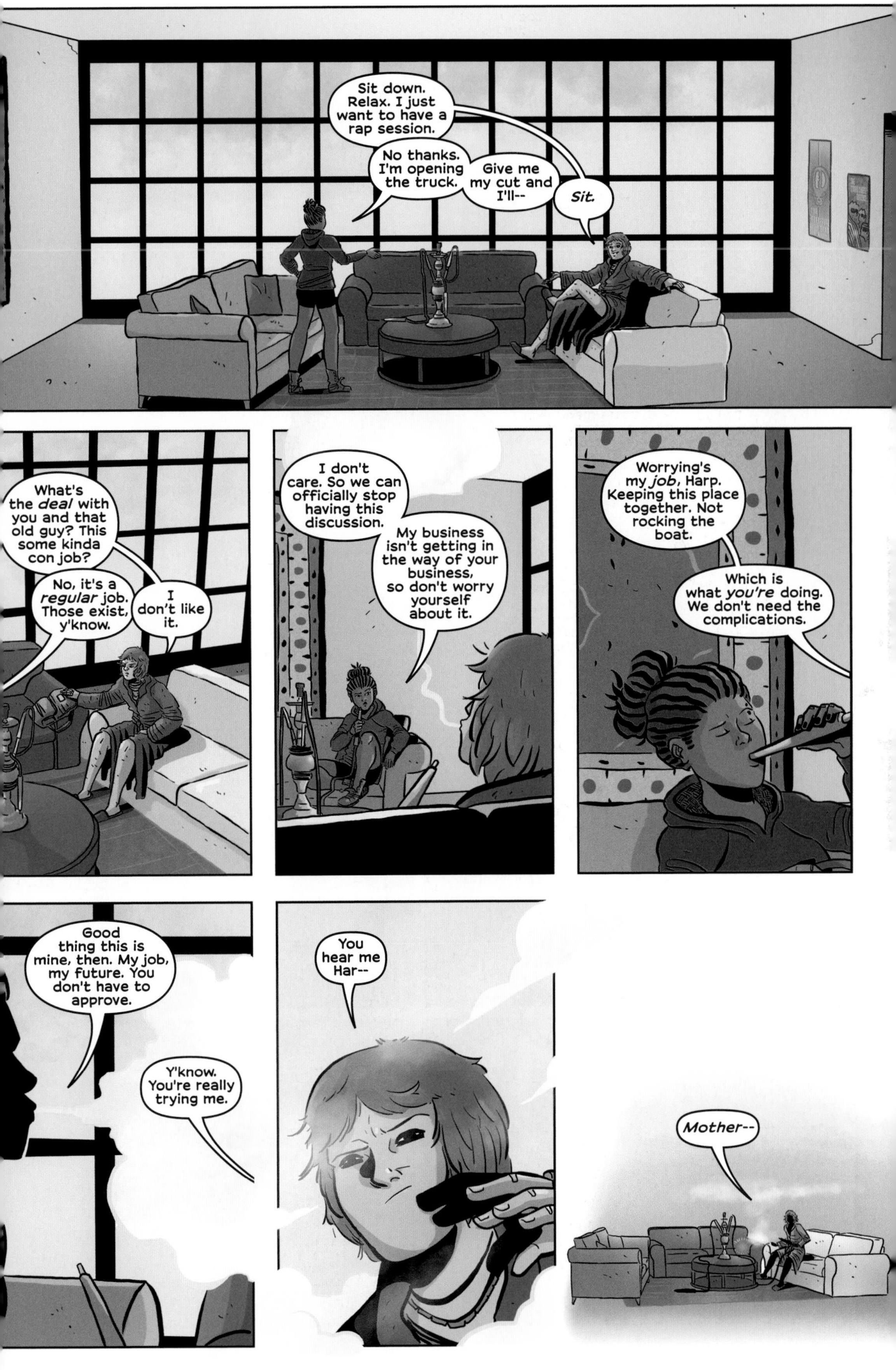
Sit down. Relax. I just want to have a rap session.
No thanks. I'm opening the truck.
Give me my cut and I'll--
Sit.
What's the deal with you and that old guy? This some kinda con job?
No, it's a regular job. Those exist, y'know.
I don't like it.
I don't care. So we can officially stop having this discussion.
My business isn't getting in the way of your business, so don't worry yourself about it.
Worrying's my job, Harp. Keeping this place together. Not rocking the boat.
Which is what you're doing. We don't need the complications.
Good thing this is mine, then. My job, my future. You don't have to approve.
Y'know. You're really trying me.
You hear me Har--
Mother--

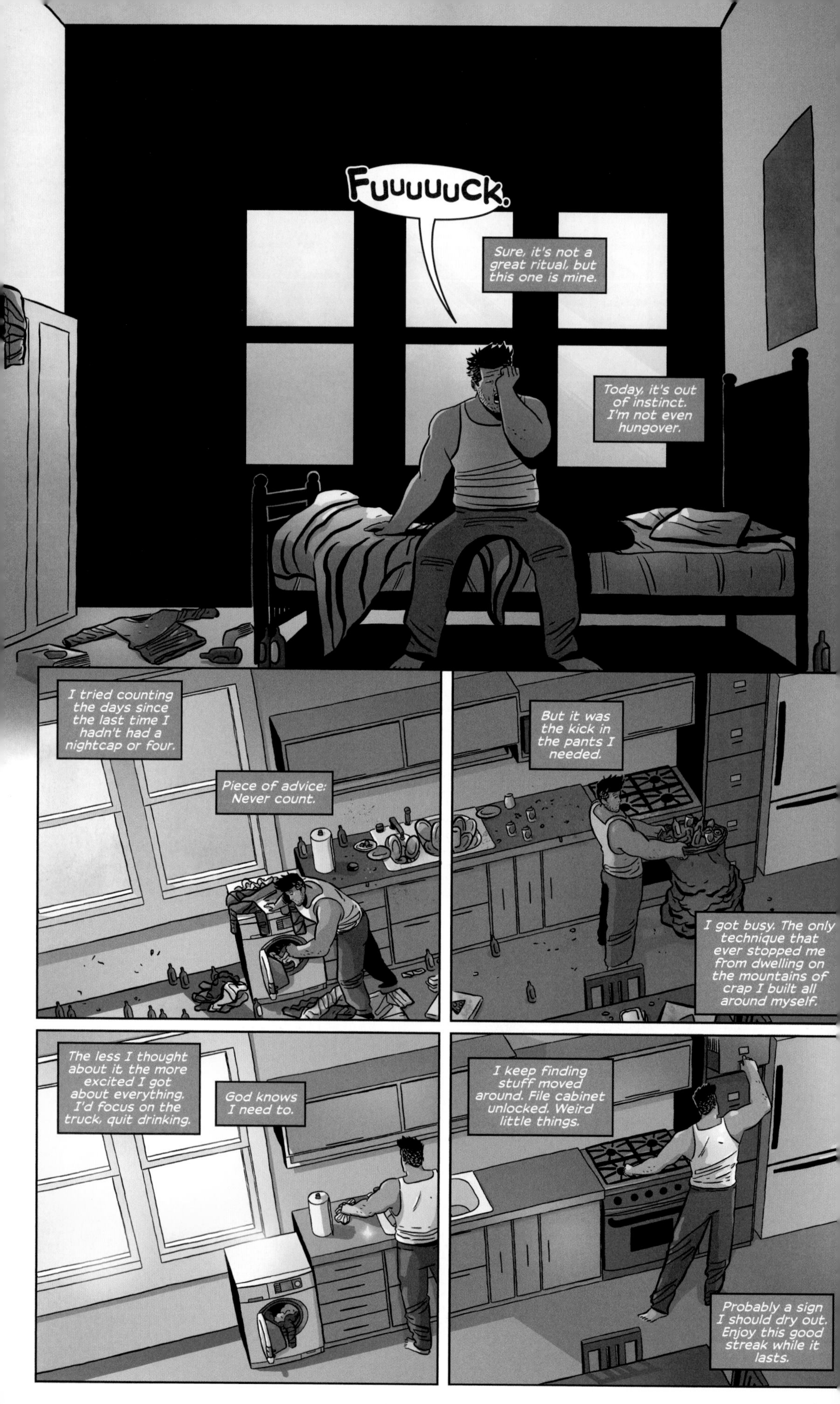

Fuuuuuck.
Sure, it's not a great ritual, but this one is mine.
Today, it's out of instinct. I'm not even hungover.
I tried counting the days since the last time I hadn't had a nightcap or four.
Piece of advice: Never count.
But it was the kick in the pants I needed.
I got busy. The only technique that ever stopped me from dwelling on the mountains of crap I built all around myself.
The less I thought about it the more excited I got about everything. I'd focus on the truck, quit drinking.
God knows I need to.
I keep finding stuff moved around. File cabinet unlocked. Weird little things.
Probably a sign I should dry out. Enjoy this good streak while it lasts.

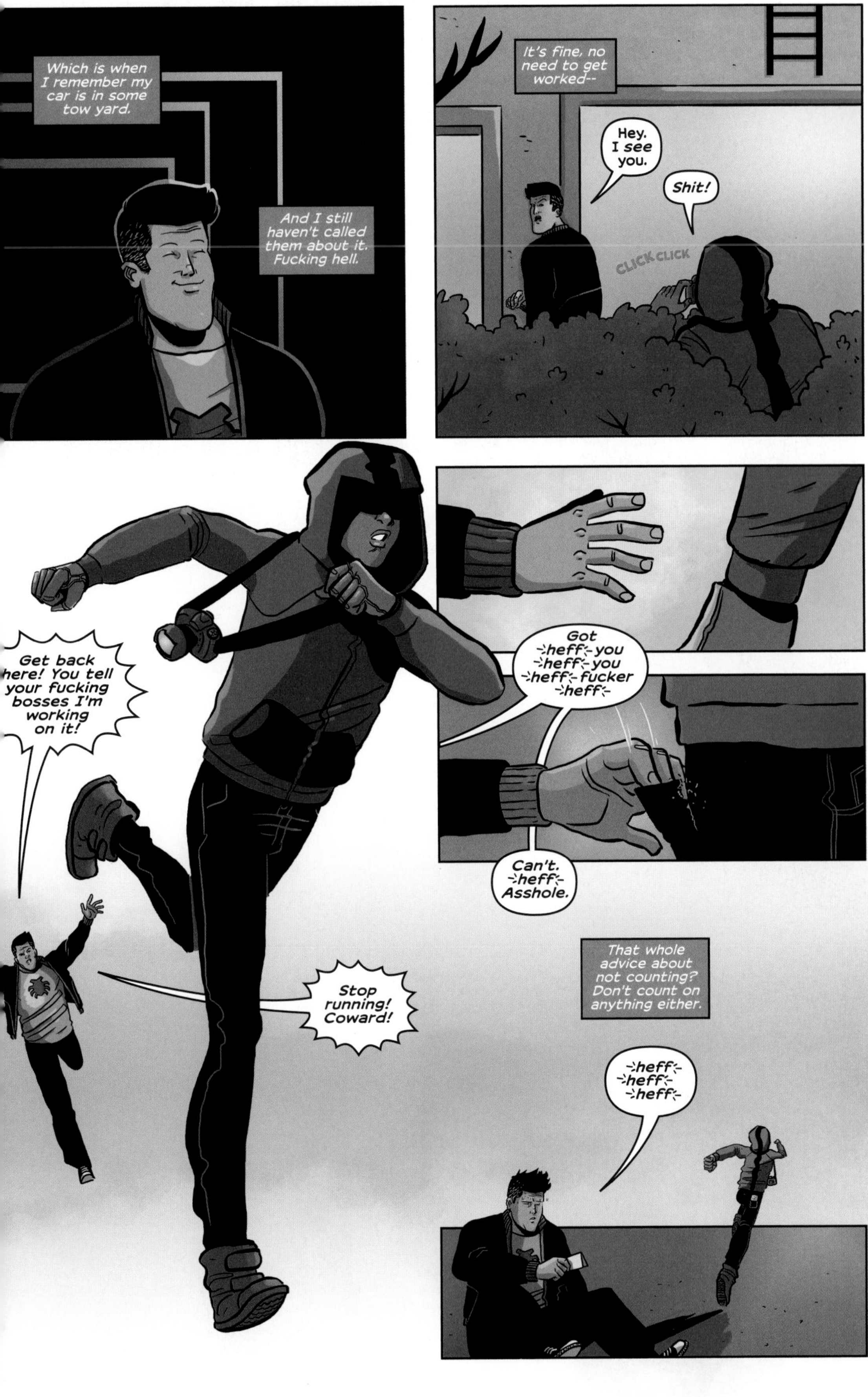

Which is when I remember my car is in some tow yard.
And I still haven't called them about it. Fucking hell.
It's fine, no need to get worked--
Hey. I see you.
Shit!
CLICK CLICK
Get back here! You tell your fucking bosses I'm working on it!
Got -heff- you -heff- you -heff- fucker -heff-
Can't. -heff- Asshole.
Stop running! Coward!
That whole advice about not counting? Don't count on anything either.
-heff- -heff- -heff-

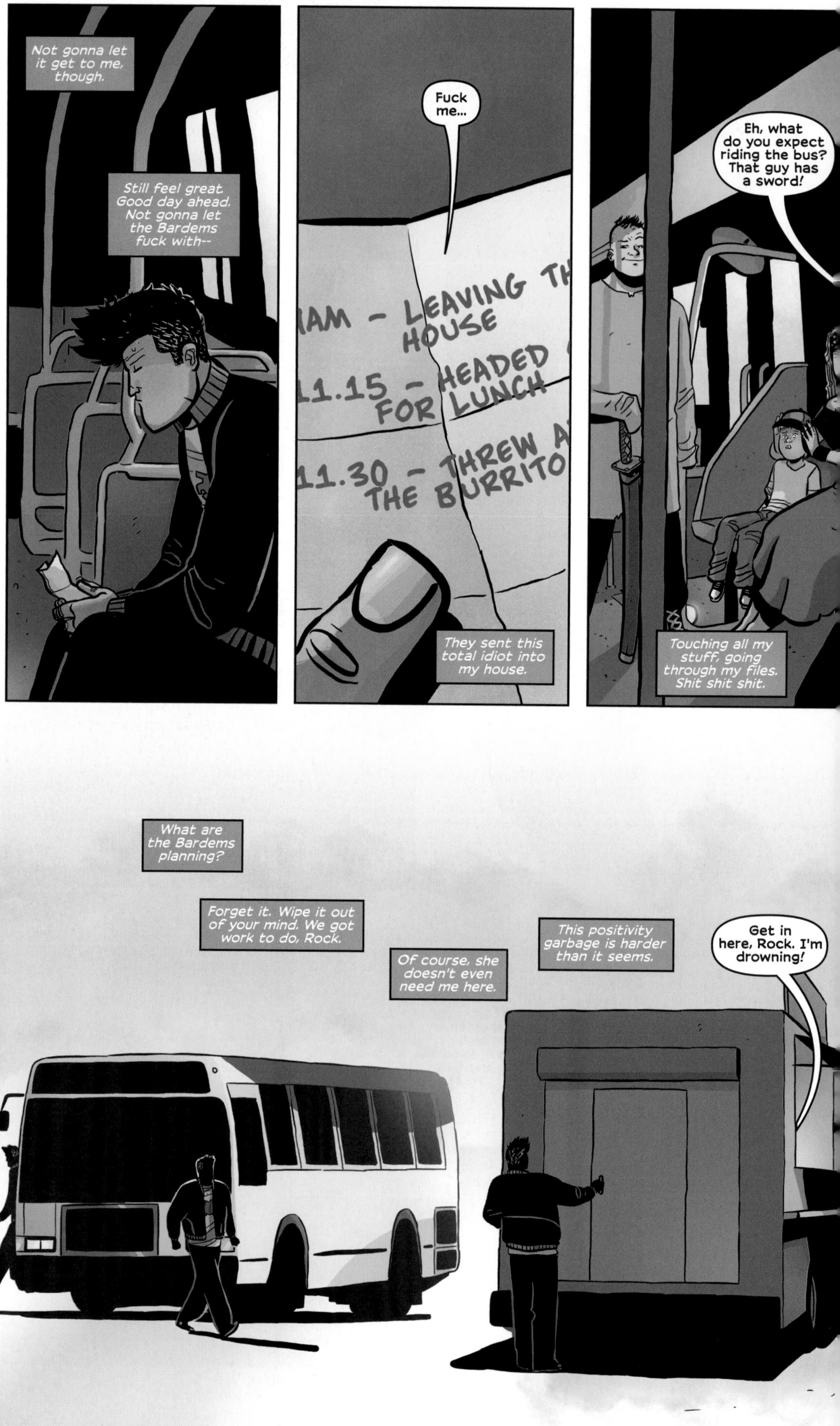
Not gonna let it get to me, though.
Still feel great. Good day ahead. Not gonna let the Bardems fuck with--
Fuck me...
IAM - LEAVING TH HOUSE
11.15 - HEADED FOR LUNCH
11.30 - THREW A THE BURRITO
They sent this total idiot into my house.
Eh, what do you expect riding the bus? That guy has a sword!
Touching all my stuff, going through my files. Shit shit shit.
What are the Bardems planning?
Forget it. Wipe it out of your mind. We got work to do, Rock.
Of course, she doesn't even need me here.
This positivity garbage is harder than it seems.
Get in here, Rock. I'm drowning!

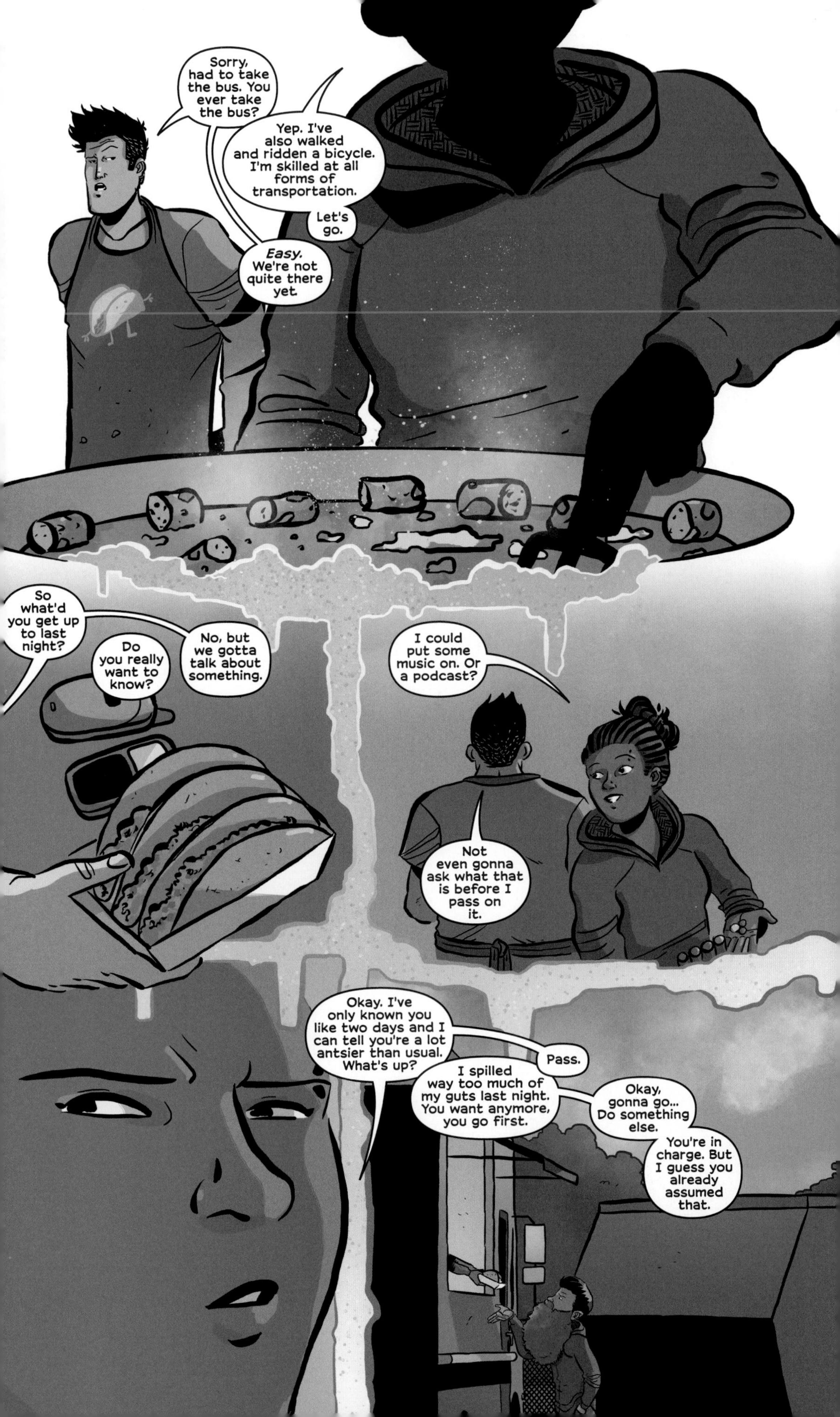
Sorry, had to take the bus. You ever take the bus?
Yep. I've also walked and ridden a bicycle. I'm skilled at all forms of transportation.
Let's go.
Easy. We're not quite there yet.
So what'd you get up to last night?
Do you really want to know?
No, but we gotta talk about something.
I could put some music on. Or a podcast?
Not even gonna ask what that is before I pass on it.
Okay. I've only known you like two days and I can tell you're a lot antsier than usual. What's up?
Pass.
I spilled way too much of my guts last night. You want anymore, you go first.
Okay, gonna go... Do something else.
You're in charge. But I guess you already assumed that.

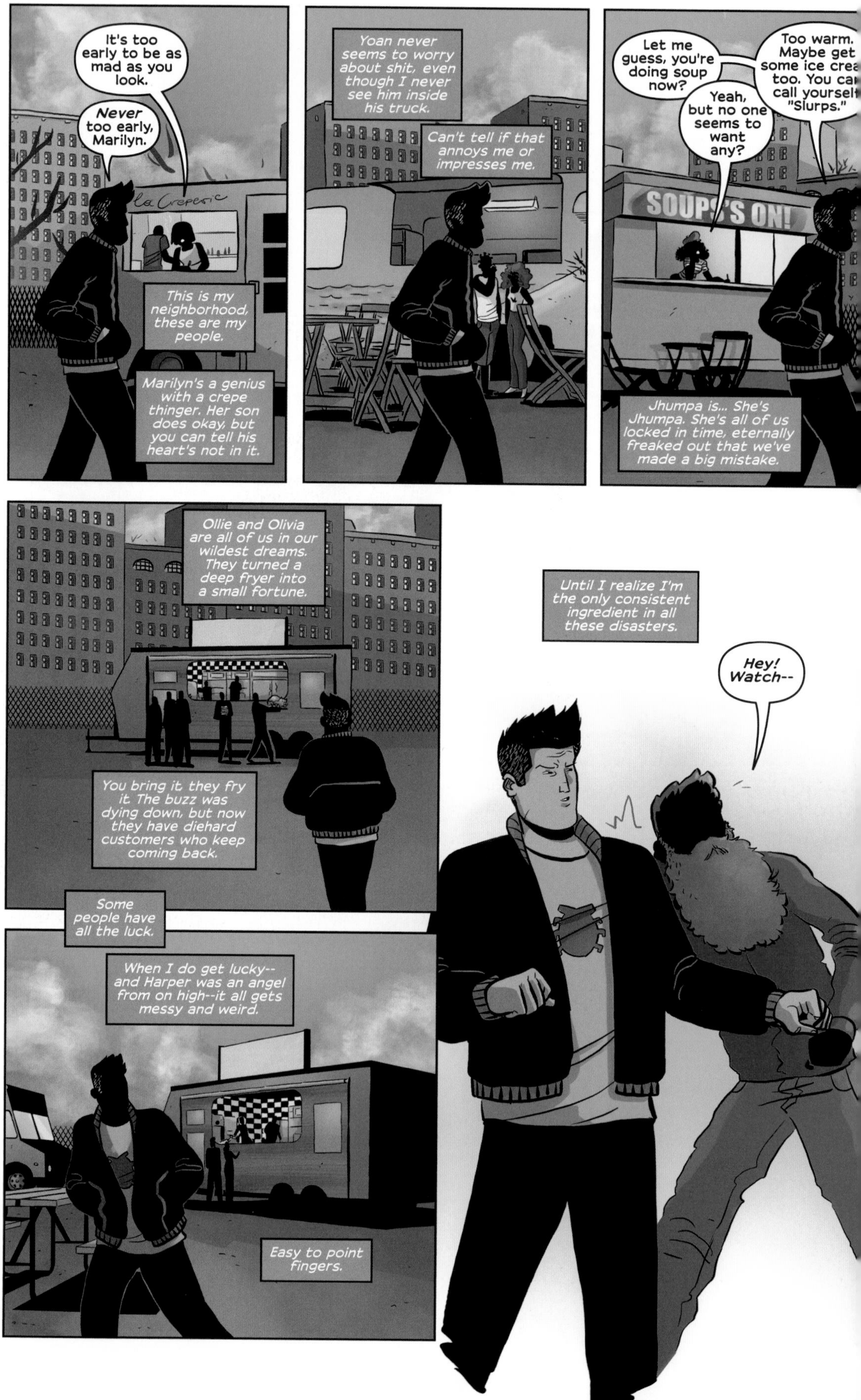
It's too early to be as mad as you look.
Never too early, Marilyn.
This is my neighborhood, these are my people.
Marilyn's a genius with a crepe thinger. Her son does okay, but you can tell his heart's not in it.
Yoan never seems to worry about shit, even though I never see him inside his truck.
Can't tell if that annoys me or impresses me.
Let me guess, you're doing soup now?
Yeah, but no one seems to want any?
Too warm. Maybe get some ice crea too. You ca call yoursel "Slurps."
SOUPS'S ON!
Jhumpa is... She's Jhumpa. She's all of us locked in time, eternally freaked out that we've made a big mistake.
Ollie and Olivia are all of us in our wildest dreams. They turned a deep fryer into a small fortune.
You bring it they fry it. The buzz was dying down, but now they have diehard customers who keep coming back.
Some people have all the luck.
When I do get lucky-- and Harper was an angel from on high--it all gets messy and weird.
Easy to point fingers.
Until I realize I'm the only consistent ingredient in all these disasters.
Hey! Watch--

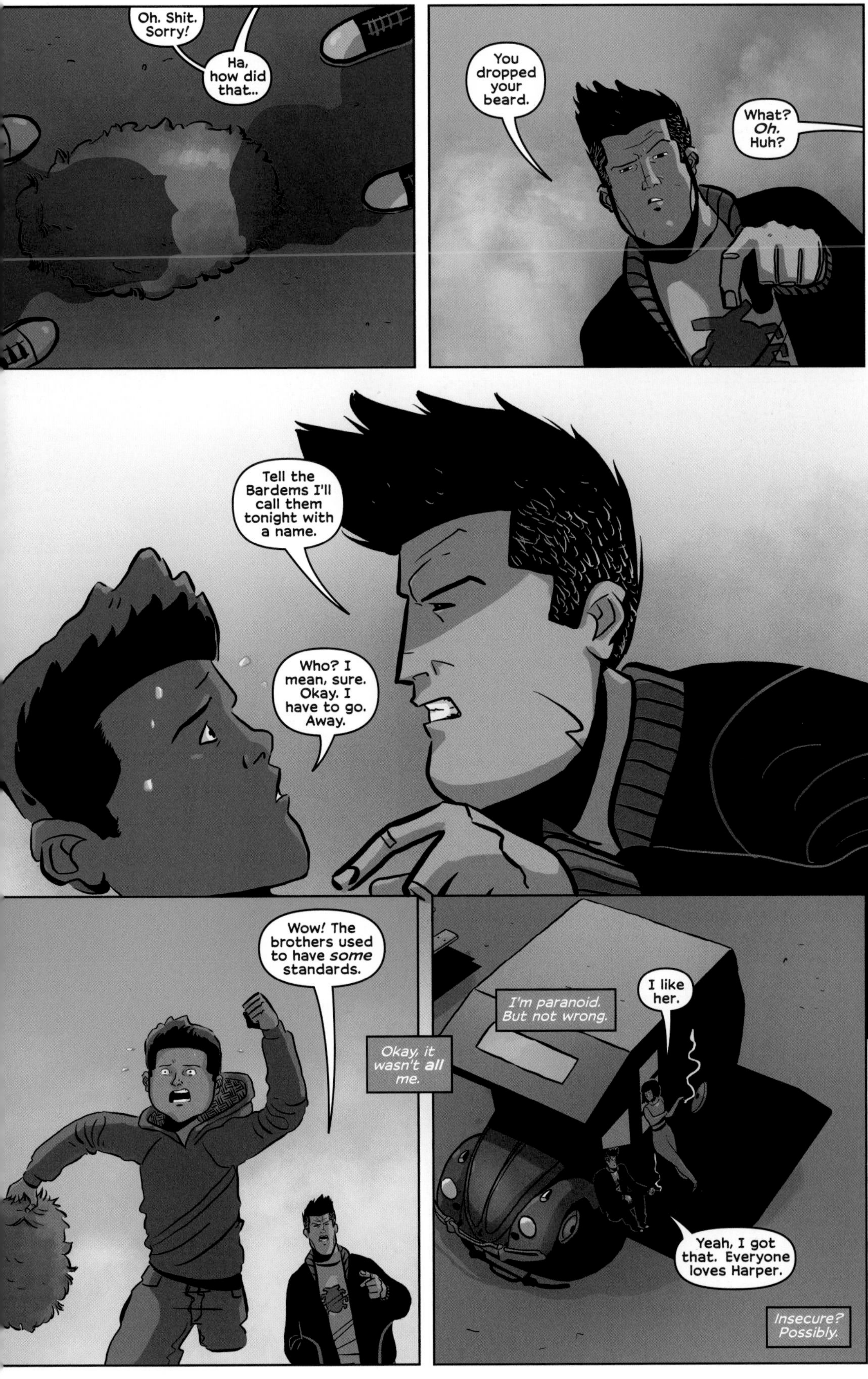
Oh. Shit. Sorry!
Ha, how did that..
You dropped your beard.
What? *Oh.* Huh?
Tell the Bardems I'll call them tonight with a name.
Who? I mean, sure. Okay. I have to go. Away.
Wow! The brothers used to have *some* standards.
*Okay, it wasn't **all** me.*
I'm paranoid. But not wrong.
I like her.
Yeah, I got that. Everyone loves Harper.
Insecure? Possibly.

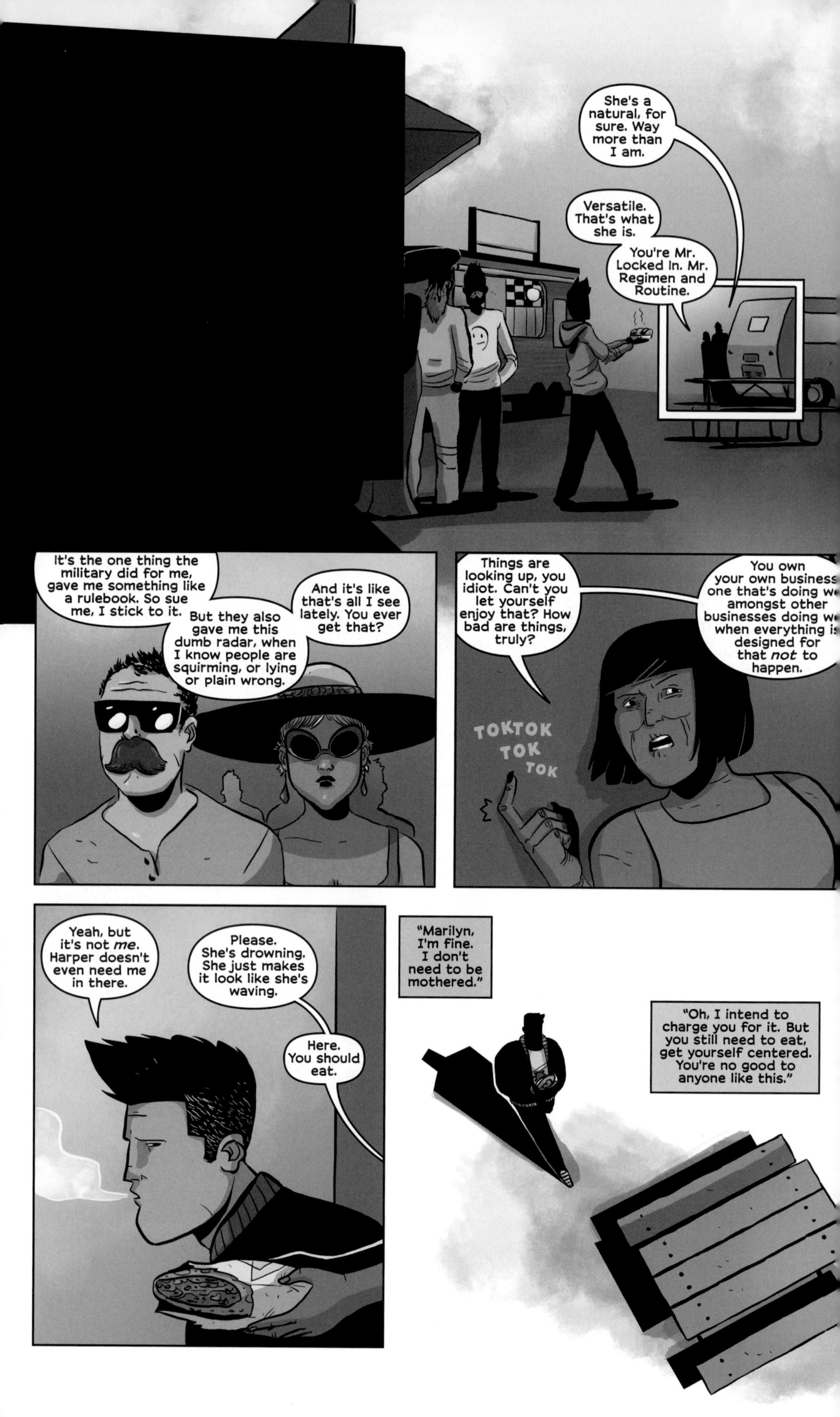

She's a natural, for sure. Way more than I am.
Versatile. That's what she is.
You're Mr. Locked In. Mr. Regimen and Routine.
It's the one thing the military did for me, gave me something like a rulebook. So sue me, I stick to it.
But they also gave me this dumb radar, when I know people are squirming, or lying or plain wrong.
And it's like that's all I see lately. You ever get that?
Things are looking up, you idiot. Can't you let yourself enjoy that? How bad are things, truly?
You own your own business one that's doing w amongst other businesses doing w when everything is designed for that *not* to happen.
TOKTOK TOK TOK
Yeah, but it's not *me*. Harper doesn't even need me in there.
Please. She's drowning. She just makes it look like she's waving.
Here. You should eat.
"Marilyn, I'm fine. I don't need to be mothered."
"Oh, I intend to charge you for it. But you still need to eat, get yourself centered. You're no good to anyone like this."

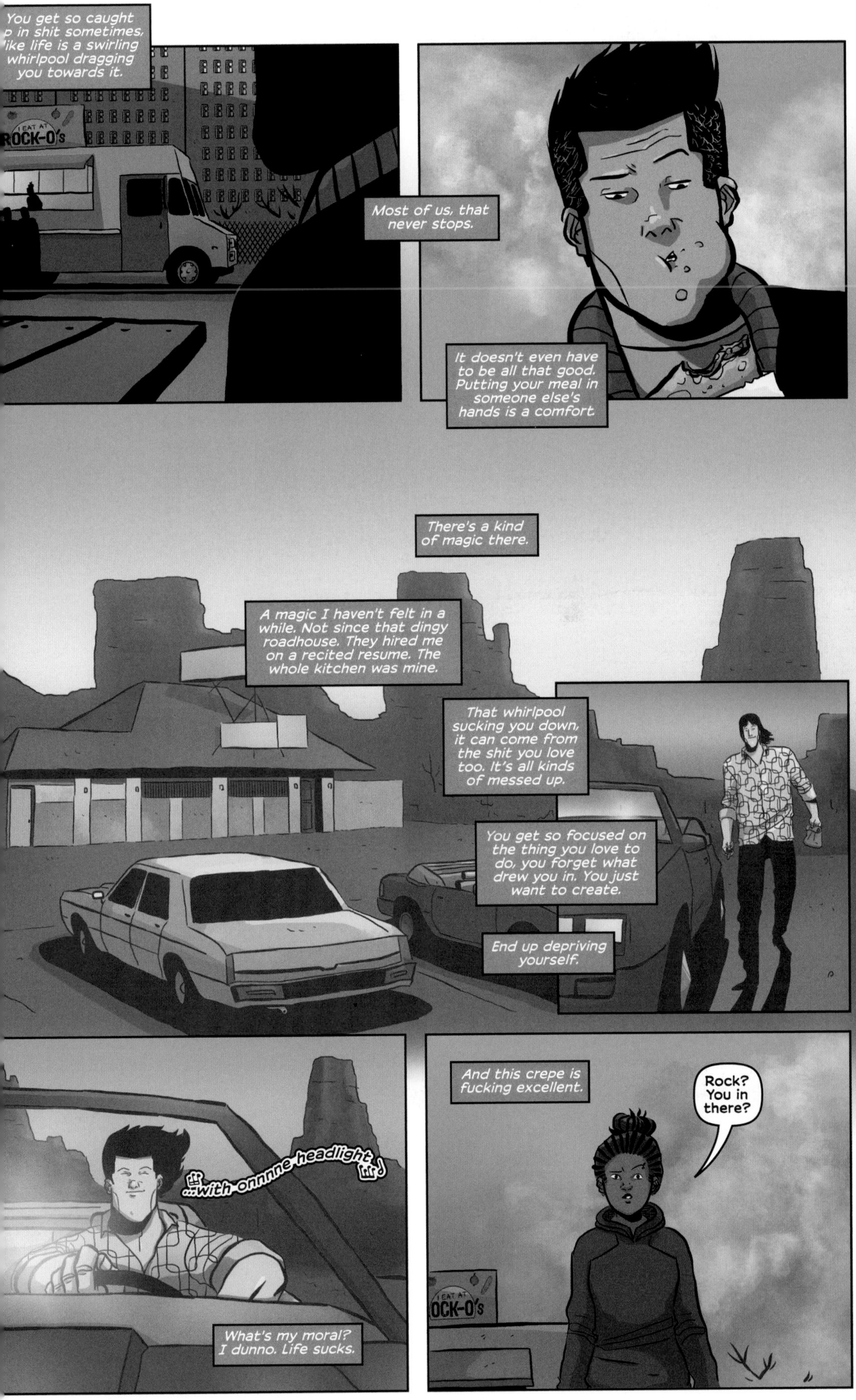
You get so caught
p in shit sometimes,
ike life is a swirling
whirlpool dragging
you towards it.
I EAT AT ROCK-O's
Most of us, that never stops.
It doesn't even have to be all that good. Putting your meal in someone else's hands is a comfort.
There's a kind of magic there.
A magic I haven't felt in a while. Not since that dingy roadhouse. They hired me on a recited resume. The whole kitchen was mine.
That whirlpool sucking you down, it can come from the shit you love too. It's all kinds of messed up.
You get so focused on the thing you love to do, you forget what drew you in. You just want to create.
End up depriving yourself.
...with-onnnne-headlight
What's my moral? I dunno. Life sucks.
And this crepe is fucking excellent.
Rock? You in there?
I EAT AT ROCK-O's

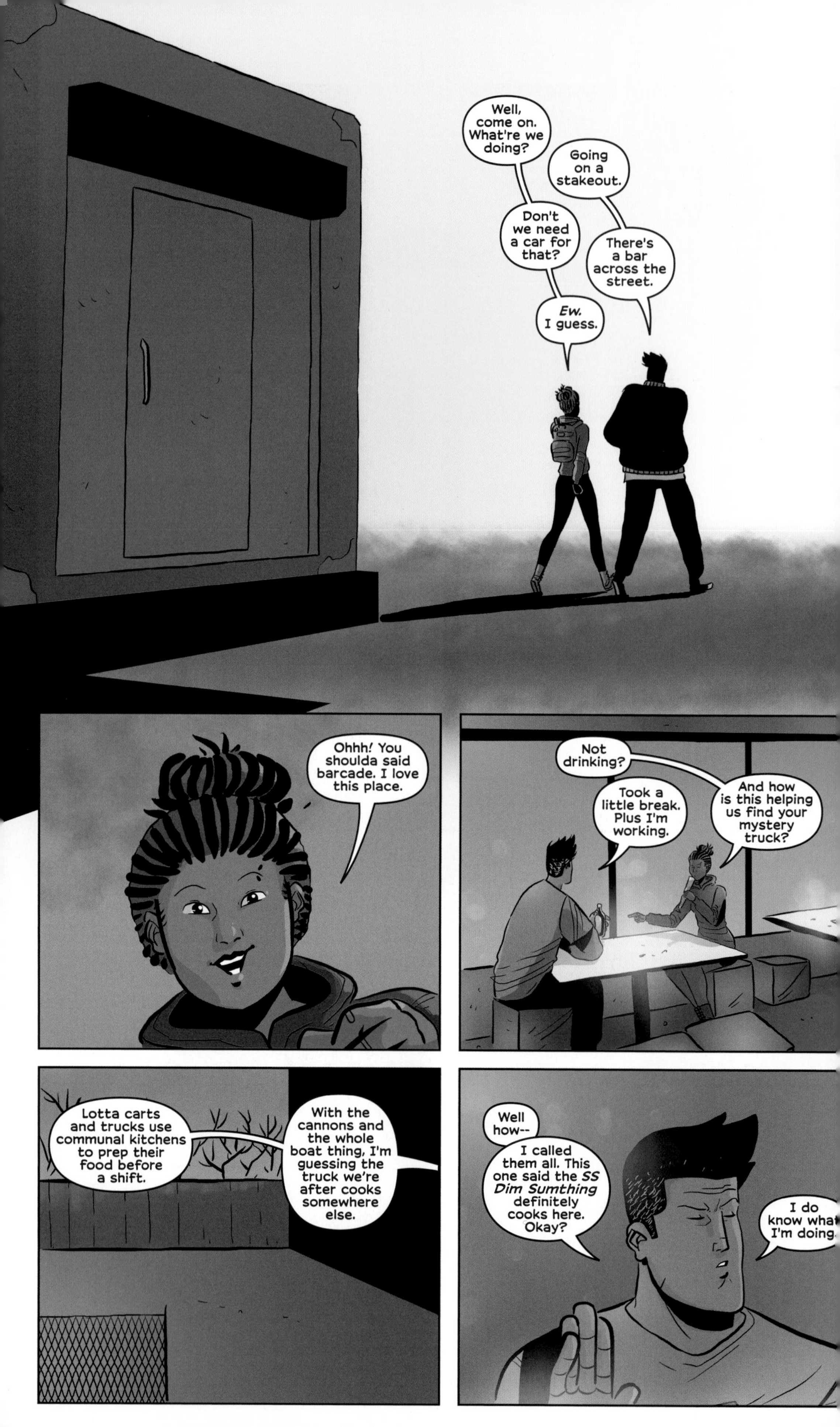
Well, come on. What're we doing?
Going on a stakeout.
Don't we need a car for that?
There's a bar across the street.
Ew. I guess.
Ohhh! You shoulda said barcade. I love this place.
Not drinking?
Took a little break. Plus I'm working.
And how is this helping us find your mystery truck?
Lotta carts and trucks use communal kitchens to prep their food before a shift.
With the cannons and the whole boat thing, I'm guessing the truck we're after cooks somewhere else.
Well how--
I called them all. This one said the *SS Dim Sumthing* definitely cooks here. Okay?

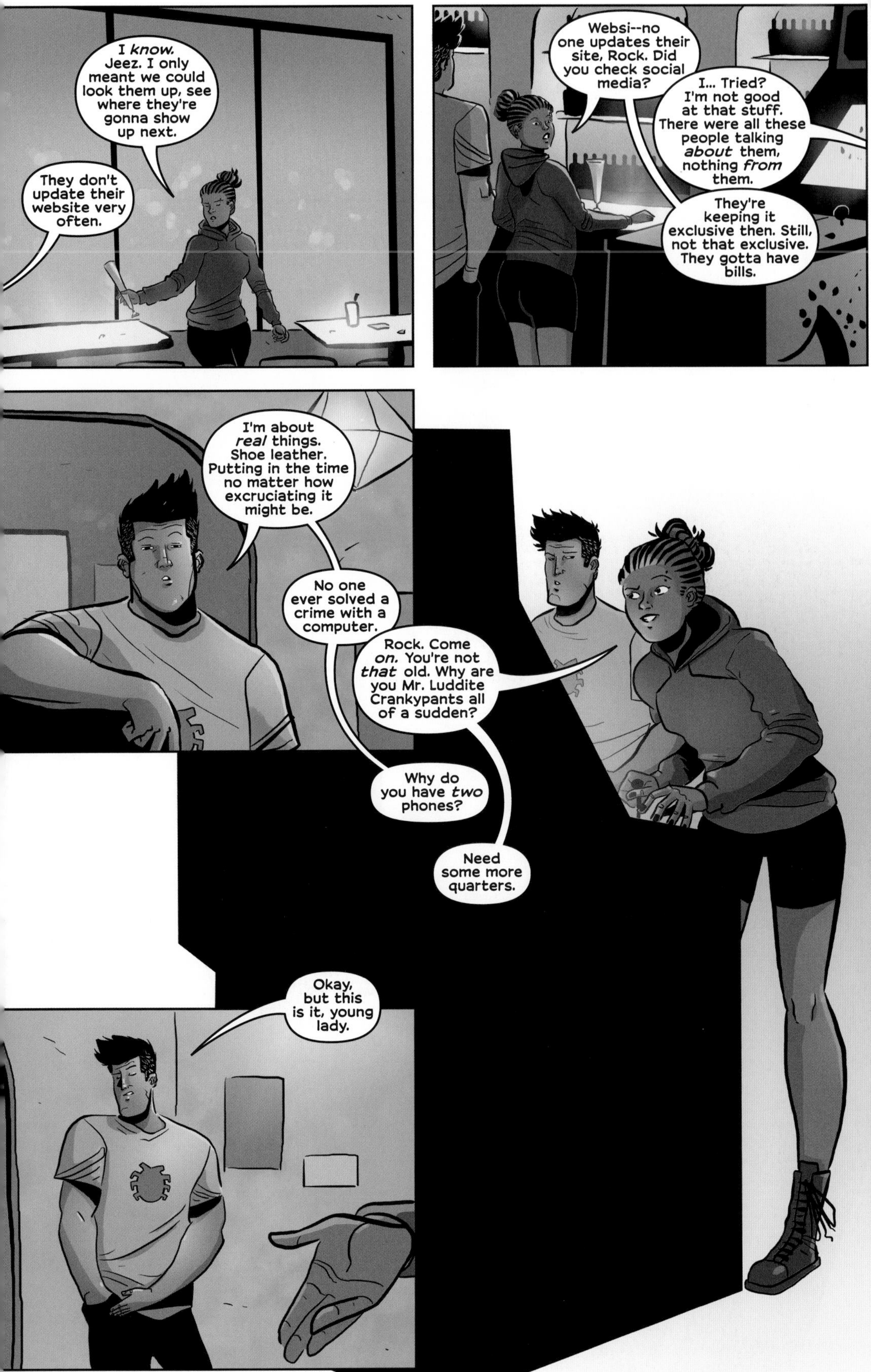
I know. Jeez. I only meant we could look them up, see where they're gonna show up next.
They don't update their website very often.
Websi--no one updates their site, Rock. Did you check social media?
I... Tried? I'm not good at that stuff. There were all these people talking about them, nothing from them.
They're keeping it exclusive then. Still, not that exclusive. They gotta have bills.
I'm about real things. Shoe leather. Putting in the time no matter how excruciating it might be.
No one ever solved a crime with a computer.
Rock. Come on. You're not that old. Why are you Mr. Luddite Crankypants all of a sudden?
Why do you have two phones?
Need some more quarters.
Okay, but this is it, young lady.

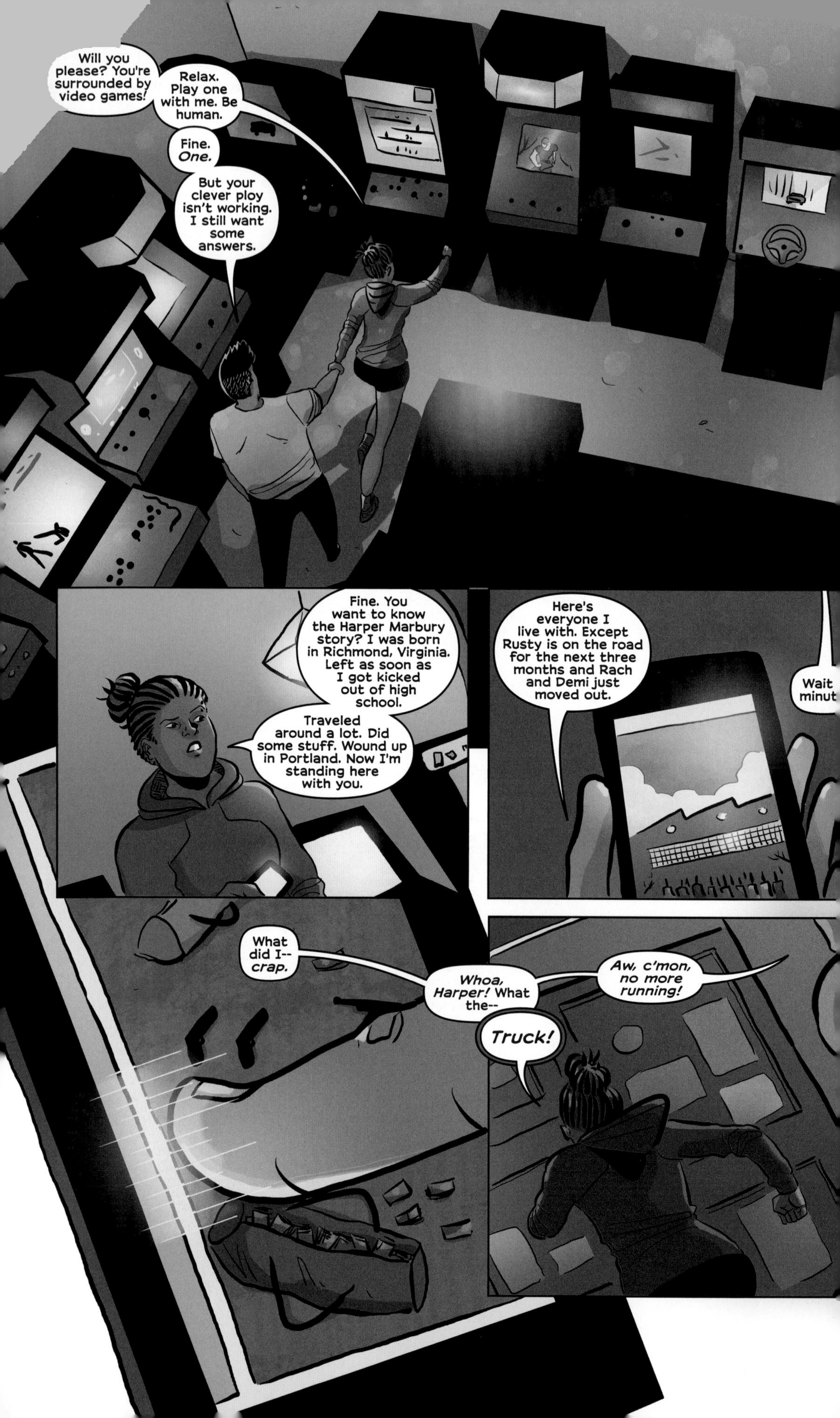
Will you please? You're surrounded by video games!
Relax. Play one with me. Be human.
Fine. One.
But your clever ploy isn't working. I still want some answers.
Fine. You want to know the Harper Marbury story? I was born in Richmond, Virginia. Left as soon as I got kicked out of high school.
Traveled around a lot. Did some stuff. Wound up in Portland. Now I'm standing here with you.
Here's everyone I live with. Except Rusty is on the road for the next three months and Rach and Demi just moved out.
Wait minut
What did I-- crap.
Whoa, Harper! What the--
Aw, c'mon, no more running!
Truck!

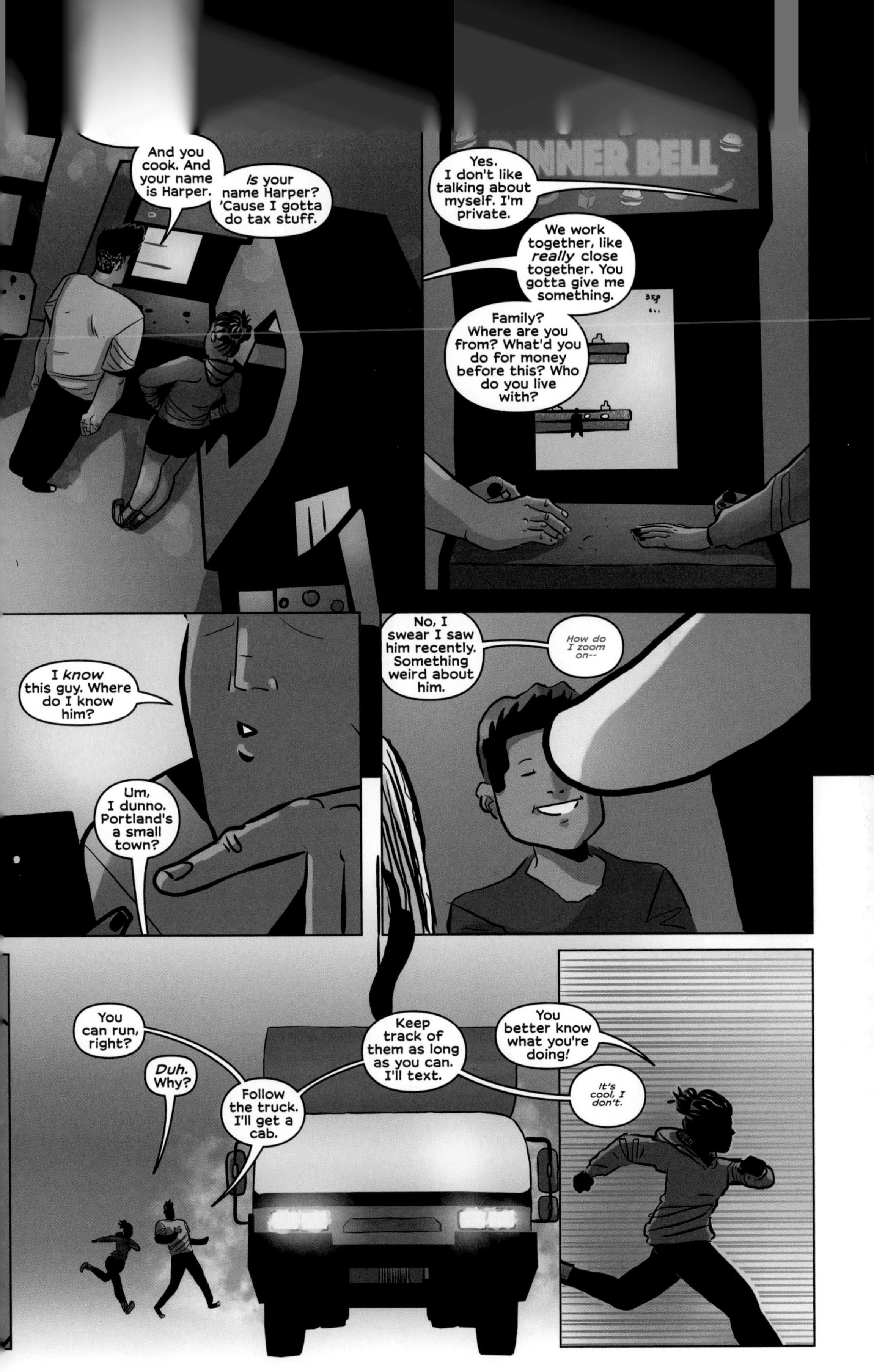

And you cook. And your name is Harper.
Is your name Harper? 'Cause I gotta do tax stuff.
Yes. I don't like talking about myself. I'm private.
We work together, like *really* close together. You gotta give me something.
Family? Where are you from? What'd you do for money before this? Who do you live with?
I *know* this guy. Where do I know him?
Um, I dunno. Portland's a small town?
No, I swear I saw him recently. Something weird about him.
How do I zoom on--
You can run, right?
Duh. Why?
Follow the truck. I'll get a cab.
Keep track of them as long as you can. I'll text.
You better know what you're doing!
It's cool, I don't.

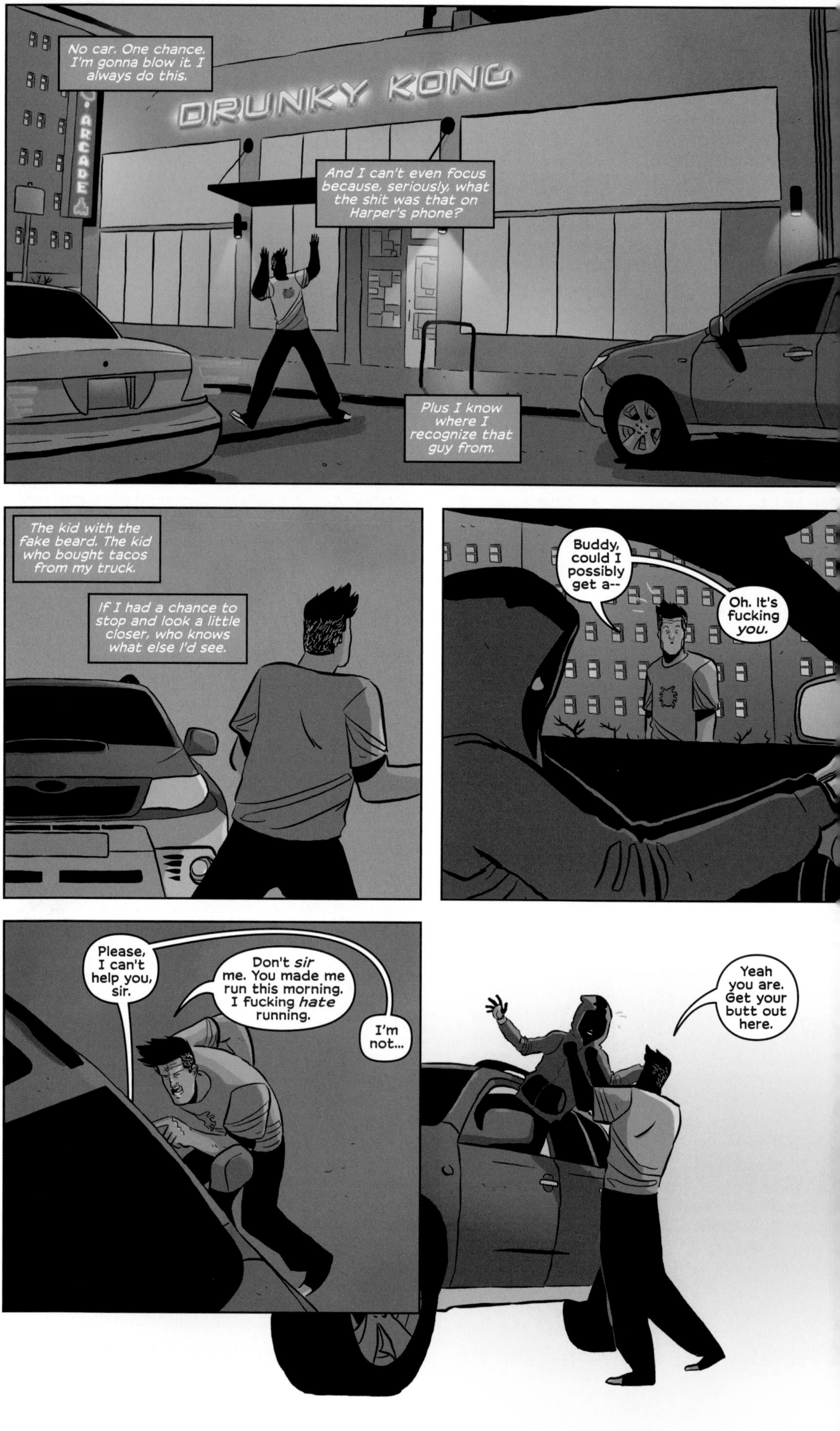
No car. One chance. I'm gonna blow it. I always do this.
DRUNKY KONG
ARCADE
And I can't even focus because, seriously, what the shit was that on Harper's phone?
Plus I know where I recognize that guy from.
The kid with the fake beard. The kid who bought tacos from my truck.
If I had a chance to stop and look a little closer, who knows what else I'd see.
Buddy, could I possibly get a--
Oh. It's fucking *you*.
Please, I can't help you, sir.
Don't *sir* me. You made me run this morning. I fucking *hate* running.
I'm not...
Yeah you are. Get your butt out here.

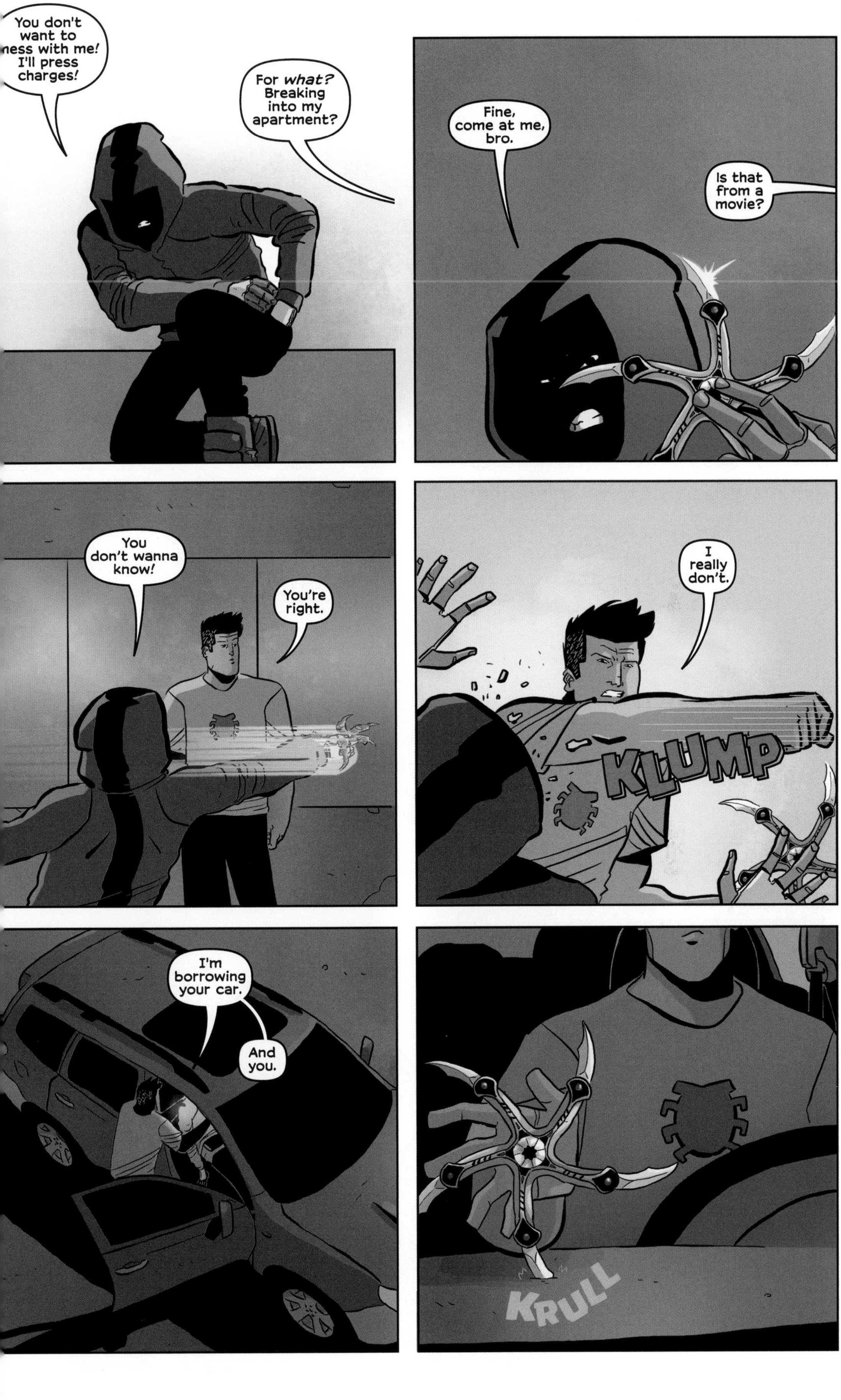
You don't want to ness with me! I'll press charges!
For what? Breaking into my apartment?
Fine, come at me, bro.
Is that from a movie?
You don't wanna know!
You're right.
I really don't.
KLUMP
I'm borrowing your car.
And you.
KRULL

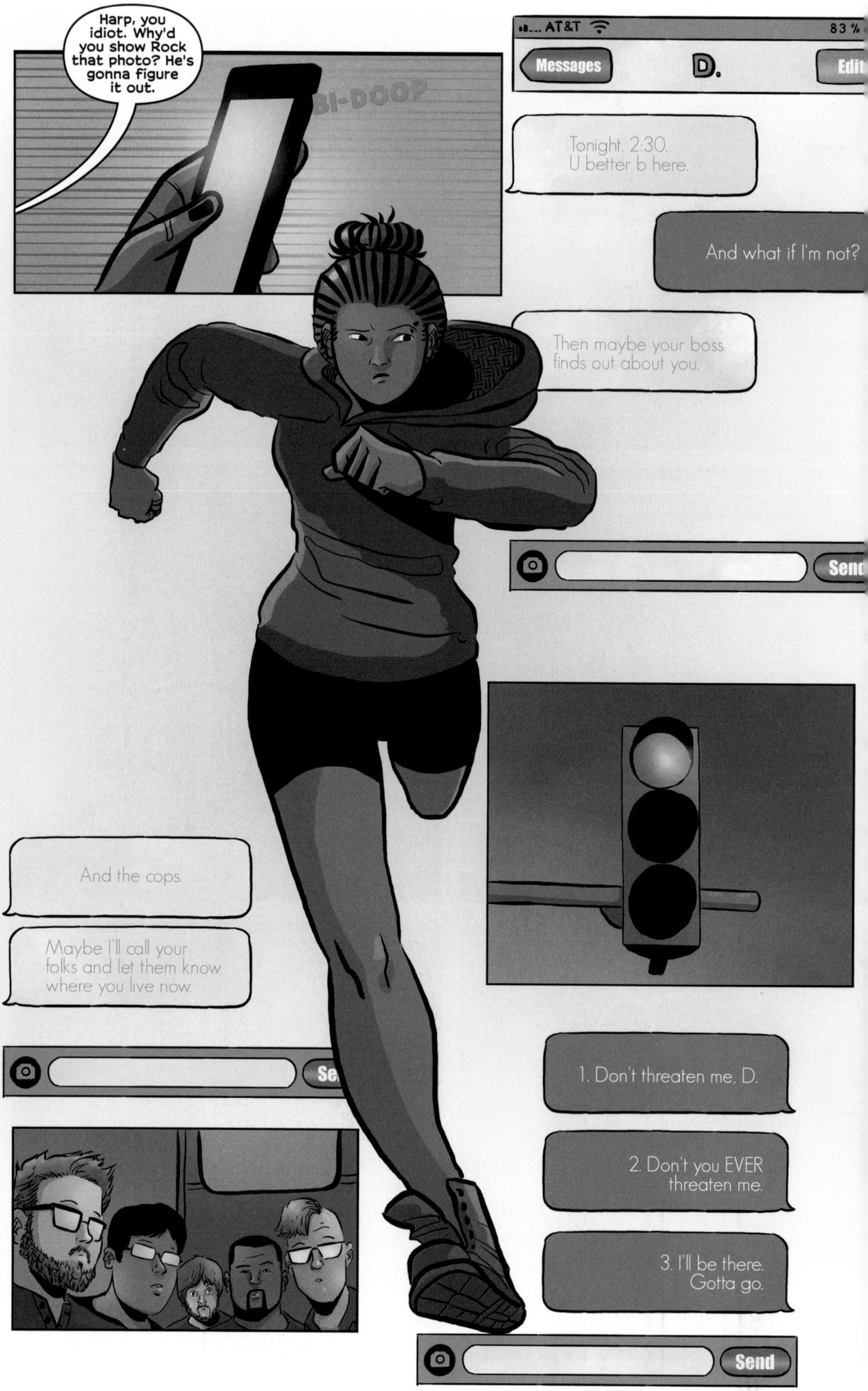
Harp, you idiot. Why'd you show Rock that photo? He's gonna figure it out.
BI-DOOP
AT&T
83 %
Messages
D.
Edit
Tonight. 2:30.
U better b here.
And what if I'm not?
Then maybe your boss finds out about you.
Send
And the cops.
Maybe I'll call your folks and let them know where you live now.
1. Don't threaten me, D.
2. Don't you EVER threaten me.
3. I'll be there. Gotta go.
Send

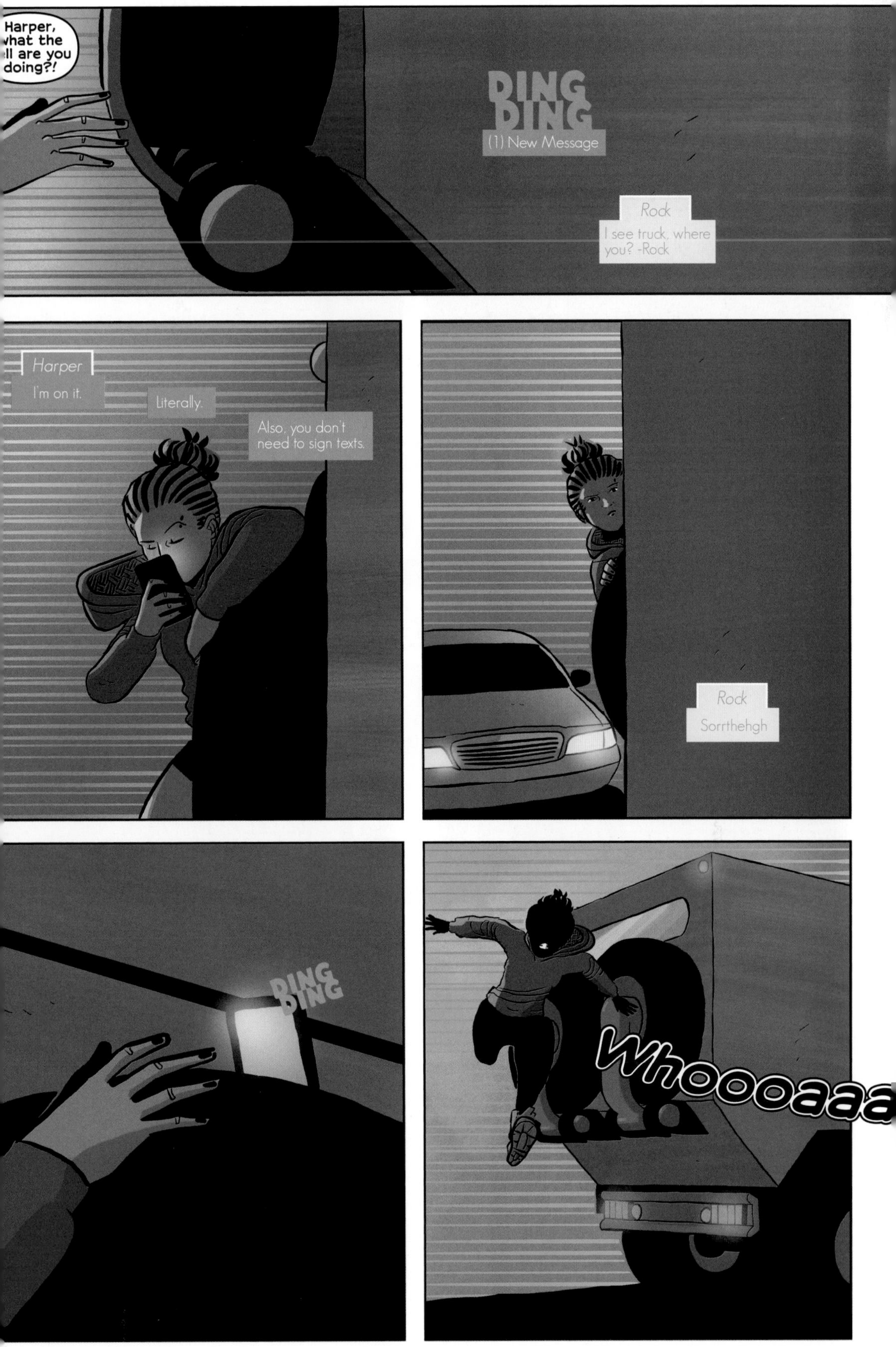

Harper, what the ell are you doing?!
DING DING
(1) New Message
Rock
I see truck, where you? -Rock
Harper
I'm on it.
Literally.
Also, you don't need to sign texts.
Rock
Sorrthehgh
DING DING
Whoooaaa

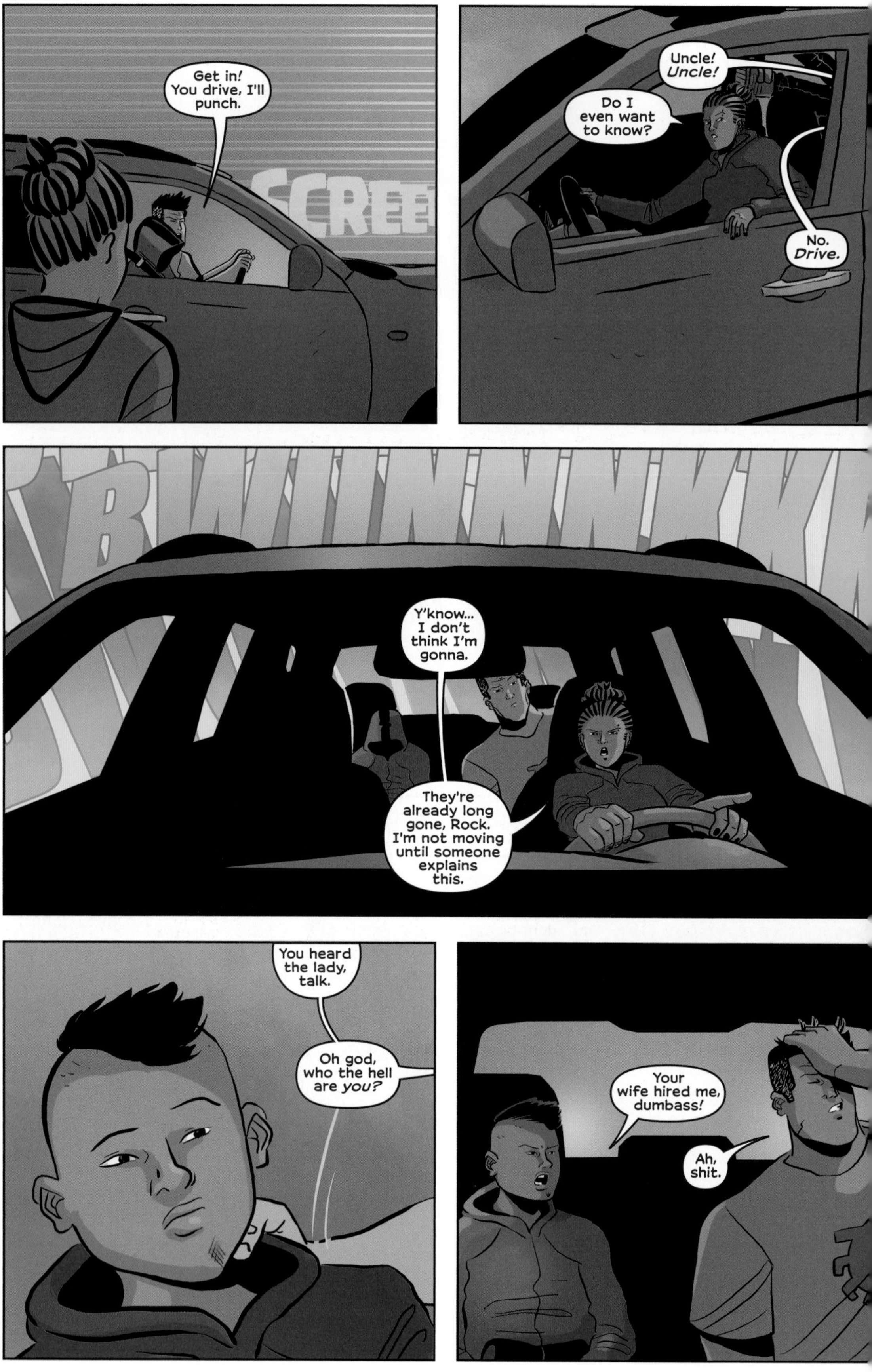
Get in! You drive, I'll punch.
SCREE
Uncle! *Uncle!*
Do I even want to know?
No. *Drive.*
Y'know... I don't think I'm gonna.
They're already long gone, Rock. I'm not moving until someone explains this.
You heard the lady, talk.
Oh god, who the hell are *you?*
Your wife hired me, dumbass!
Ah, shit.

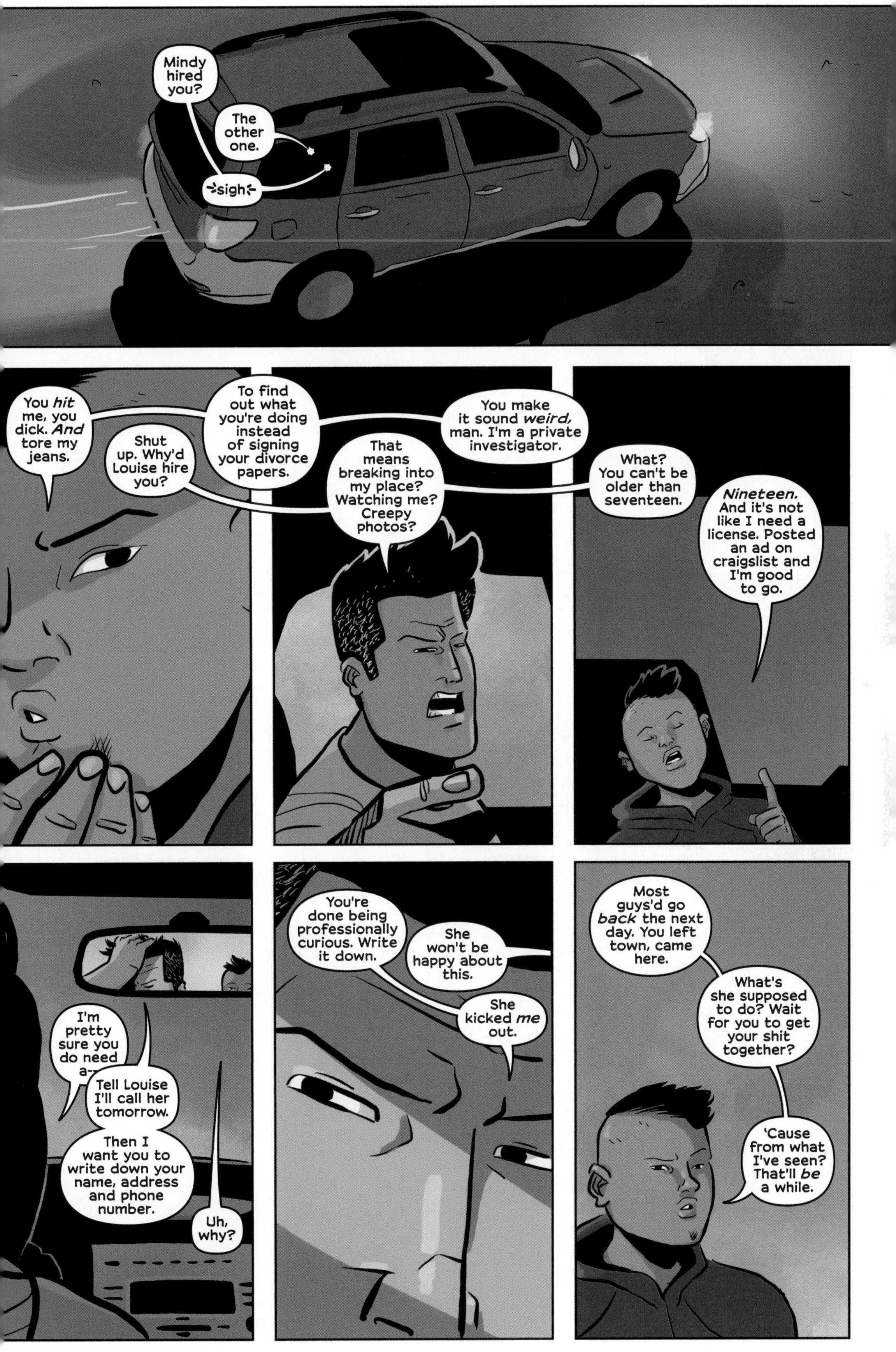
Mindy hired you?
The other one.
sigh
You *hit* me, you dick. *And* tore my jeans.
To find out what you're doing instead of signing your divorce papers.
Shut up. Why'd Louise hire you?
You make it sound *weird*, man. I'm a private investigator.
That means breaking into my place? Watching me? Creepy photos?
What? You can't be older than seventeen.
Nineteen. And it's not like I need a license. Posted an ad on craigslist and I'm good to go.
I'm pretty sure you do need a--
Tell Louise I'll call her tomorrow.
Then I want you to write down your name, address and phone number.
Uh, why?
You're done being professionally curious. Write it down.
She won't be happy about this.
She kicked *me* out.
Most guys'd go *back* the next day. You left town, came here.
What's she supposed to do? Wait for you to get your shit together?
'Cause from what I've seen? That'll *be* a while.

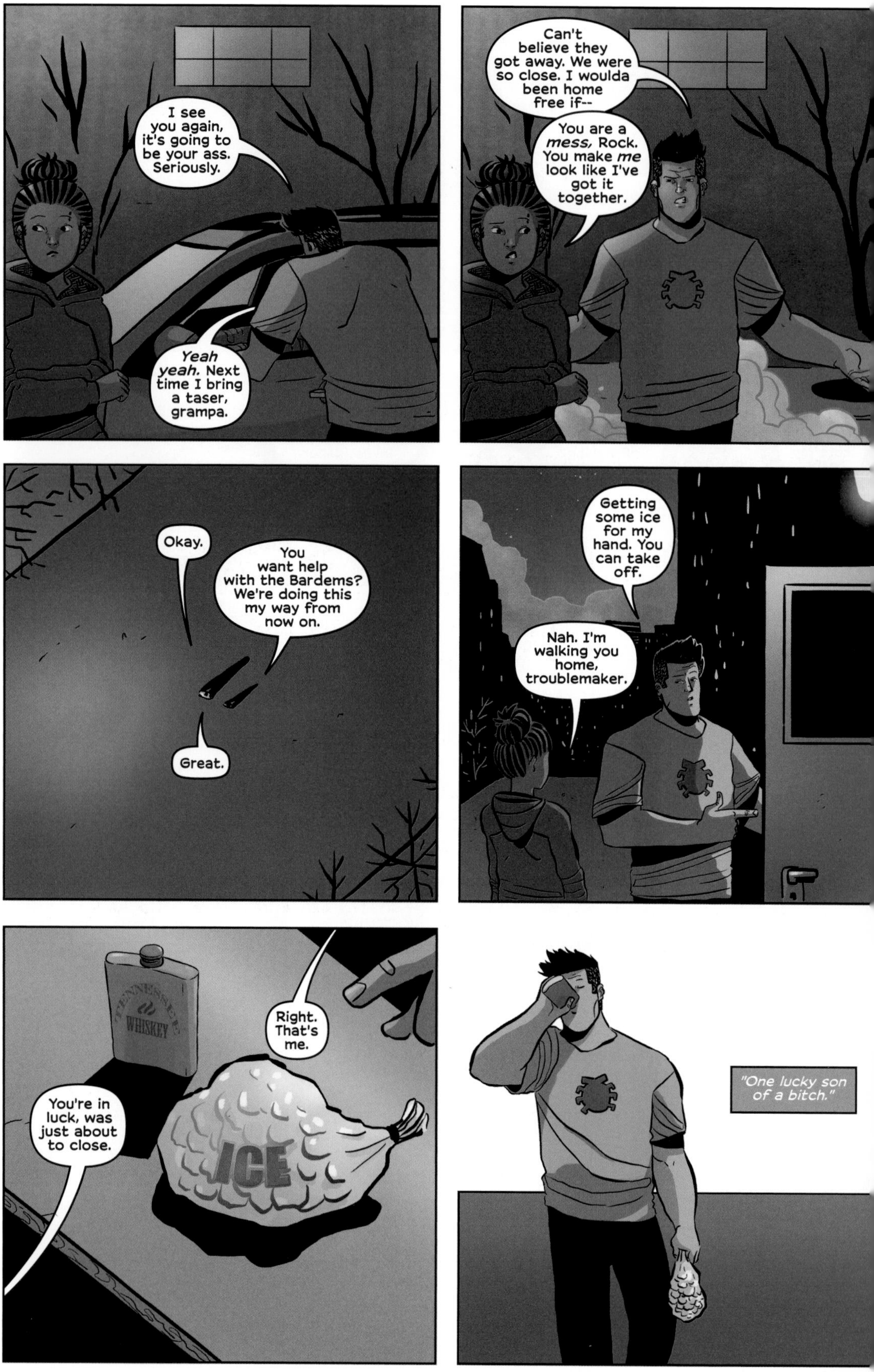
I see you again, it's going to be your ass. Seriously.
Yeah yeah. Next time I bring a taser, grampa.
Can't believe they got away. We were so close. I woulda been home free if--
You are a *mess,* Rock. You make *me* look like I've got it together.
Okay.
You want help with the Bardems? We're doing this my way from now on.
Great.
Getting some ice for my hand. You can take off.
Nah. I'm walking you home, troublemaker.
TENNESSEE WHISKEY
Right. That's me.
You're in luck, was just about to close.
ICE
"One lucky son of a bitch."

My Standard Split Apple Breakfast

preparation - about 10 mins.
cook time - 15ish mins.

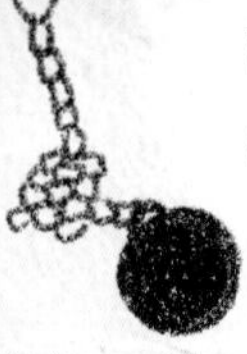

by Harper Marbury, to prove to Rock that I can use proper recipes and measurements and all that other boring stuff for cheaters

(this recipe makes enough to serve around 6 - for Split Apple-sized crowds, I quadruple it all)

INGREDIENTS (Don't ask where I get them)

- 14 ounces medium tofu - drained and crumbled
  (we make our own in a bathtub in the kitchen. lotta science projects going on around here. but i guess you could buy it from a store?)
- 1 medium/larger red bell pepper - diced
- 1 small carrot - diced
  (personally i am not a carrot fan but i grudgingly acknowledge they're good for you, plus they add the right color to the dish. you could sub in orange bell peppers but those are crazy hard to find when dumpster diving for some reason)
- 4 green onions - chopped
- 1 clove garlic - minced
- ½ tsp. ground cumin
- ¼ tsp. ground turmeric
- ½ tsp. hot sauce - dealer's choice
  (slightly related, but a guy who lives here sometimes who calls himself J-Zazz, he has this sauce he calls "Illusion of Control" that's so hot it makes you hallucinate for 6 hours straight. it might not technically be legal. or hot sauce.)

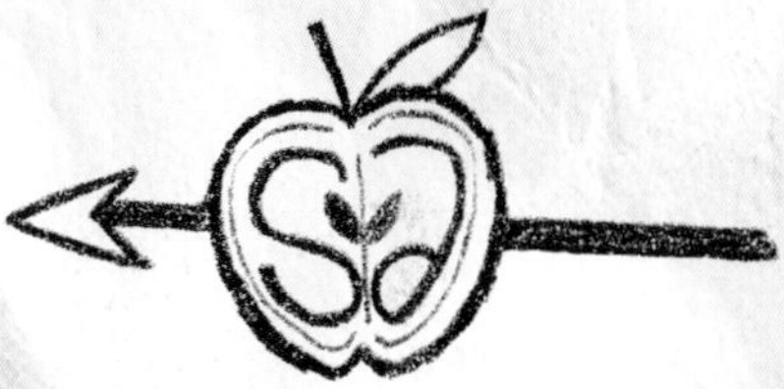

- 2 Tbsp. chopped cilantro
  (you will get pushback from those mutants who think cilantro tastes like soap, so maybe skip it altogether? Or stick to the purity of your vision. you choose.)

Get your butt outta bed, get annoyed, get cooking

- Okay, so, ideally you've done all that chopping and mincing and stuff in advance. And in a perfect world, you have your tofu ready to use. It's Orlando's job to tend to the tofu tub, but sometimes he gets distracted and you're outta luck.
- Heat a large skillet over medium. Use oil or cooking spray if you care about your skillet. This one belongs to an ex-roommate, so I don't give a shit about it.
- Add the bell pepper and carrot to the skillet, cooking them for about 7 minutes or until they get tender. The smell of food cooking will cause most of the Split Apple residents to begin waking up. You don't have a long time now before they come looking for the source of it.
- Stir in the green onions and garlic. Add the cumin and tumeric, i like to drizzle it from above in a spiral. Cook it for another minute.
- Now add the tofu and hot sauce to the mix. Everyone has started forming lines for the bathroom, you better hurry.
- Cook it all for 5 minutes, or until everything is heated all the way thru and the liquidy stuff has cooked off. Now stir in the cilantro and dump the finished product in a big glass baking dish or a giant bowl or whatever is handy and clean. Back away as the jackals move in on their prey.

  Serve with salsa, if you have it. Or don't! Trust me, they'll only notice if you don't, and they won't thank you if you do. Dicks.

4: COOKING WITH GAS

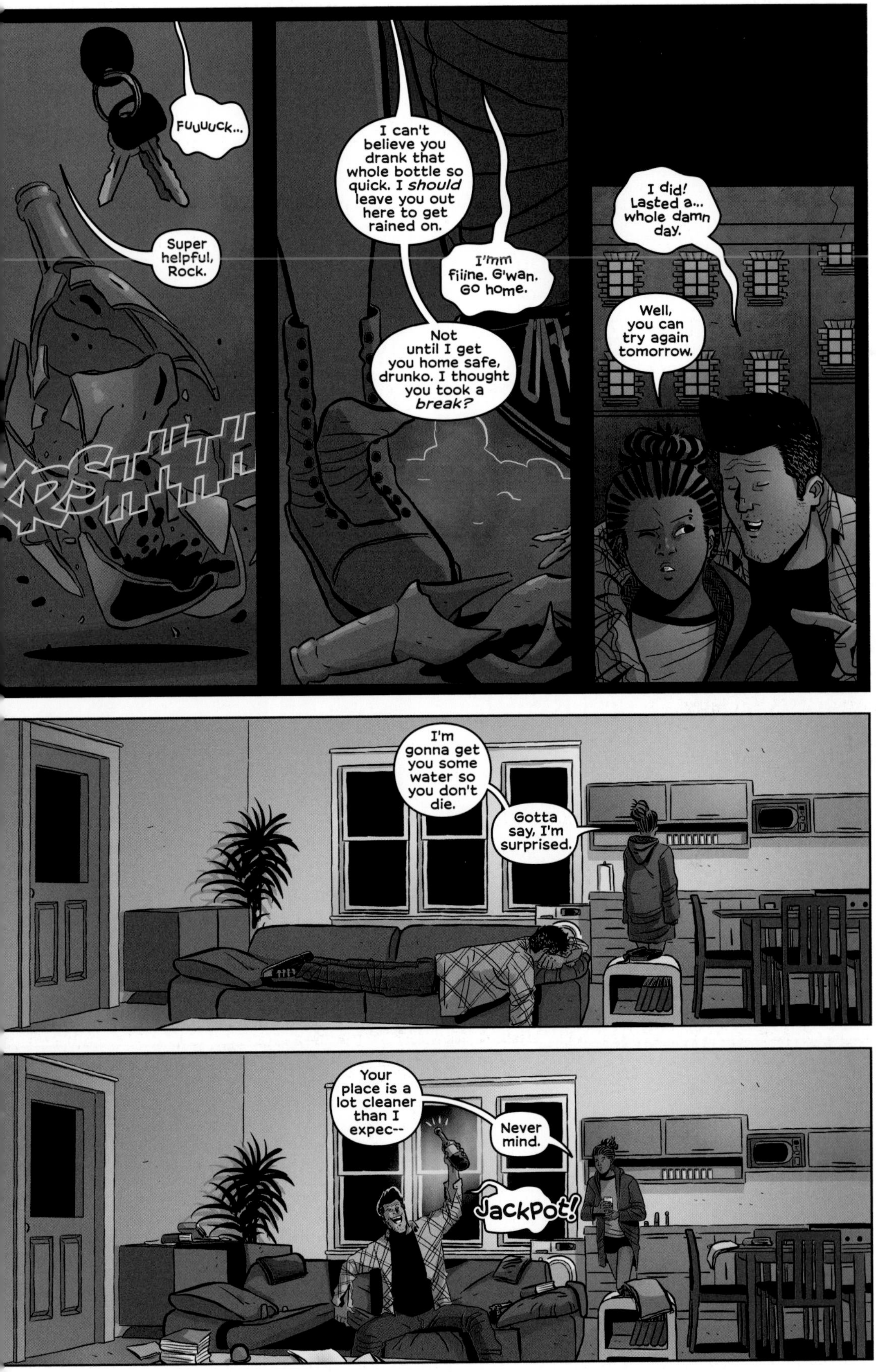
FUUUUCK...
Super helpful, Rock.
KRSHHHH
I can't believe you drank that whole bottle so quick. I *should* leave you out here to get rained on.
I'mm fiiine. G'wan. Go home.
Not until I get you home safe, drunko. I thought you took a *break?*
I did! Lasted a... whole damn day.
Well, you can try again tomorrow.
I'm gonna get you some water so you don't die.
Gotta say, I'm surprised.
Your place is a lot cleaner than I expec--
Never mind.
JACKPOT!

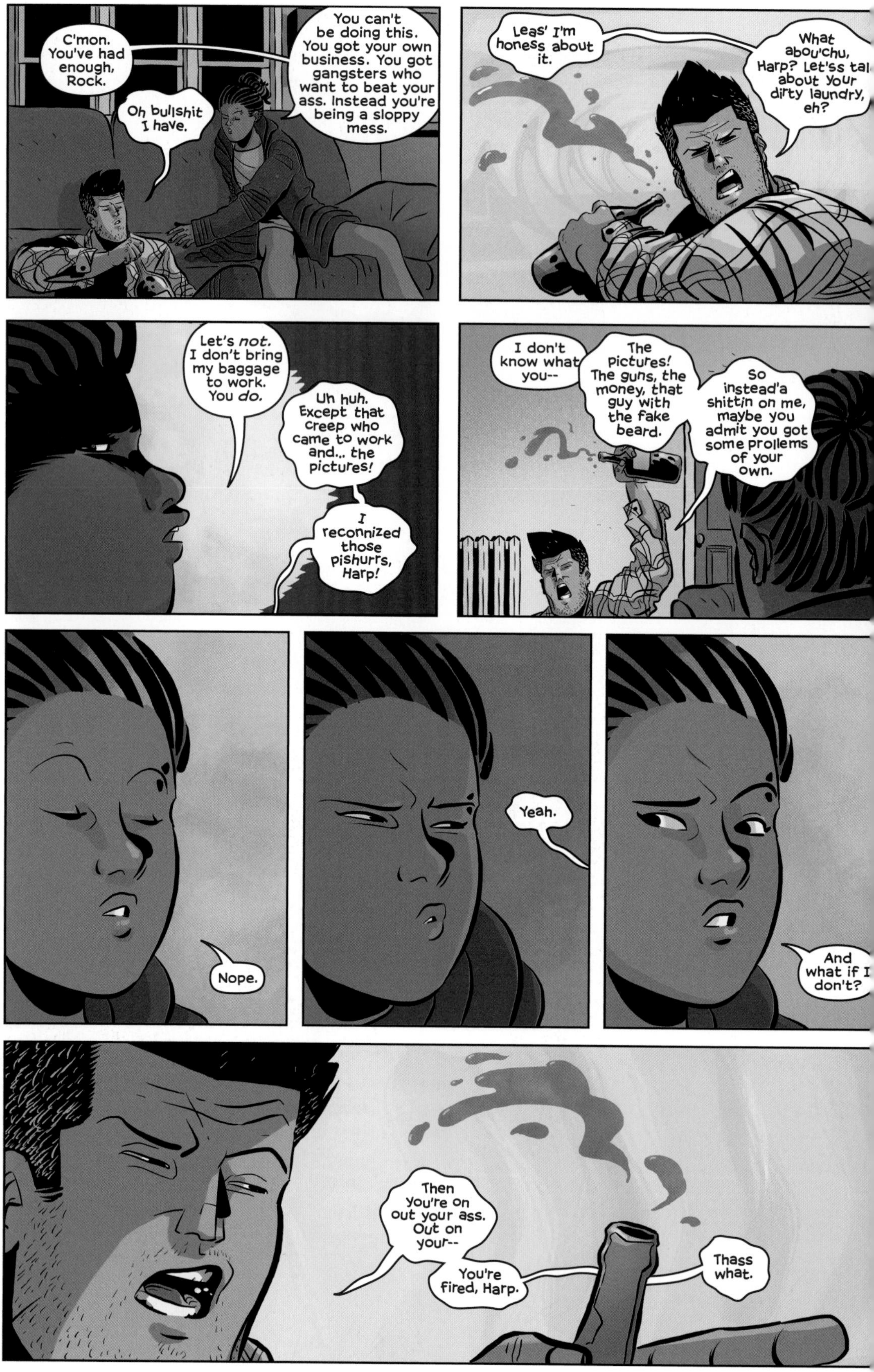
C'mon. You've had enough, Rock.
Oh bullshit I have.
You can't be doing this. You got your own business. You got gangsters who want to beat your ass. Instead you're being a sloppy mess.
Leas' I'm honess about it.
What abou'chu, Harp? Let'ss tal about your dirty laundry, eh?
Let's *not.* I don't bring my baggage to work. You *do.*
Uh huh. Except that creep who came to work and... the pictures!
I reconnized those pishurrs, Harp!
I don't know what you--
The pictures! The guns, the money, that guy with the fake beard.
So instead'a shittin on me, maybe you admit you got some prollems of your own.
Nope.
Yeah.
And what if I don't?
Then you're on out your ass. Out on your--
You're fired, Harp.
Thass what.

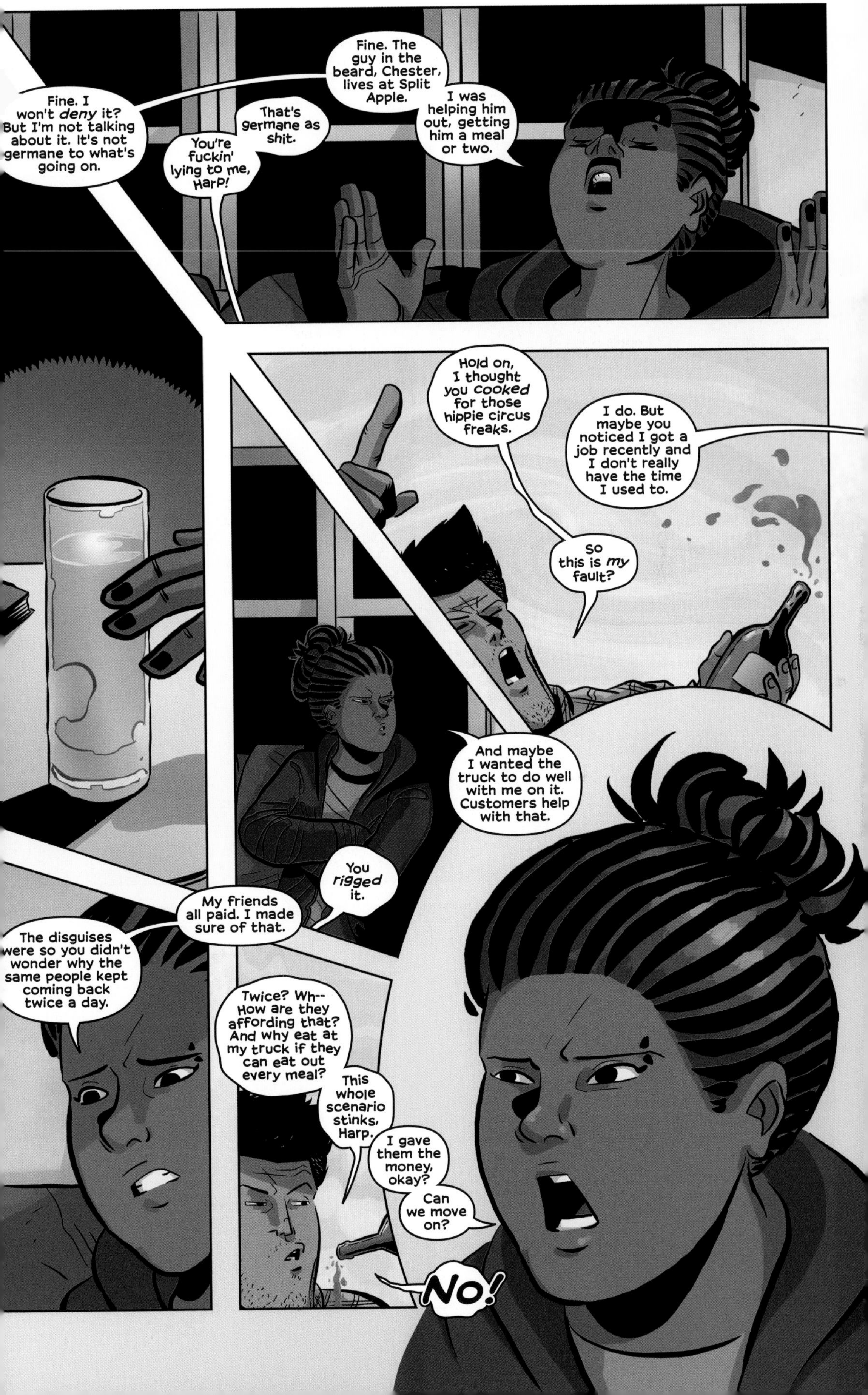
Fine. I won't *deny* it? But I'm not talking about it. It's not germane to what's going on.
Fine. The guy in the beard, Chester, lives at Split Apple.
I was helping him out, getting him a meal or two.
That's germane as shit.
You're fuckin' lying to me, Harp!
Hold on, I thought you *cooked* for those hippie circus freaks.
I do. But maybe you noticed I got a job recently and I don't really have the time I used to.
So this is *my* fault?
And maybe I wanted the truck to do well with me on it. Customers help with that.
You *rigged* it.
My friends all paid. I made sure of that.
The disguises were so you didn't wonder why the same people kept coming back twice a day.
Twice? Wh-- How are they affording that? And why eat at my truck if they can eat out every meal?
This whole scenario stinks, Harp.
I gave them the money, okay?
Can we move on?
No!

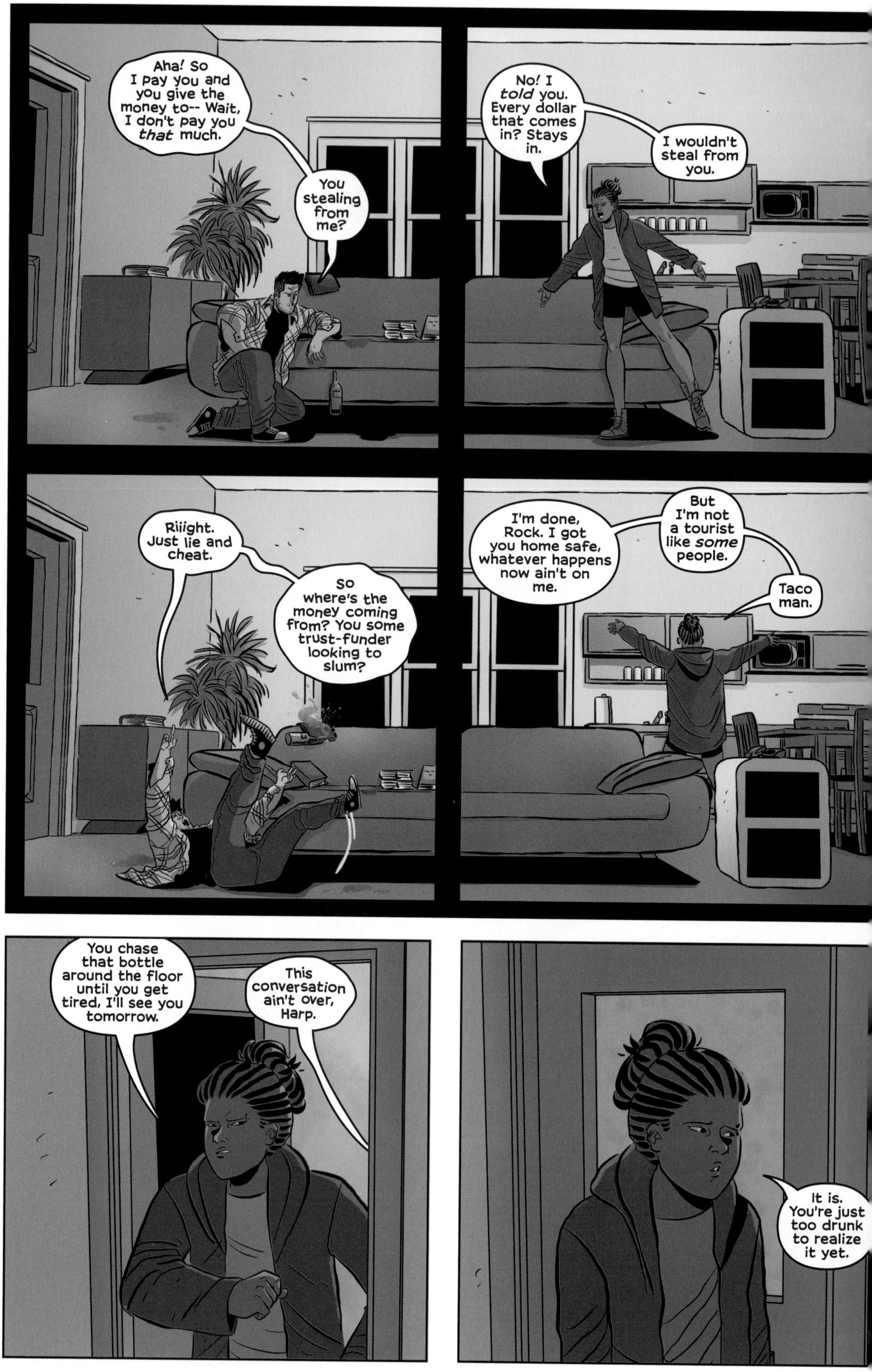
Aha! So I pay you and you give the money to-- Wait, I don't pay you *that* much.
You stealing from me?
No! I *told* you. Every dollar that comes in? Stays in.
I wouldn't steal from you.
Riiight. Just lie and cheat.
So where's the money coming from? You some trust-funder looking to slum?
I'm done, Rock. I got you home safe, whatever happens now ain't on me.
But I'm not a tourist like *some* people.
Taco man.
You chase that bottle around the floor until you get tired, I'll see you tomorrow.
This conversation ain't over, Harp.
It is. You're just too drunk to realize it yet.

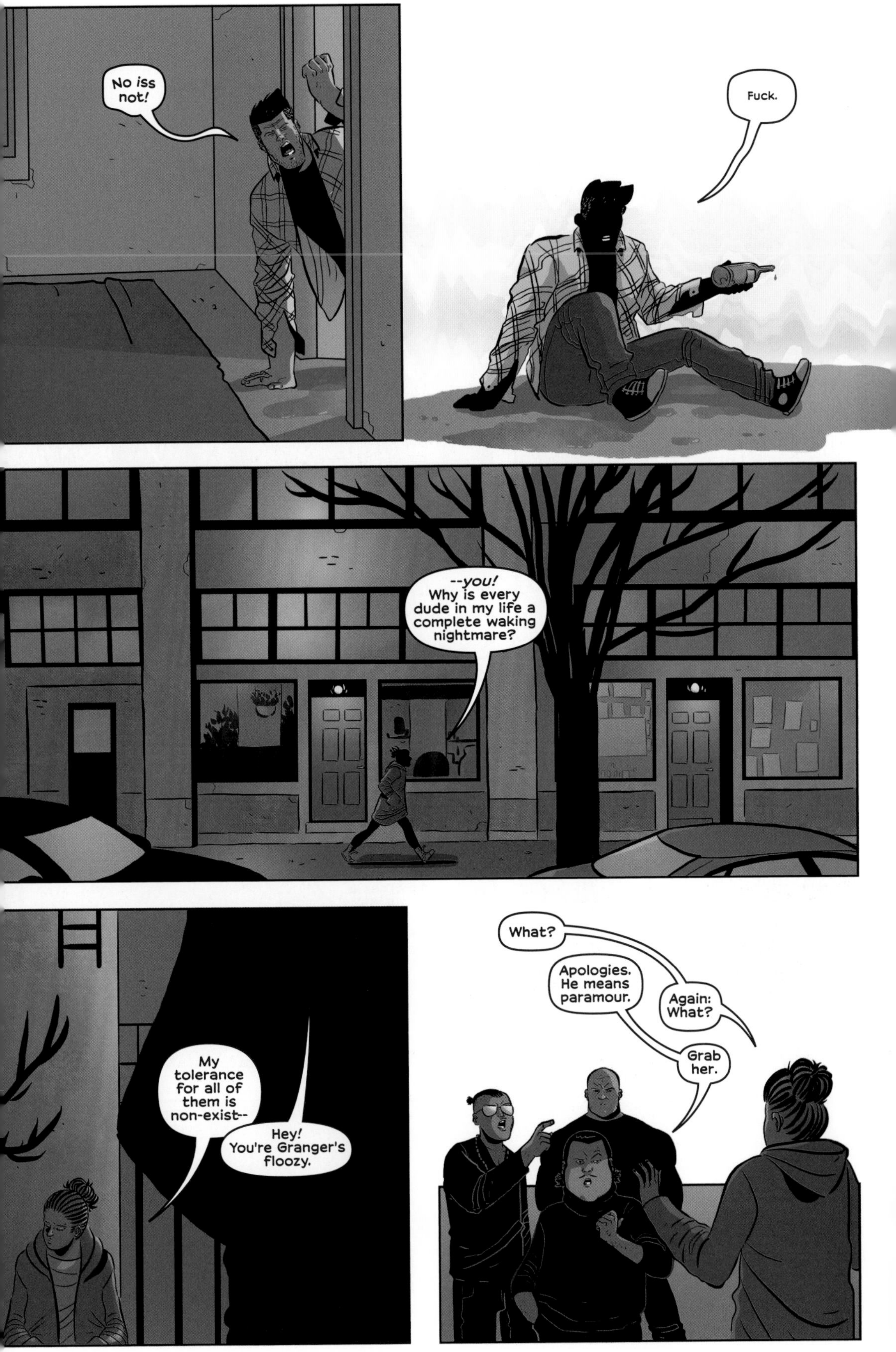
No iss not!
Fuck.
--you! Why is every dude in my life a complete waking nightmare?
My tolerance for all of them is non-exist--
Hey! You're Granger's floozy.
What?
Apologies. He means paramour.
Again: What?
Grab her.

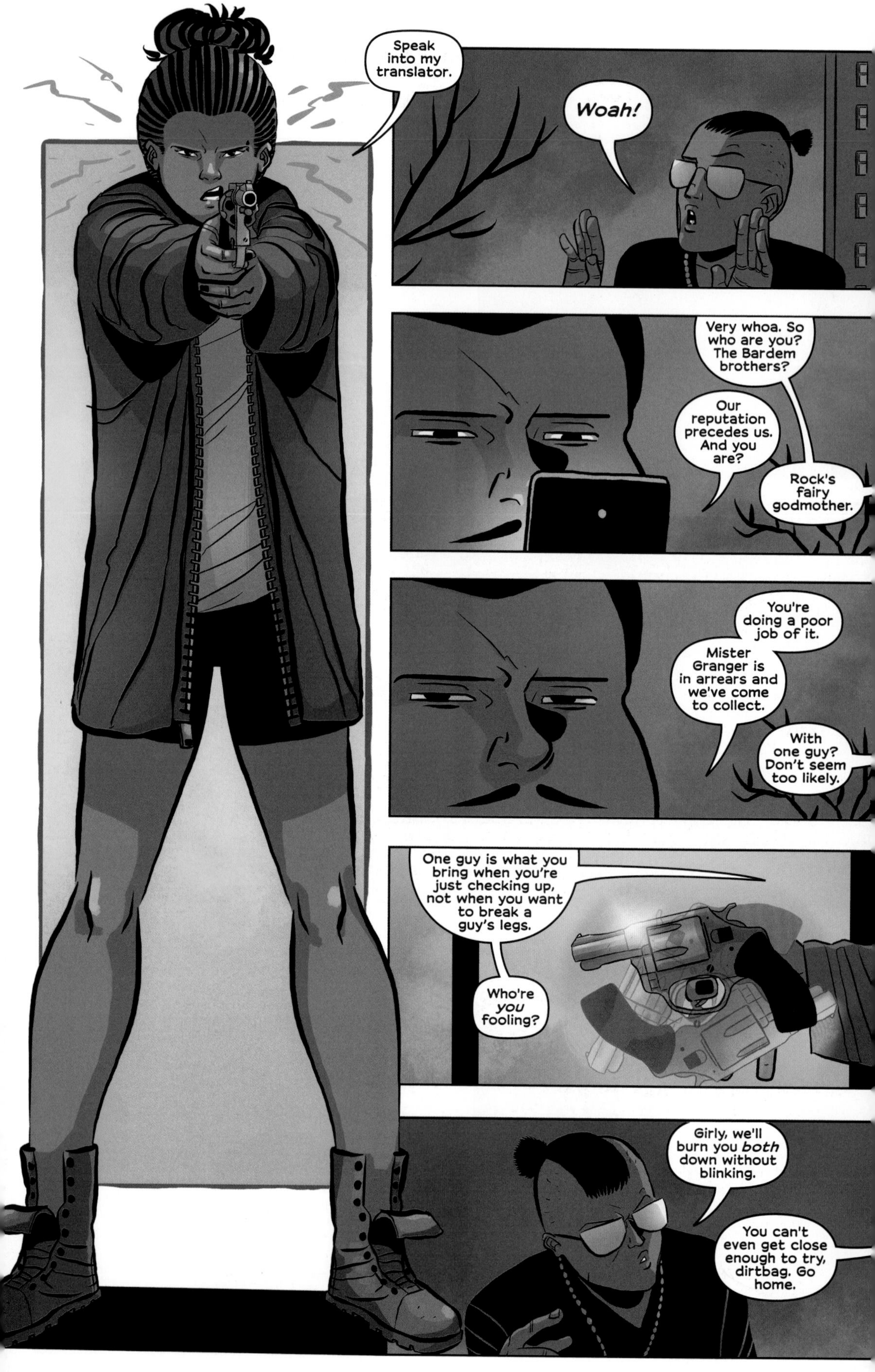
Speak into my translator.
Woah!
Very whoa. So who are you? The Bardem brothers?
Our reputation precedes us. And you are?
Rock's fairy godmother.
You're doing a poor job of it.
Mister Granger is in arrears and we've come to collect.
With one guy? Don't seem too likely.
One guy is what you bring when you're just checking up, not when you want to break a guy's legs.
Who're *you* fooling?
Girly, we'll burn you *both* down without blinking.
You can't even get close enough to try, dirtbag. Go home.

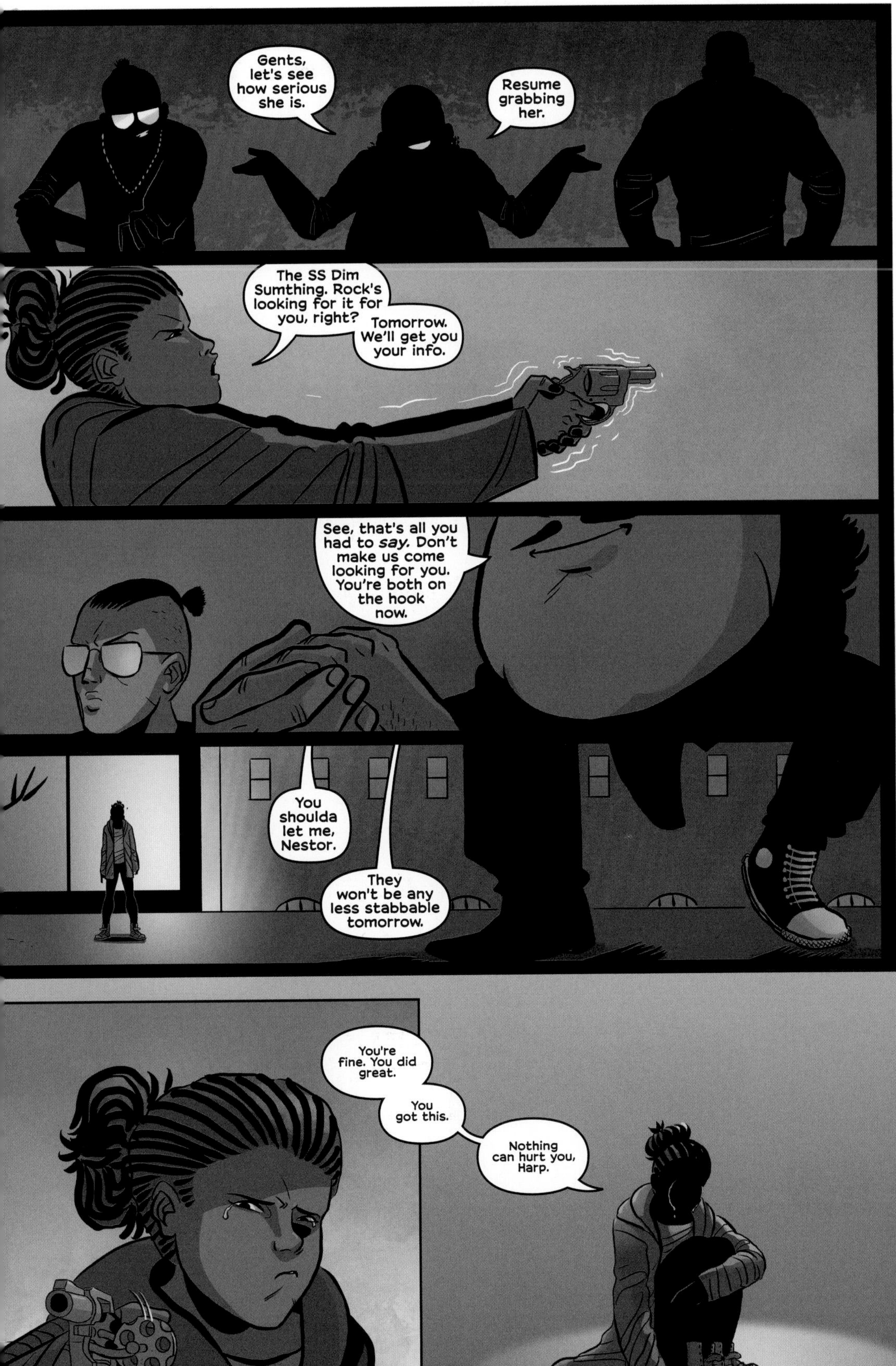
Gents, let's see how serious she is.
Resume grabbing her.
The SS Dim Sumthing. Rock's looking for it for you, right?
Tomorrow. We'll get you your info.
See, that's all you had to *say.* Don't make us come looking for you. You're both on the hook now.
You shoulda let me, Nestor.
They won't be any less stabbable tomorrow.
You're fine. You did great.
You got this.
Nothing can hurt you, Harp.

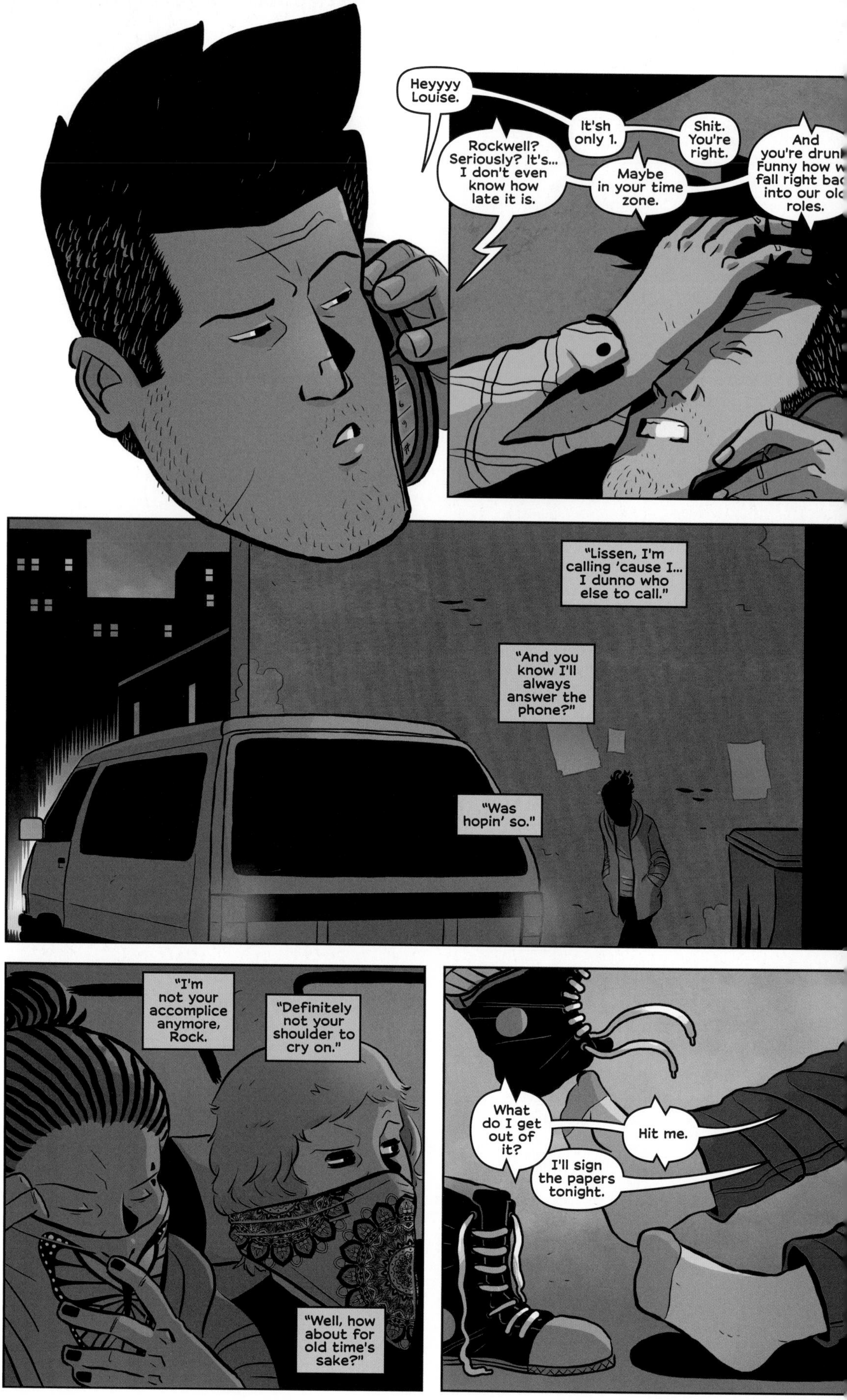
Heyyyy Louise.
Rockwell? Seriously? It's... I don't even know how late it is.
It'sh only 1.
Maybe in your time zone.
Shit. You're right.
And you're drun Funny how w fall right bac into our old roles.
"Lissen, I'm calling 'cause I... I dunno who else to call."
"And you know I'll always answer the phone?"
"Was hopin' so."
"I'm not your accomplice anymore, Rock.
"Definitely not your shoulder to cry on."
"Well, how about for old time's sake?"
What do I get out of it?
Hit me.
I'll sign the papers tonight.

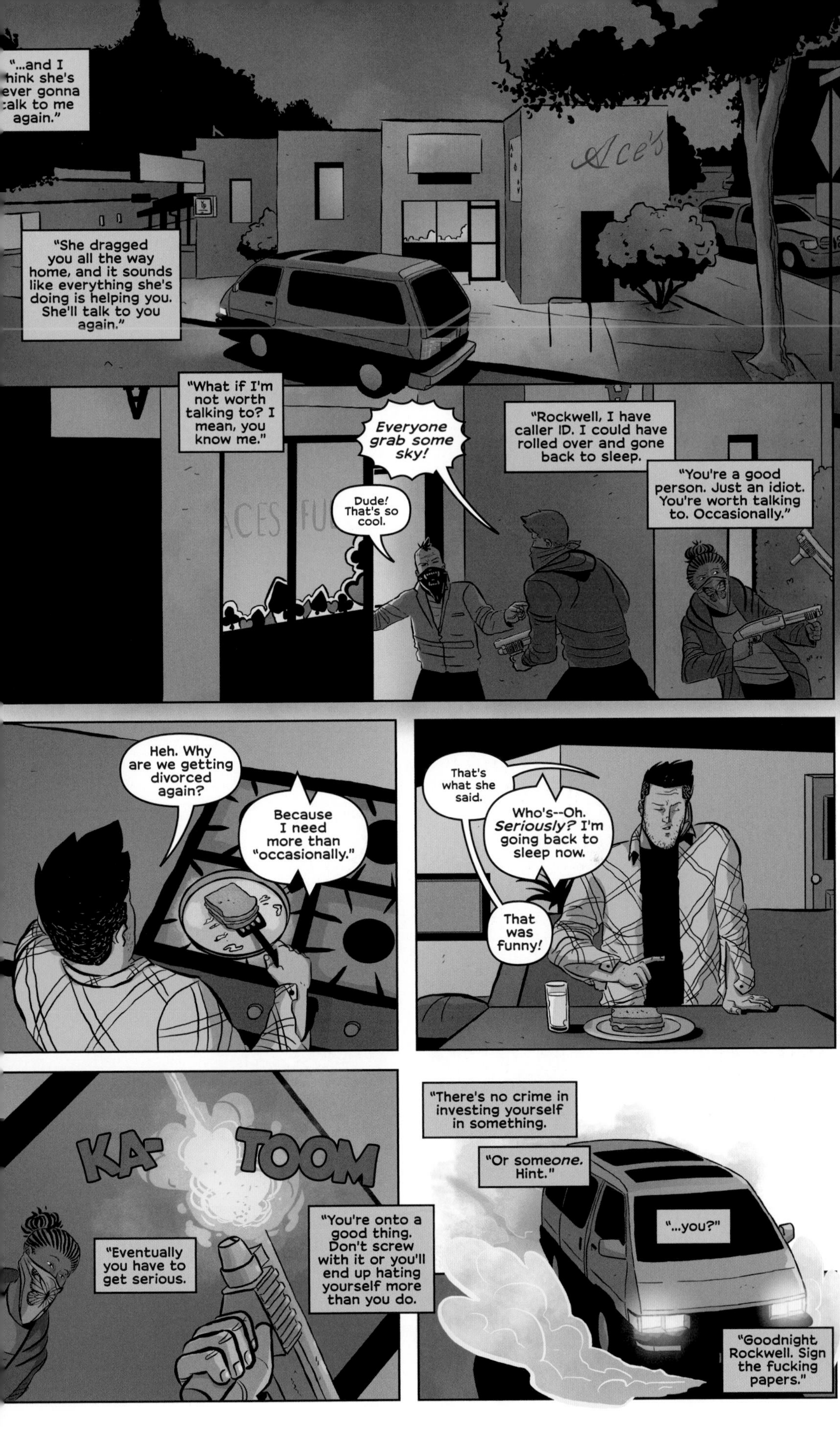
"...and I
hink she's
ever gonna
talk to me
again."
"She dragged you all the way home, and it sounds like everything she's doing is helping you. She'll talk to you again."
Ace's
"What if I'm not worth talking to? I mean, you know me."
Everyone grab some sky!
Dude! That's so cool.
"Rockwell, I have caller ID. I could have rolled over and gone back to sleep.
"You're a good person. Just an idiot. You're worth talking to. Occasionally."
Heh. Why are we getting divorced again?
Because I need more than "occasionally."
That's what she said.
Who's--Oh. Seriously? I'm going back to sleep now.
That was funny!
KA-TOOM
"Eventually you have to get serious.
"You're onto a good thing. Don't screw with it or you'll end up hating yourself more than you do.
"There's no crime in investing yourself in something.
"Or someone. Hint."
"...you?"
"Goodnight Rockwell. Sign the fucking papers."

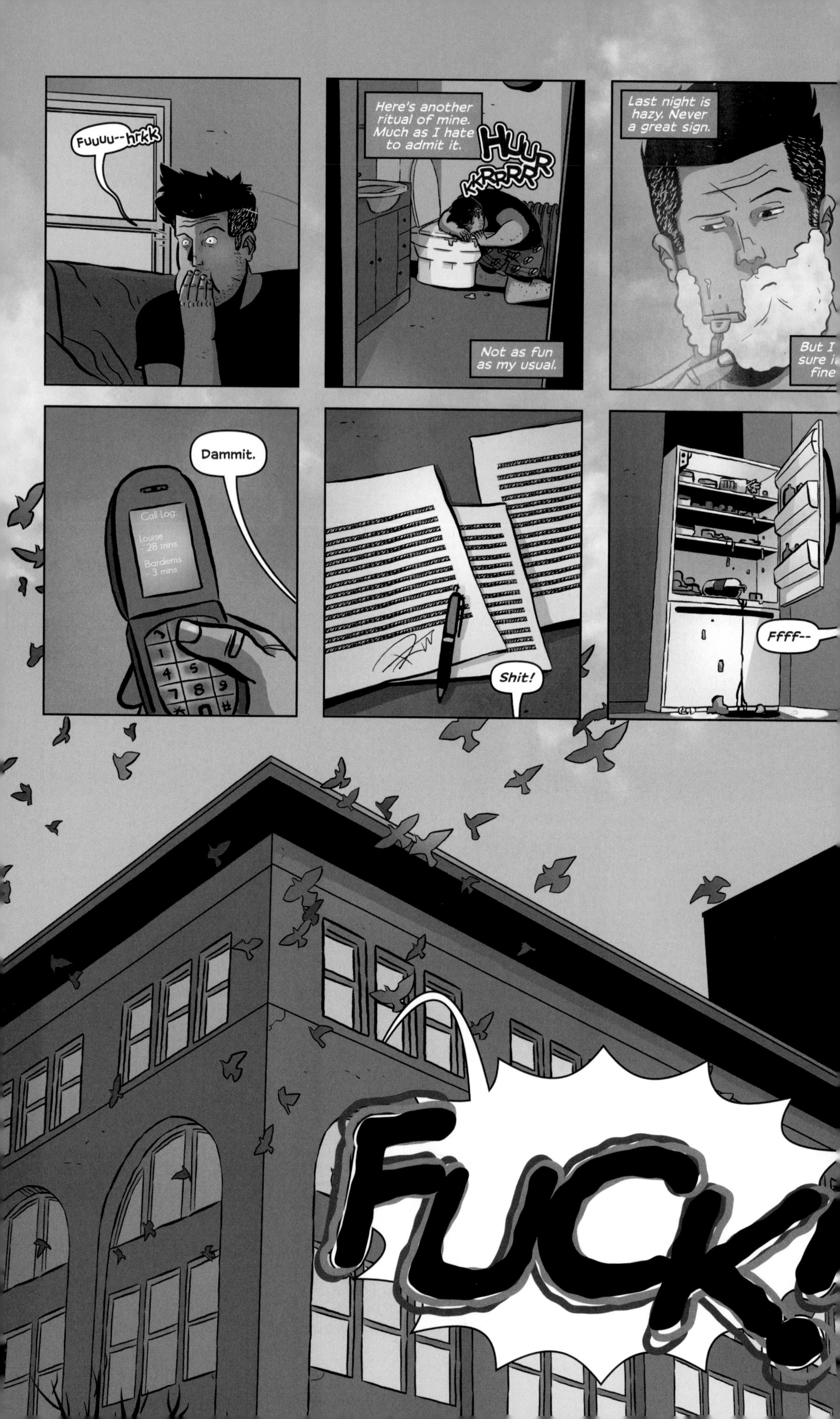
Fuuuu--hrkk
Here's another ritual of mine. Much as I hate to admit it.
HUUR KKRRRRR
Not as fun as my usual.
Last night is hazy. Never a great sign.
But I sure i fine
Call Log:
Louise - 28 mins
Bardems - 3 mins
Dammit.
Shit!
Ffff--
FUCK!

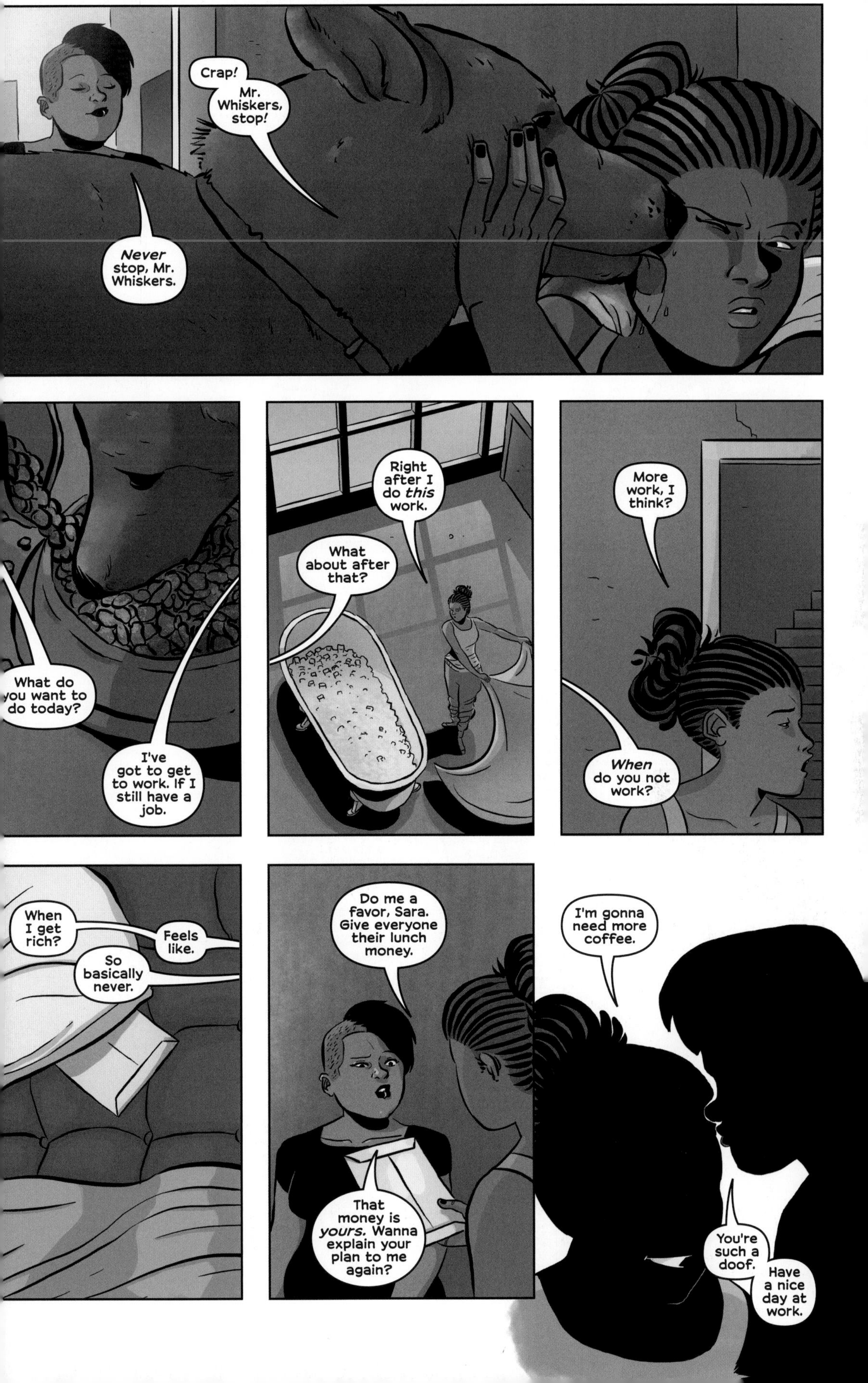
Crap! Mr. Whiskers, stop!
Never stop, Mr. Whiskers.
What do you want to do today?
I've got to get to work. If I still have a job.
What about after that?
Right after I do this work.
More work, I think?
When do you not work?
When I get rich?
Feels like.
So basically never.
Do me a favor, Sara. Give everyone their lunch money.
That money is yours. Wanna explain your plan to me again?
I'm gonna need more coffee.
You're such a doof.
Have a nice day at work.

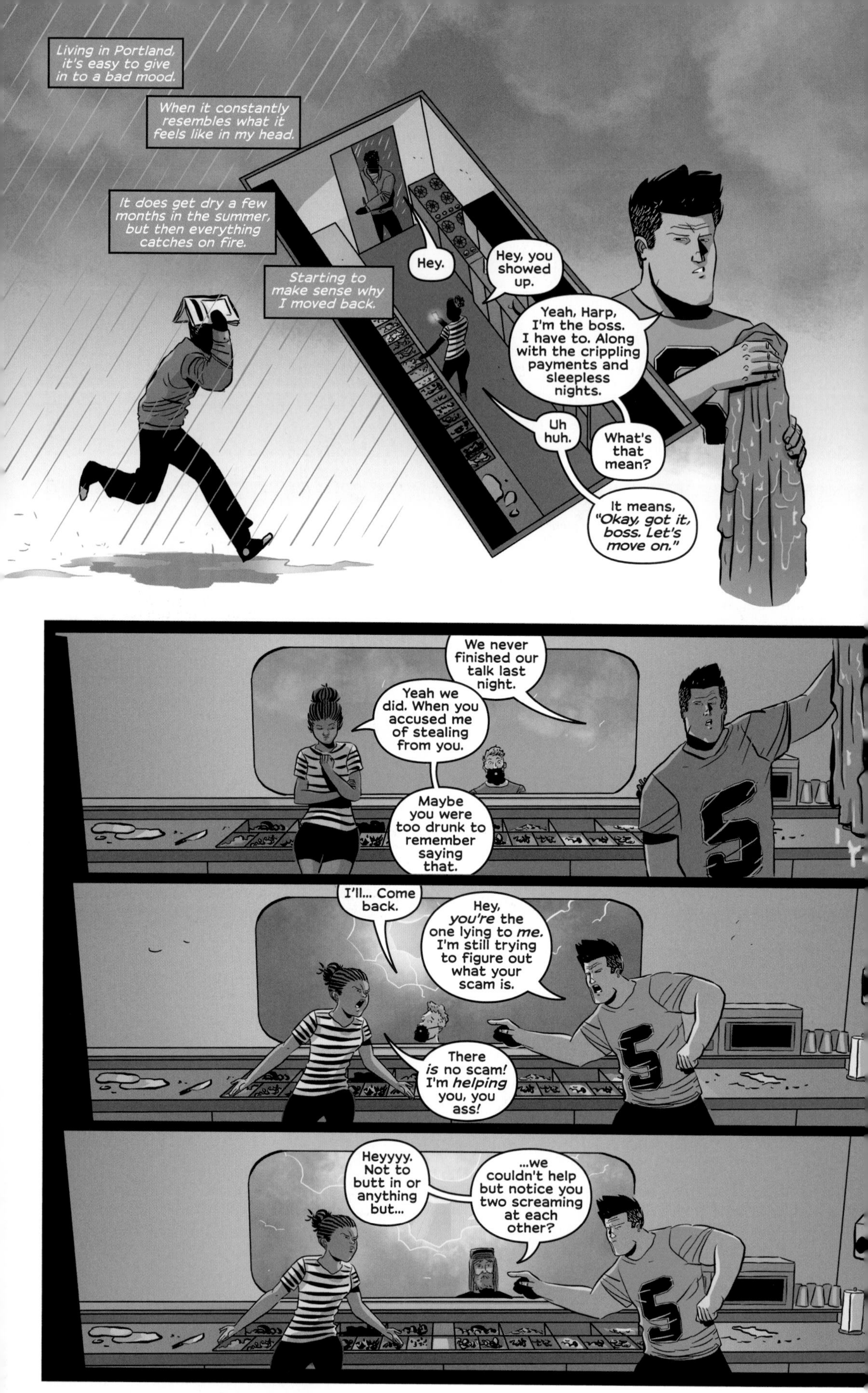
Living in Portland, it's easy to give in to a bad mood.
When it constantly resembles what it feels like in my head.
It does get dry a few months in the summer, but then everything catches on fire.
Starting to make sense why I moved back.
Hey.
Hey, you showed up.
Yeah, Harp, I'm the boss. I have to. Along with the crippling payments and sleepless nights.
Uh huh.
What's that mean?
It means, "Okay, got it, boss. Let's move on."
We never finished our talk last night.
Yeah we did. When you accused me of stealing from you.
Maybe you were too drunk to remember saying that.
I'll... Come back.
Hey, you're the one lying to me. I'm still trying to figure out what your scam is.
There is no scam! I'm helping you, you ass!
Heyyyy. Not to butt in or anything but...
...we couldn't help but notice you two screaming at each other?

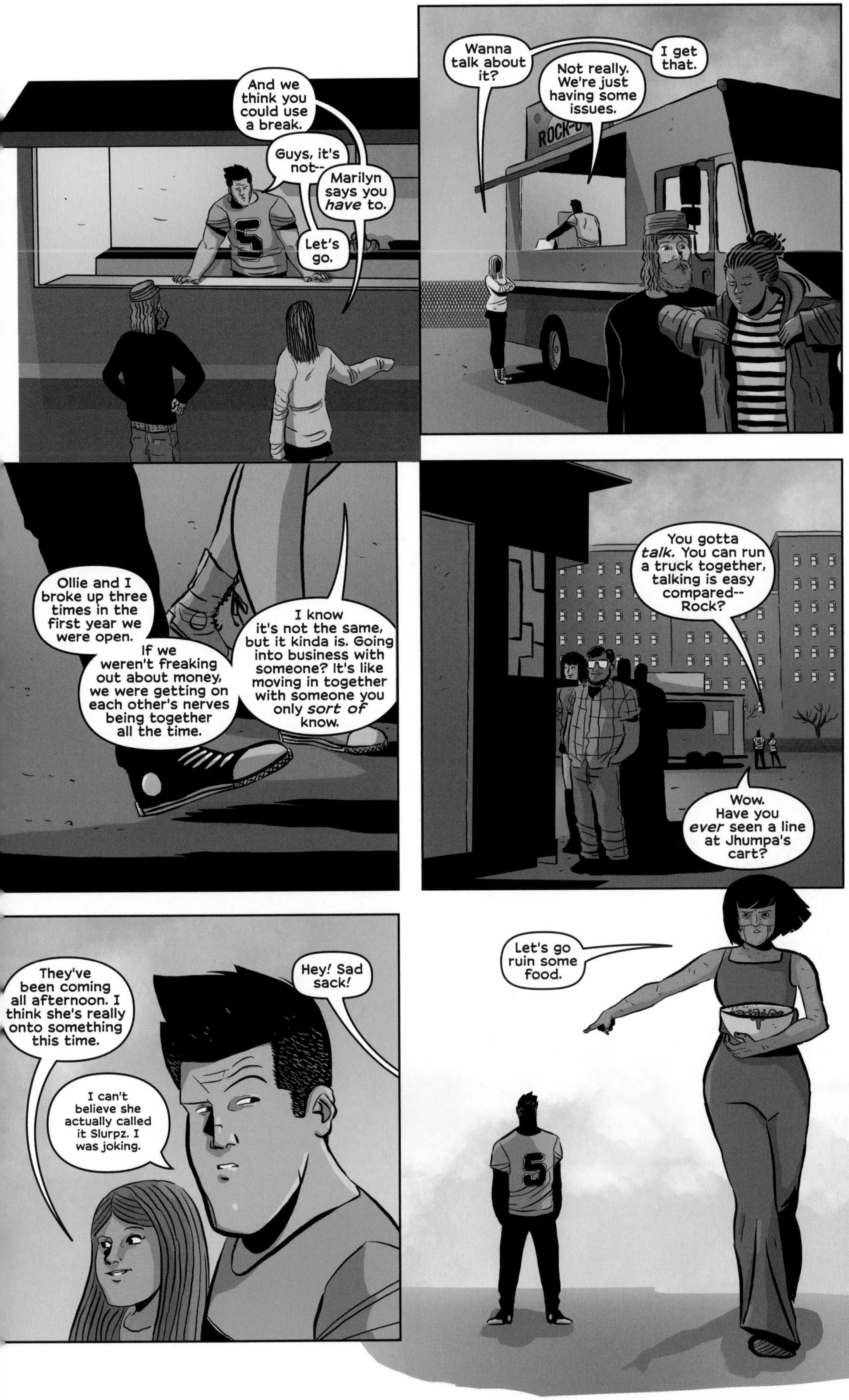
And we think you could use a break.
Guys, it's not--
Marilyn says you *have* to.
Let's go.
Wanna talk about it?
Not really. We're just having some issues.
I get that.
ROCK-O
Ollie and I broke up three times in the first year we were open.
If we weren't freaking out about money, we were getting on each other's nerves being together all the time.
I know it's not the same, but it kinda is. Going into business with someone? It's like moving in together with someone you only *sort of* know.
You gotta *talk*. You can run a truck together, talking is easy compared-- Rock?
Wow. Have you *ever* seen a line at Jhumpa's cart?
They've been coming all afternoon. I think she's really onto something this time.
I can't believe she actually called it Slurpz. I was joking.
Hey! Sad sack!
Let's go ruin some food.

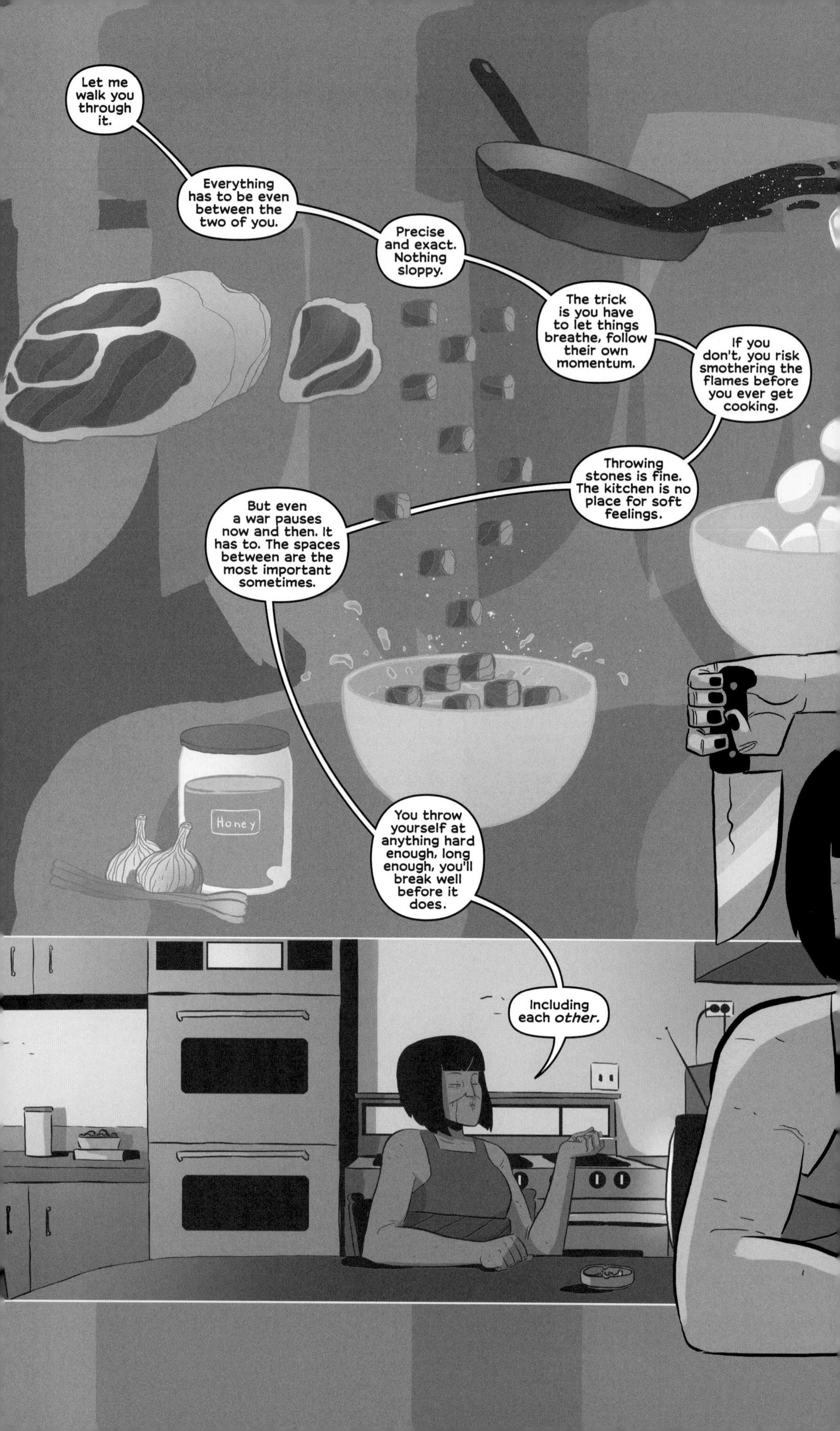
Let me walk you through it.
Everything has to be even between the two of you.
Precise and exact. Nothing sloppy.
The trick is you have to let things breathe, follow their own momentum.
If you don't, you risk smothering the flames before you ever get cooking.
Throwing stones is fine. The kitchen is no place for soft feelings.
But even a war pauses now and then. It has to. The spaces between are the most important sometimes.
Honey
You throw yourself at anything hard enough, long enough, you'll break well before it does.
Including each *other.*

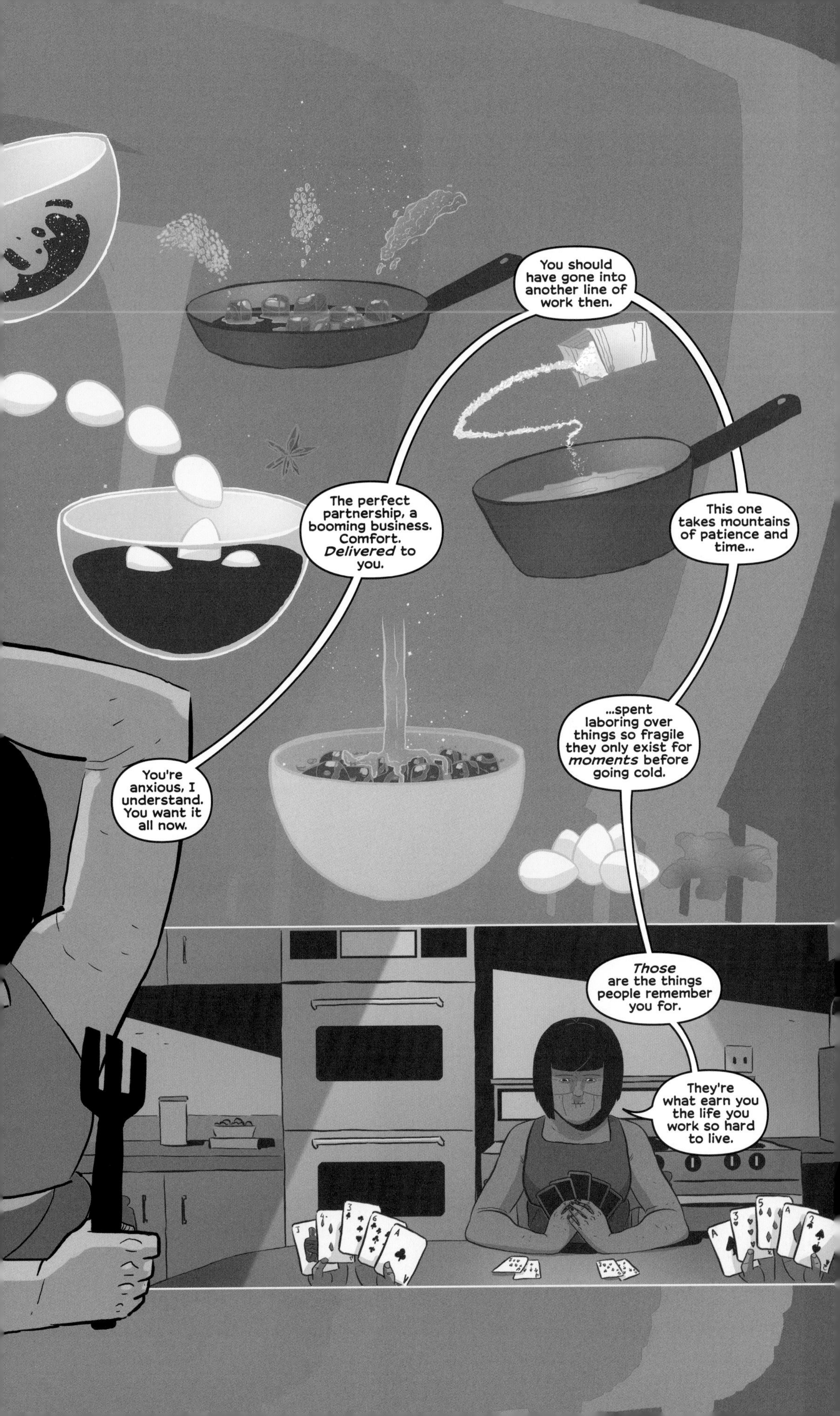

You should have gone into another line of work then.
The perfect partnership, a booming business. Comfort. *Delivered* to you.
You're anxious, I understand. You want it all now.
This one takes mountains of patience and time...
...spent laboring over things so fragile they only exist for *moments* before going cold.
Those are the things people remember you for.
They're what earn you the life you work so hard to live.

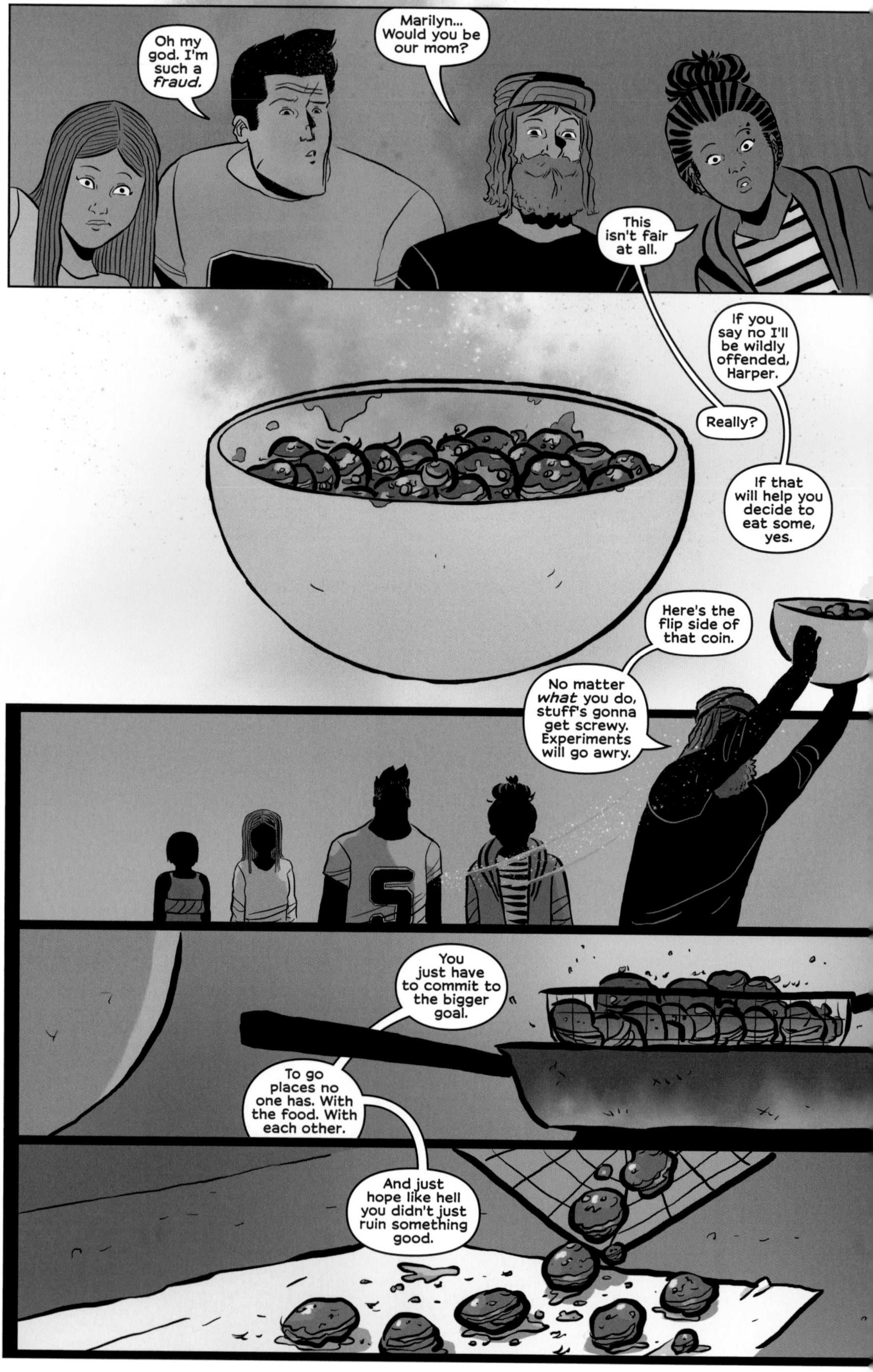
Oh my god. I'm such a *fraud.*
Marilyn... Would you be our mom?
This isn't fair at all.
If you say no I'll be wildly offended, Harper.
Really?
If that will help you decide to eat some, yes.
Here's the flip side of that coin.
No matter *what* you do, stuff's gonna get screwy. Experiments will go awry.
You just have to commit to the bigger goal.
To go places no one has. With the food. With each other.
And just hope like hell you didn't just ruin something good.

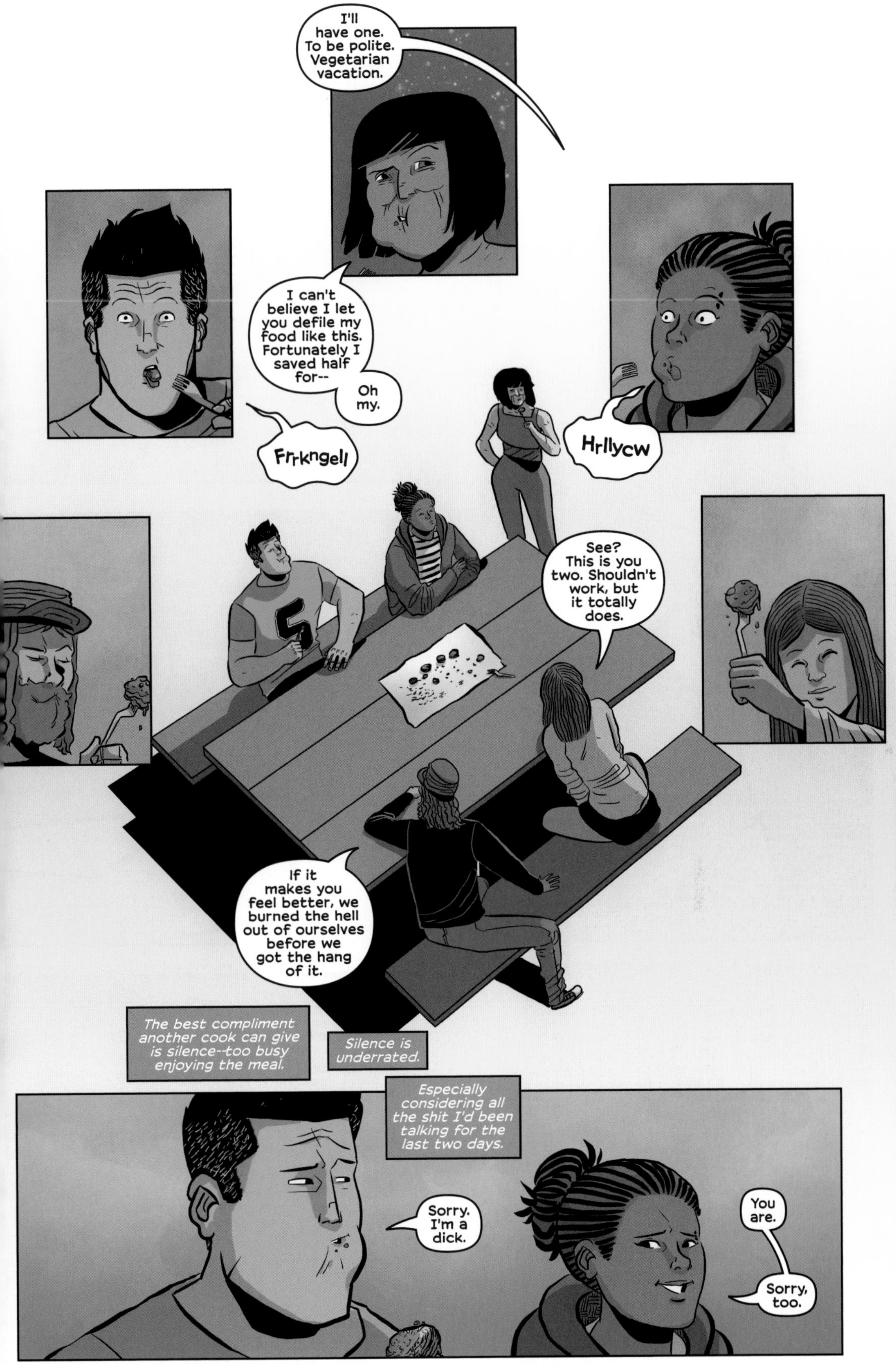

I'll have one. To be polite. Vegetarian vacation.
I can't believe I let you defile my food like this. Fortunately I saved half for--
Oh my.
Frrkngell
Hrllycw
See? This is you two. Shouldn't work, but it totally does.
If it makes you feel better, we burned the hell out of ourselves before we got the hang of it.
The best compliment another cook can give is silence--too busy enjoying the meal.
Silence is underrated.
Especially considering all the shit I'd been talking for the last two days.
Sorry. I'm a dick.
You are.
Sorry, too.

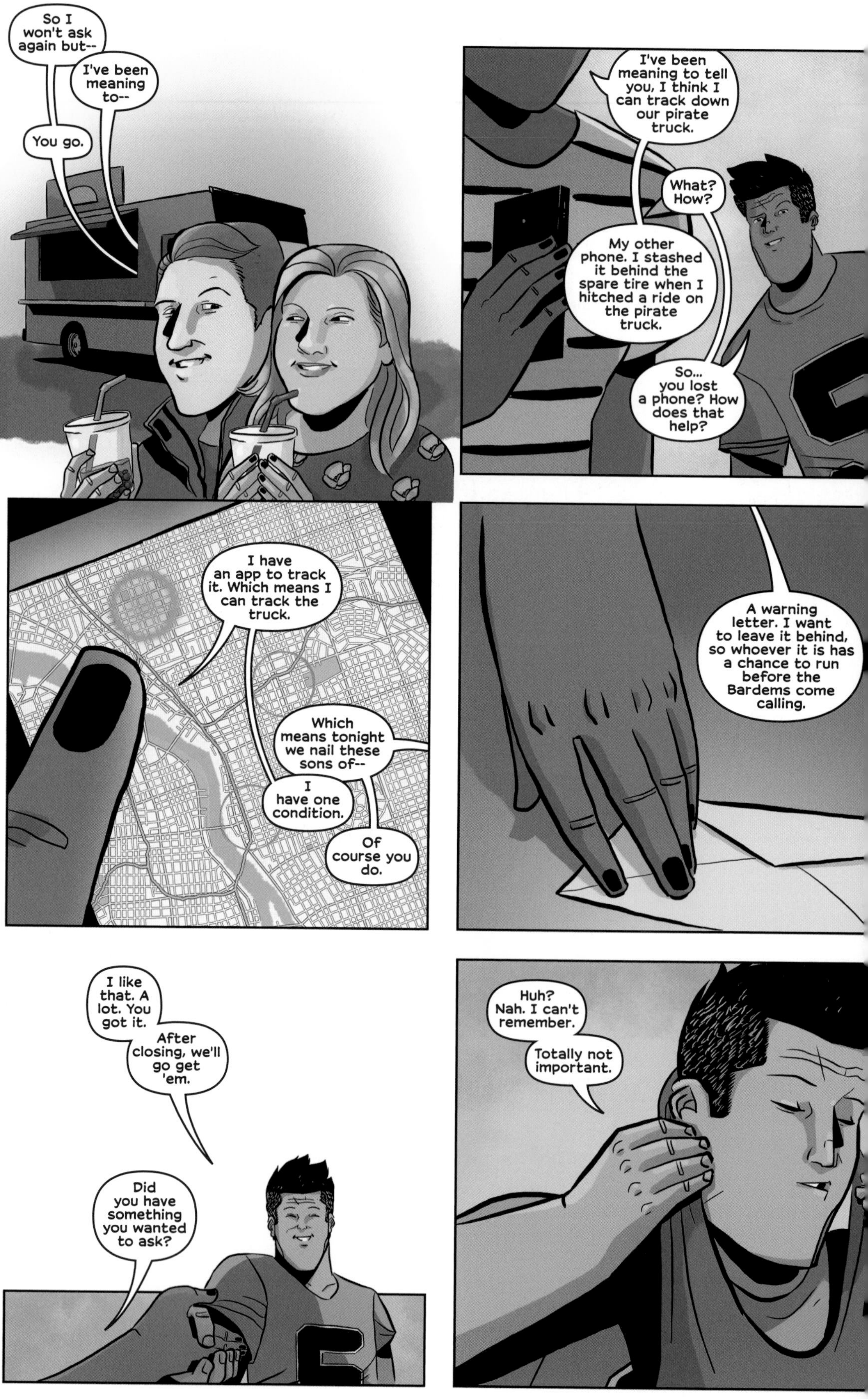
So I won't ask again but--
I've been meaning to--
You go.
I've been meaning to tell you, I think I can track down our pirate truck.
What? How?
My other phone. I stashed it behind the spare tire when I hitched a ride on the pirate truck.
So... you lost a phone? How does that help?
I have an app to track it. Which means I can track the truck.
Which means tonight we nail these sons of--
I have one condition.
Of course you do.
A warning letter. I want to leave it behind, so whoever it is has a chance to run before the Bardems come calling.
I like that. A lot. You got it.
After closing, we'll go get 'em.
Did you have something you wanted to ask?
Huh? Nah. I can't remember.
Totally not important.

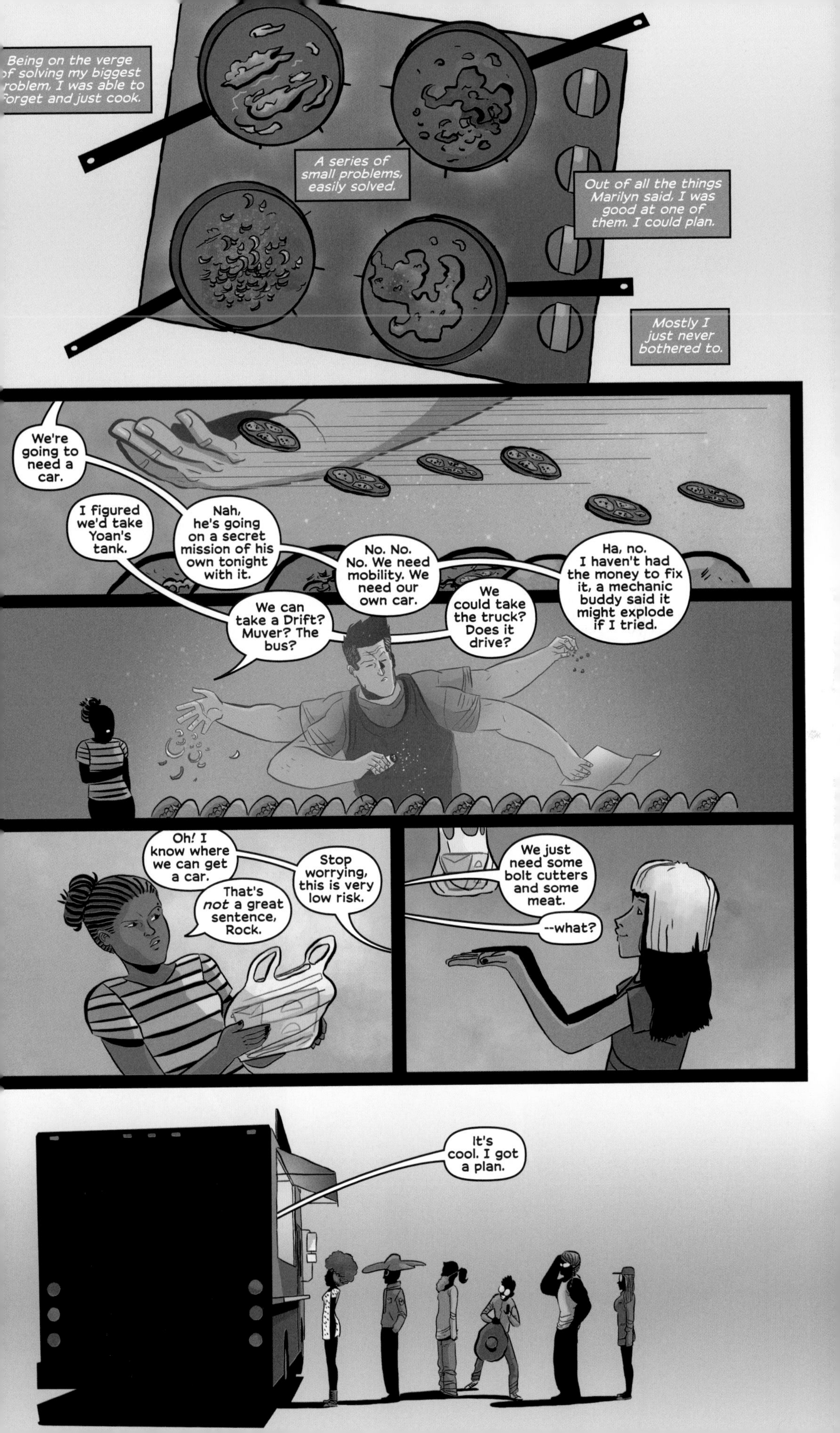
Being on the verge of solving my biggest problem, I was able to forget and just cook.
A series of small problems, easily solved.
Out of all the things Marilyn said, I was good at one of them. I could plan.
Mostly I just never bothered to.
We're going to need a car.
I figured we'd take Yoan's tank.
Nah, he's going on a secret mission of his own tonight with it.
We can take a Drift? Muver? The bus?
No. No. No. We need mobility. We need our own car.
We could take the truck? Does it drive?
Ha, no. I haven't had the money to fix it, a mechanic buddy said it might explode if I tried.
Oh! I know where we can get a car.
That's *not* a great sentence, Rock.
Stop worrying, this is very low risk.
We just need some bolt cutters and some meat.
--what?
It's cool. I got a plan.

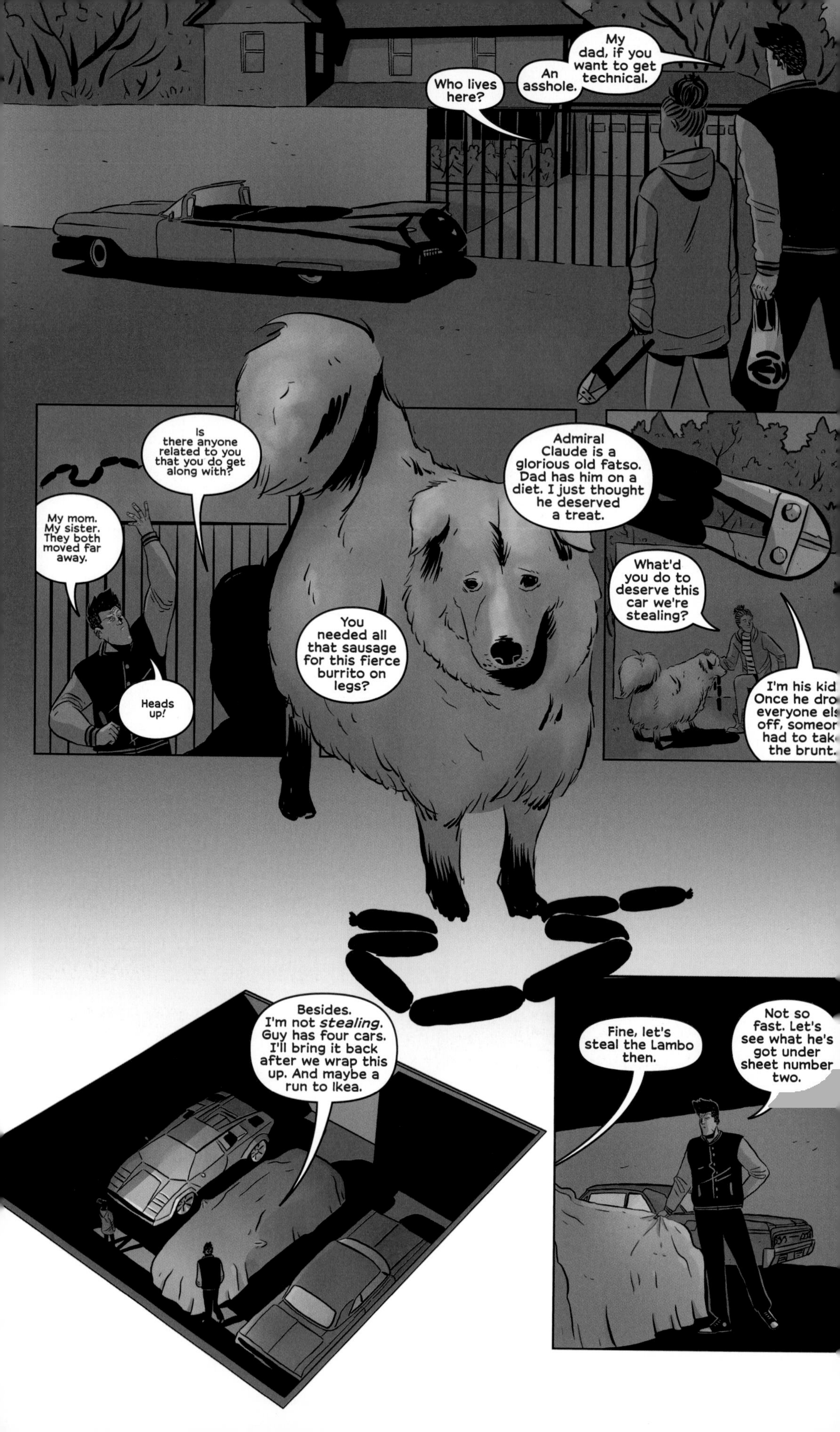
Who lives here?
An asshole.
My dad, if you want to get technical.
Is there anyone related to you that you do get along with?
My mom. My sister. They both moved far away.
Heads up!
You needed all that sausage for this fierce burrito on legs?
Admiral Claude is a glorious old fatso. Dad has him on a diet. I just thought he deserved a treat.
What'd you do to deserve this car we're stealing?
Besides. I'm not *stealing*. Guy has four cars. I'll bring it back after we wrap this up. And maybe a run to Ikea.
Fine, let's steal the Lambo then.
Not so fast. Let's see what he's got under sheet number two.

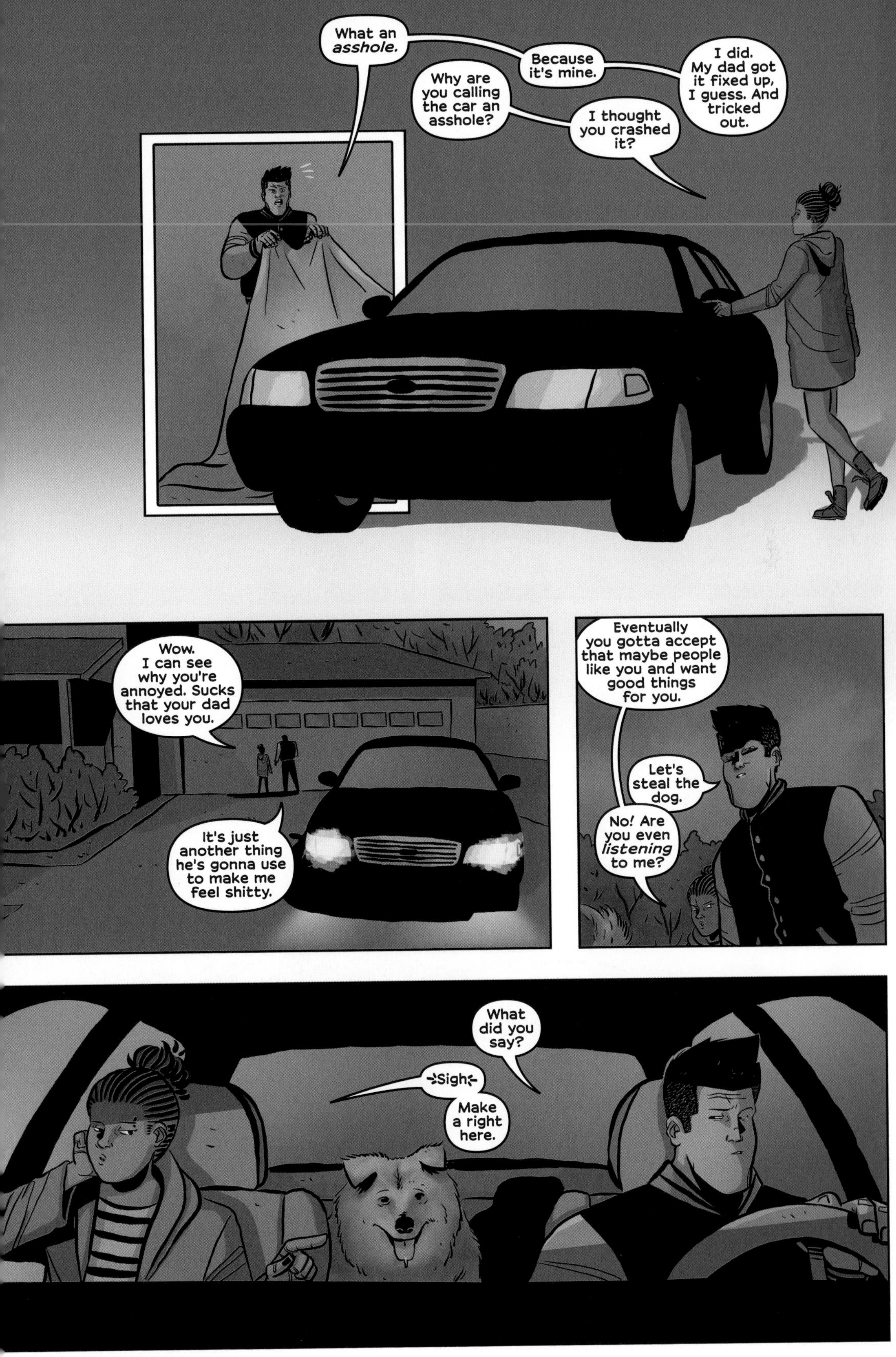
What an *asshole.*
Why are you calling the car an asshole?
Because it's mine.
I thought you crashed it?
I did. My dad got it fixed up, I guess. And tricked out.
Wow. I can see why you're annoyed. Sucks that your dad loves you.
It's just another thing he's gonna use to make me feel shitty.
Eventually you gotta accept that maybe people like you and want good things for you.
Let's steal the dog.
No! Are you even *listening* to me?
What did you say?
Sigh
Make a right here.

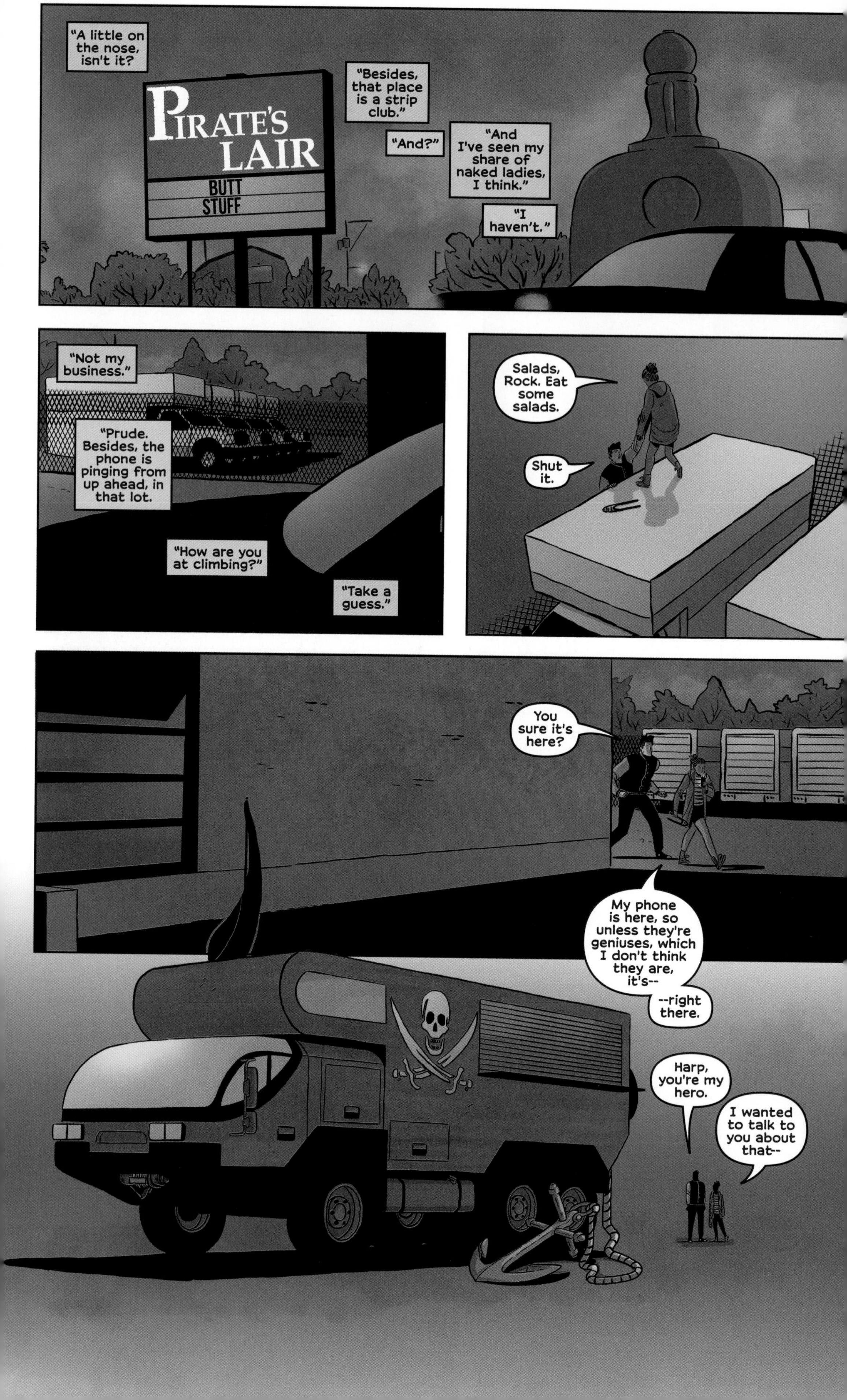

"A little on the nose, isn't it?
PIRATE'S LAIR
BUTT STUFF
"Besides, that place is a strip club."
"And?"
"And I've seen my share of naked ladies, I think."
"I haven't."
"Not my business."
"Prude. Besides, the phone is pinging from up ahead, in that lot.
"How are you at climbing?"
"Take a guess."
Salads, Rock. Eat some salads.
Shut it.
You sure it's here?
My phone is here, so unless they're geniuses, which I don't think they are, it's--
--right there.
Harp, you're my hero.
I wanted to talk to you about that--

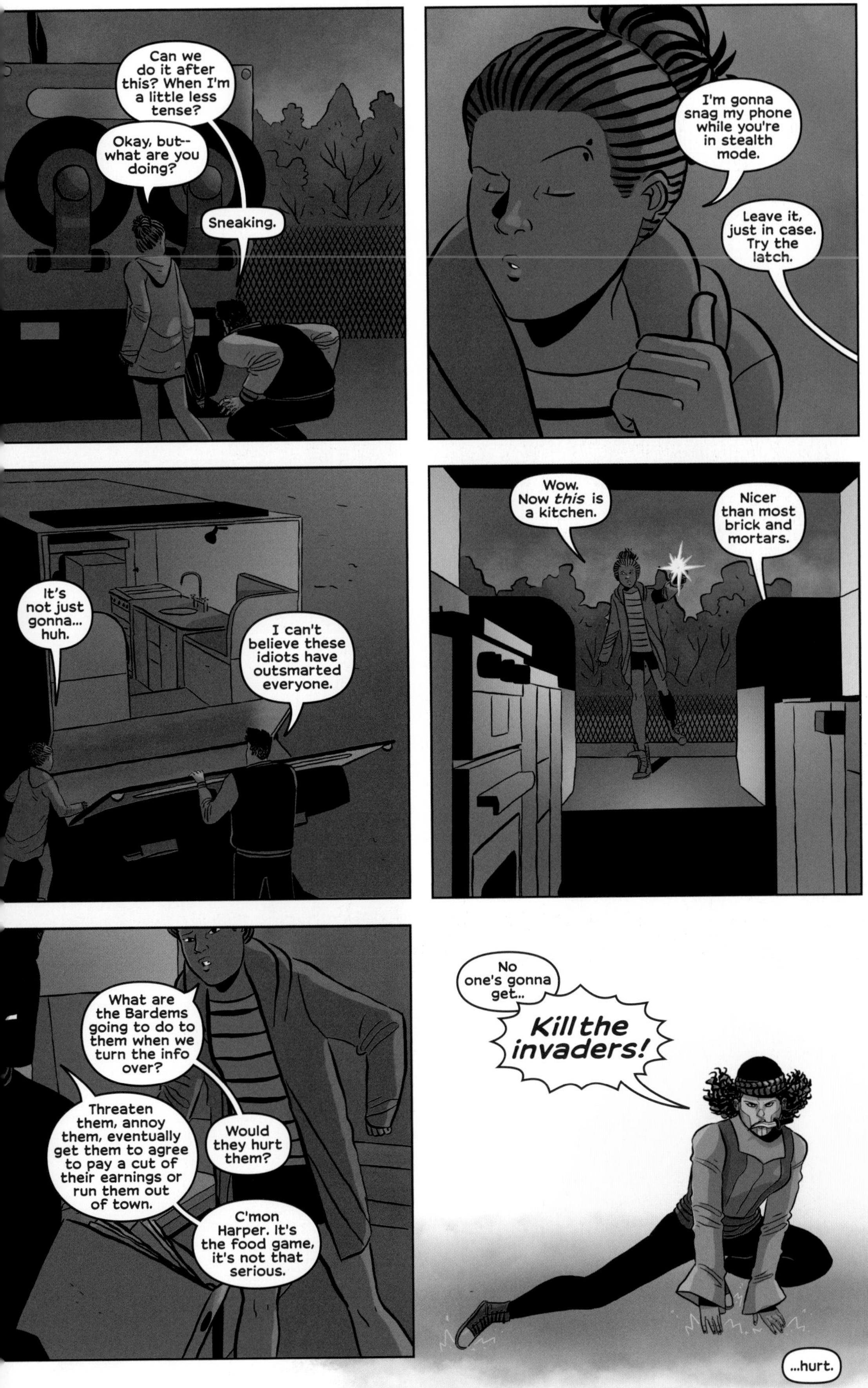
Can we do it after this? When I'm a little less tense?
Okay, but-- what are you doing?
Sneaking.
I'm gonna snag my phone while you're in stealth mode.
Leave it, just in case. Try the latch.
It's not just gonna... huh.
I can't believe these idiots have outsmarted everyone.
Wow. Now *this* is a kitchen.
Nicer than most brick and mortars.
What are the Bardems going to do to them when we turn the info over?
Threaten them, annoy them, eventually get them to agree to pay a cut of their earnings or run them out of town.
Would they hurt them?
C'mon Harper. It's the food game, it's not that serious.
No one's gonna get...
Kill the invaders!
...hurt.

Okay, I know it's fun to play dress-up but enough is enough.

Everything is harder when you have a partner.

Lone-wolfing it, I could do any stupid old shit that occurred to me.

Harp!

But now I have someone else's back to watch out for besides my own.

Can everyone just calm the fuck down?

Behind you, Rock!

On the upside, she watched mine.

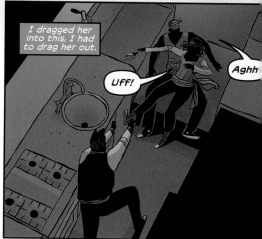

I dragged her into this, I had to drag her out.

Uff!

Aghh

I just wish someone could do the same for me.

All hands, get this ship moving!

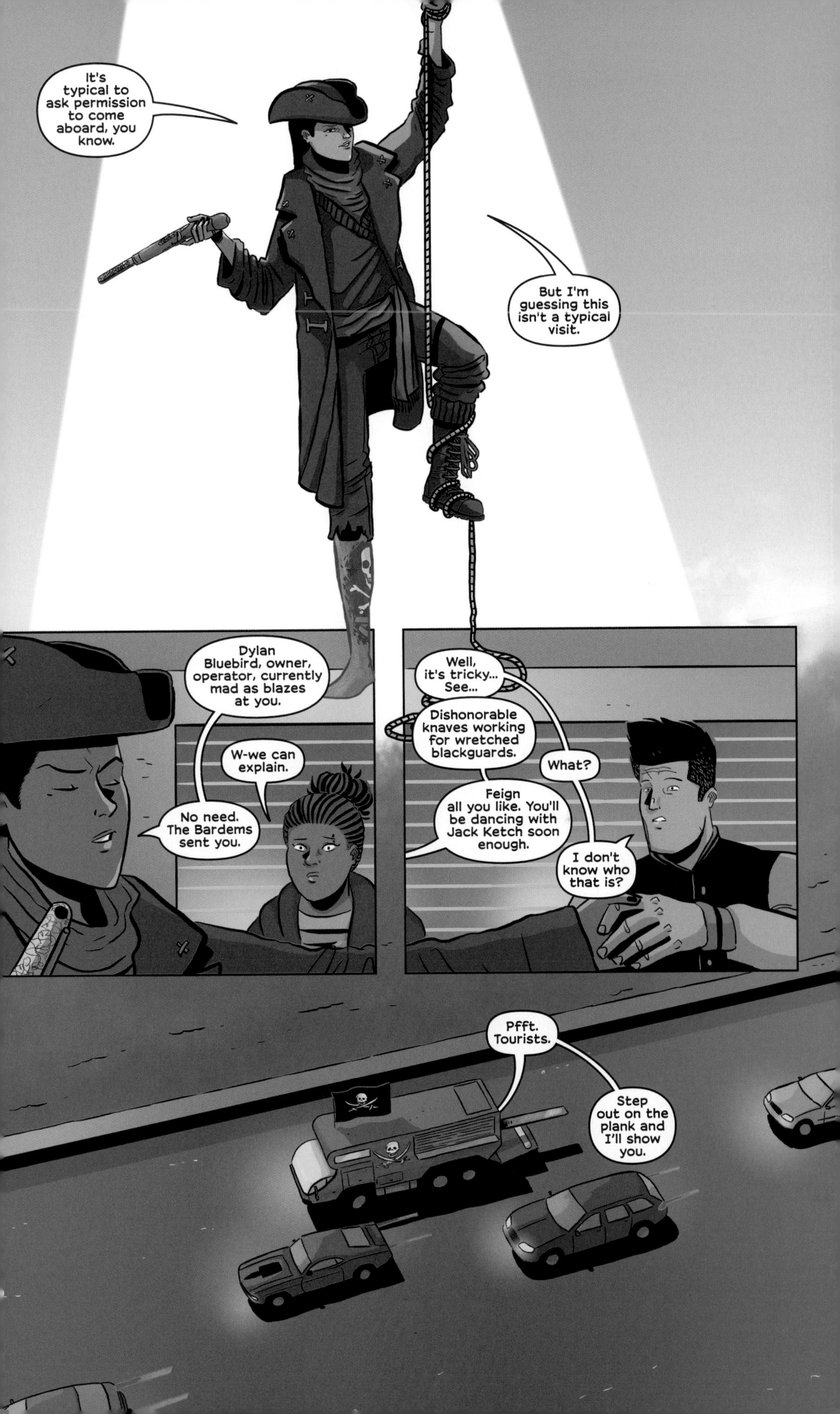
It's typical to ask permission to come aboard, you know.
But I'm guessing this isn't a typical visit.
Dylan Bluebird, owner, operator, currently mad as blazes at you.
W-we can explain.
No need. The Bardems sent you.
Well, it's tricky... See...
Dishonorable knaves working for wretched blackguards.
What?
Feign all you like. You'll be dancing with Jack Ketch soon enough.
I don't know who that is?
Pfft. Tourists.
Step out on the plank and I'll show you.

BURMESE RED PORK STEW (UNFRIED VERSION)

(AS EXPLAINED BY MARILYN IN EXCHANGE FOR SOME FUTURE FAVOR OWED. GOD HELP ME, IT WAS WORTH IT.)

INGREDIENTS

PREP TIME — LONG AS HELL
COOK TIME — 1 HR 45 MINUTES

THE STEW
- ½ CUP SOY SAUCE
- 1 TBSP TOASTED SESAME OIL
- 2 TBSP CHILI OIL
- 2 LBS PORK SHOULDER, CUT INTO 1 INCH CUBES
- 1 LB FRESH PORK BELLY, NO SKIN, CUT INTO CUBES
- 1 TBSP VEGETABLE OIL
- 8 GARLIC CLOVES, CHOPPED
- ¼ CUP FRESH GINGER (PEELED + FINELY CHOPPED)
- 3 TBSP HOT CHILI PASTE
- ½ CUPS SUGAR

PICKLED EGGS
- 1 CUP SOY SAUCE
- ¼ CUP HONEY
- 1 WHOLE STAR ANISE
- 5 LARGE EGGS (HARD-BOILED + PEELED)

ACCESSORIES
- STEAMED WHITE RICE
- CHOPPED SCALLIONS

THINGS YOU'LL NEED
- PASTRY BRUSH
- DEEP OVENPROOF SKILLET (WITH LID)
- PATIENCE

AROUND STEP 4, BRING THESE TO A BOIL IN A SAUCEPAN, STIRRING UNTIL HONEY DISSOLVES THEN LET IT COOL.

↓

POUR BRINE OVER EGGS IN BOWL, ADD WATER UNTIL THEY'RE COVERED.

↓

LET EGGS BRINE OVERNIGHT IN FRIDGE.

↓

WHILE THE STEW IS COOKING, DRAIN THE PICKLED EGGS. HALVE OR CHOP THEM UP.

DAY 1 - MARINADE DAY

1. WHISK SOY SAUCE, SESAME OIL, AND CHILI OIL IN A MEDIUM BOWL.
2. ADD CUBED PORK SHOULDER + BELLY — TOSS TO EVENLY COAT IT ALL.
3. COVER AND PUT IN FRIDGE, 6 HOURS OR MORE. BE SURE TO TOSS IT EVERY FEW HOURS TO KEEP IT FROM TURNING INTO A GIANT MEAT FRANKENSTEIN.
4. GO LIVE YOUR LIFE, GET A DRINK, WATCH THE SUNSET. ENJOY THESE LAST FEW MOMENTS BEFORE YOUR BEING ISN'T CONSUMED WITH COOKING PORK.

DAY 2 - COOK DAY

1. DRAIN THE PORK, SAVE THE LEFTOVER MARINADE, YOU'LL NEED IT IN A BIT.
2. HEAT VEGETABLE OIL IN A LARGE OVENPROOF SKILLET.
3. THIS NEXT PART'S GONNA TAKE A BIT, SO PREPARE YOURSELF FOR GRUNTWORK.
4. WORKING IN BATCHES, COOK THE MARINATED PORK CUBES, TURNING THEM, UNTIL THEY'RE BROWNED ON ALL SIDES. 5 MINUTES OR SO FOR EACH BATCH, MOVING THE BROWNED PORK TO A BAKING SHEET OR WHATEVER WORKS FOR YOUR KITCHEN SITUATION.
5. PREHEAT YOUR OVEN TO 275°. IF YOU AREN'T SWEATING YET, IT'S COMING.
6. REMOVE THE FAT FROM THE JUICES IN SKILLET WITH A SPOON AND GET RID OF IT (YOUR DOG WOULDN'T SAY NO IF ASKED TO DISPOSE OF IT).
7. PUT THE PORK AND THAT MARINADE YOU SAVED INTO YOUR OVEN-READY SKILLET. MIX IN THE GARLIC, GINGER, AND CHILI PASTE; SET IT ALL ASIDE.
8. STIR THE SUGAR AND ¼ CUP WATER TOGETHER IN A MEDIUM SAUCEPAN OVER MEDIUM-LOW HEAT UNTIL THE SUGAR DISSOLVES AND THE MIXTURE GETS SYRUPY.
9. TURN THE HEAT UP TO MEDIUM-HIGH SO THE SYRUP BOILS. SWIRL THE SAUCEPAN AND BRUSH DOWN THE SIDES WITH A WET BRUSH (DON'T STIR IT! YOU'RE BASICALLY MAKING CARAMEL AND THAT STUFF STICKS TO EVERYTHING). KEEP DOING THIS UNTIL THE SYRUP TURNS A DEEP AMBER, THEN GET READY TO MOVE QUICKLY.
10. POUR THE CARAMEL OVER THE PORK MIXTURE. IT'S GOING TO HARDEN QUICKER THAN YOU EXPECT, SO DON'T DRAG ASS.
11. ADD ½ CUP WATER TO THE SYRUP SAUCEPAN + STIR IT OVER MEDIUM HEAT TO DISSOLVE ANY REMAINING CARAMEL. POUR THIS INTO THE SKILLET AND STIR TO BLEND.
12. COVER TIGHTLY AND PUT THE OVENPROOF SKILLET IN THE OVEN. IT'LL BE IN THERE 1 HOUR AND 45 MINUTES, BUT SET SOME REMINDERS TO TAKE IT OUT AND STIR IT EVERY 30 MINUTES, UNTIL THE PORK IS SUPER TENDER. YOU'LL KNOW WHEN YOU SEE IT.
13. COOK THE RICE WHILE YOU WAIT. PUT THE RICE IN THE BOWL, THE STEW OVER THE RICE, GARNISH WITH EGGS AND SCALLIONS. EAT UNTIL YOU SEE GOD. THEN HAVE THIRDS.

5: CLEAN PLATES

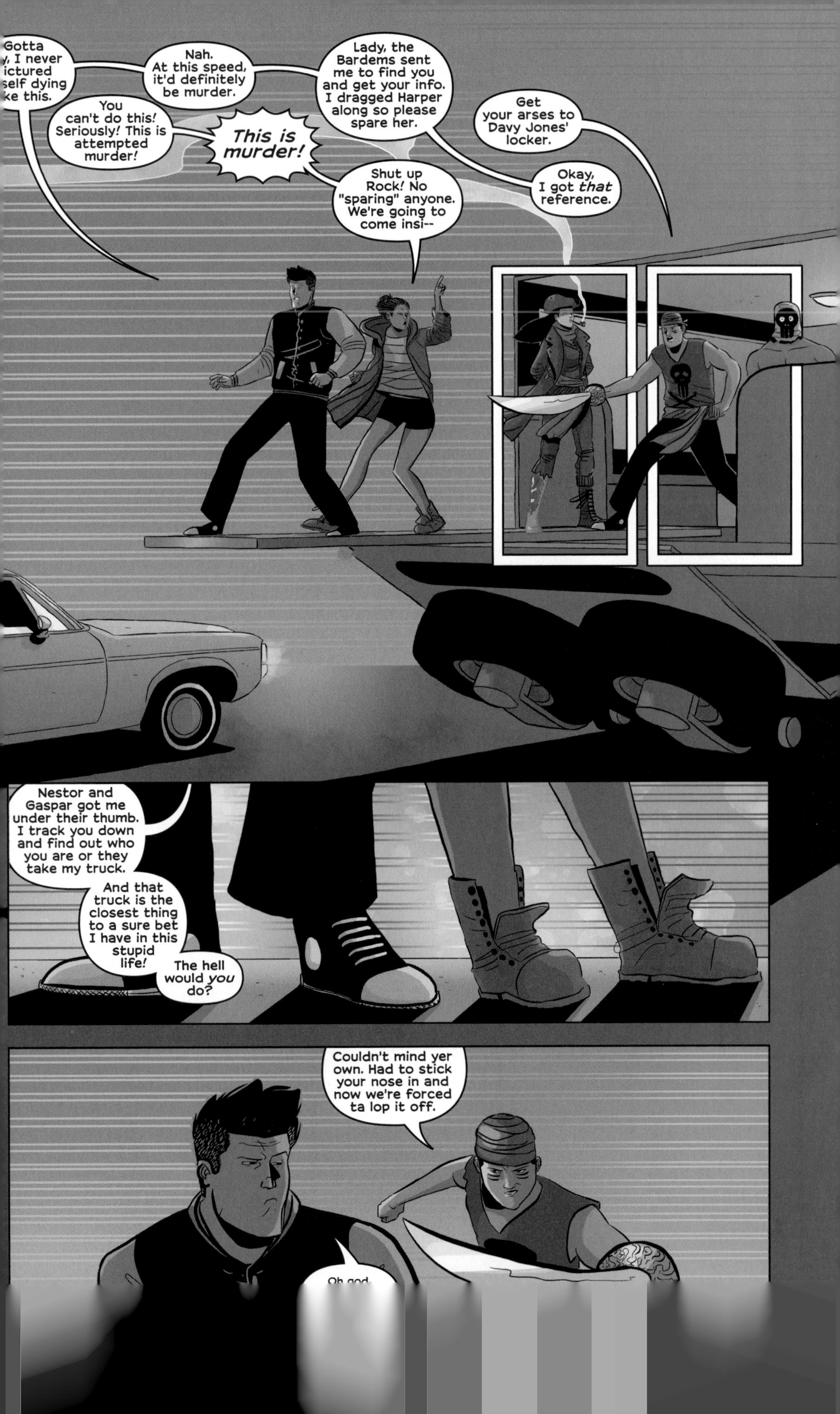
Gotta
y, I never
ictured
self dying
ke this.
Nah. At this speed, it'd definitely be murder.
Lady, the Bardems sent me to find you and get your info. I dragged Harper along so please spare her.
You can't do this! Seriously! This is attempted murder!
This is murder!
Get your arses to Davy Jones' locker.
Shut up Rock! No "sparing" anyone. We're going to come insi--
Okay, I got *that* reference.
Nestor and Gaspar got me under their thumb. I track you down and find out who you are or they take my truck.
And that truck is the closest thing to a sure bet I have in this stupid life!
The hell would *you* do?
Couldn't mind yer own. Had to stick your nose in and now we're forced ta lop it off.
Oh god.

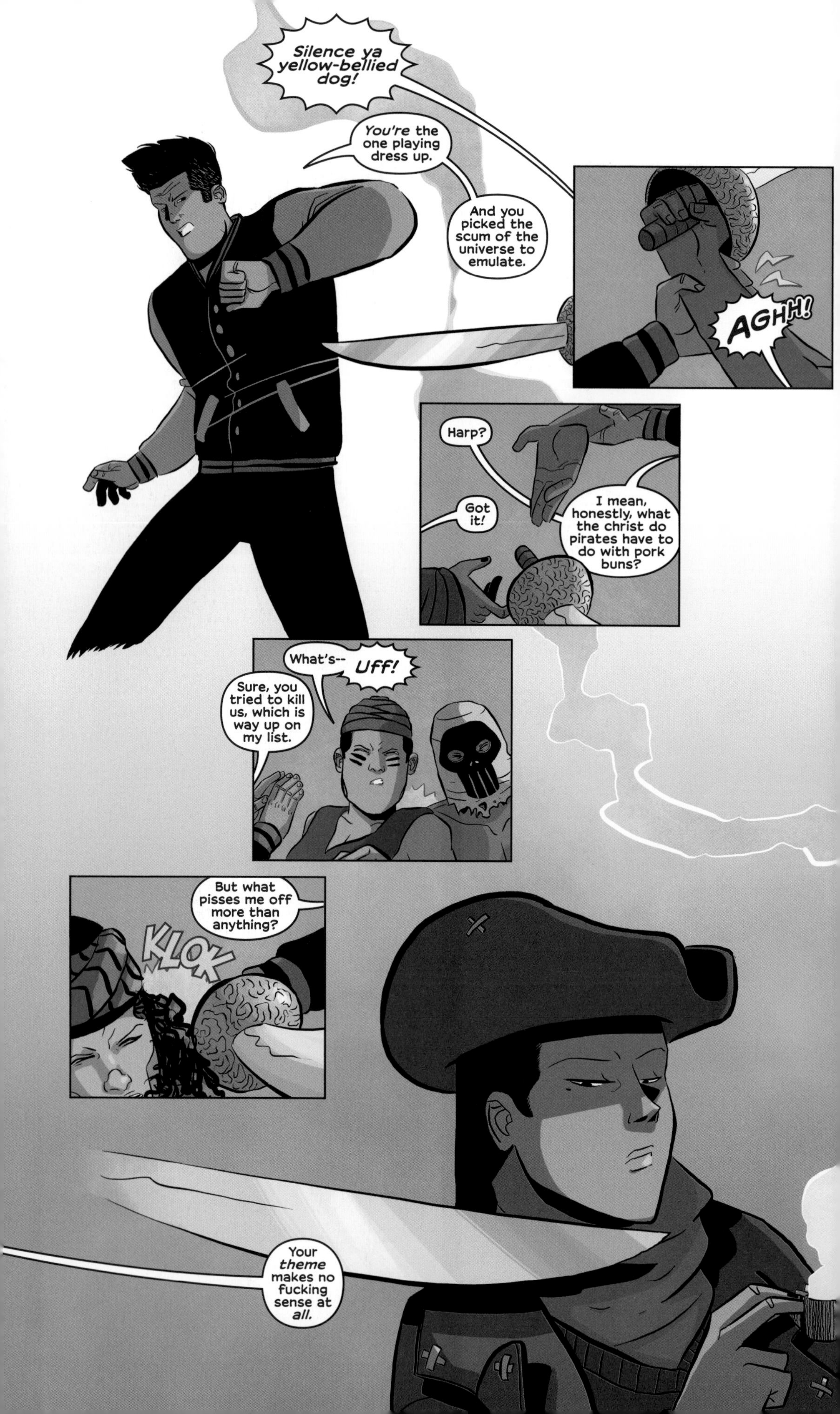
Silence ya yellow-bellied dog!
You're the one playing dress up.
And you picked the scum of the universe to emulate.
AGHH!
Harp?
Got it!
I mean, honestly, what the christ do pirates have to do with pork buns?
What's--
UFF!
Sure, you tried to kill us, which is way up on my list.
But what pisses me off more than anything?
KLOK
Your theme makes no fucking sense at all.

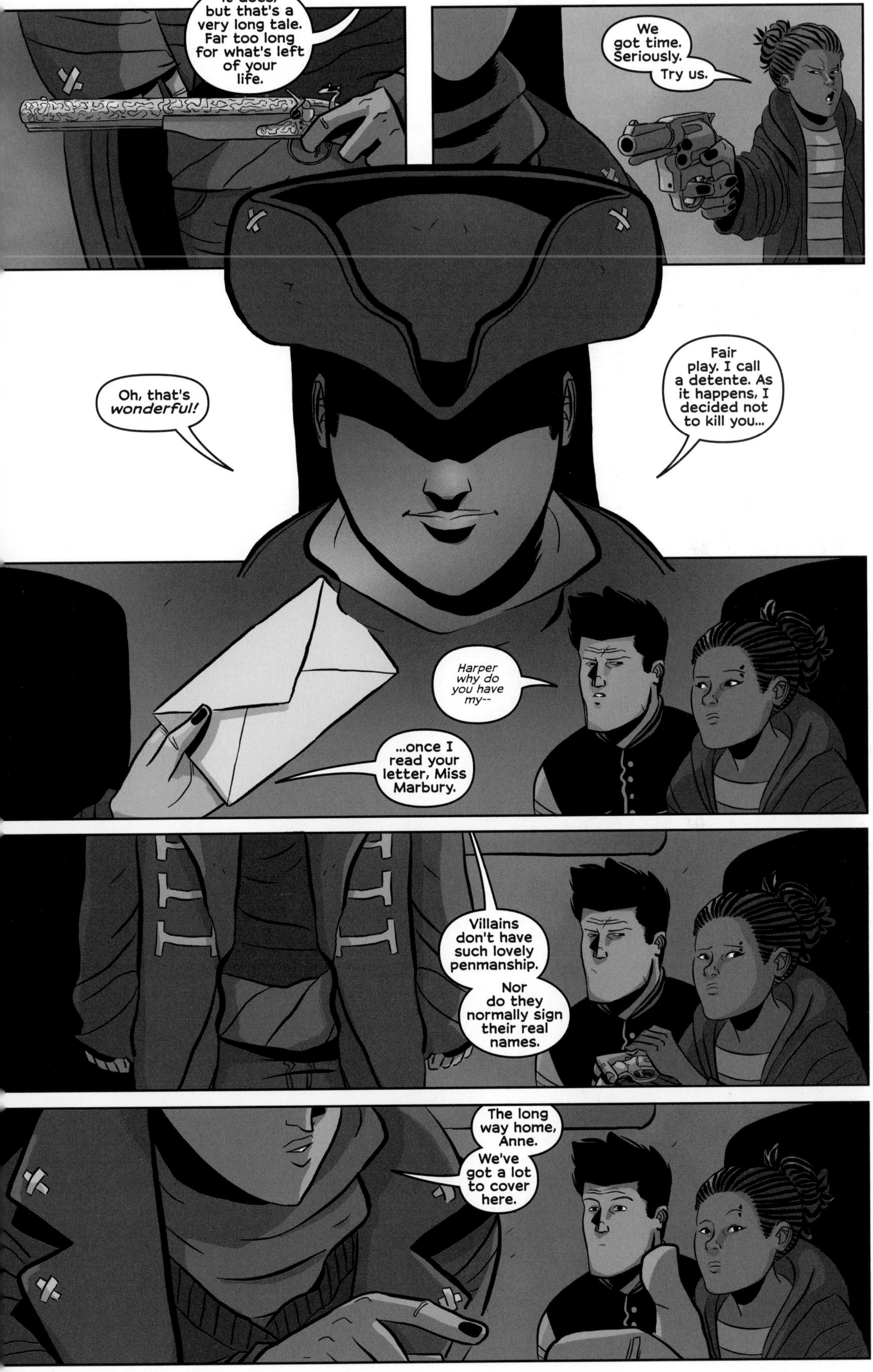
It does, but that's a very long tale. Far too long for what's left of your life.
We got time. Seriously.
Try us.
Oh, that's *wonderful!*
Fair play. I call a detente. As it happens, I decided not to kill you...
Harper why do you have my--
...once I read your letter, Miss Marbury.
Villains don't have such lovely penmanship.
Nor do they normally sign their real names.
The long way home, Anne.
We've got a lot to cover here.

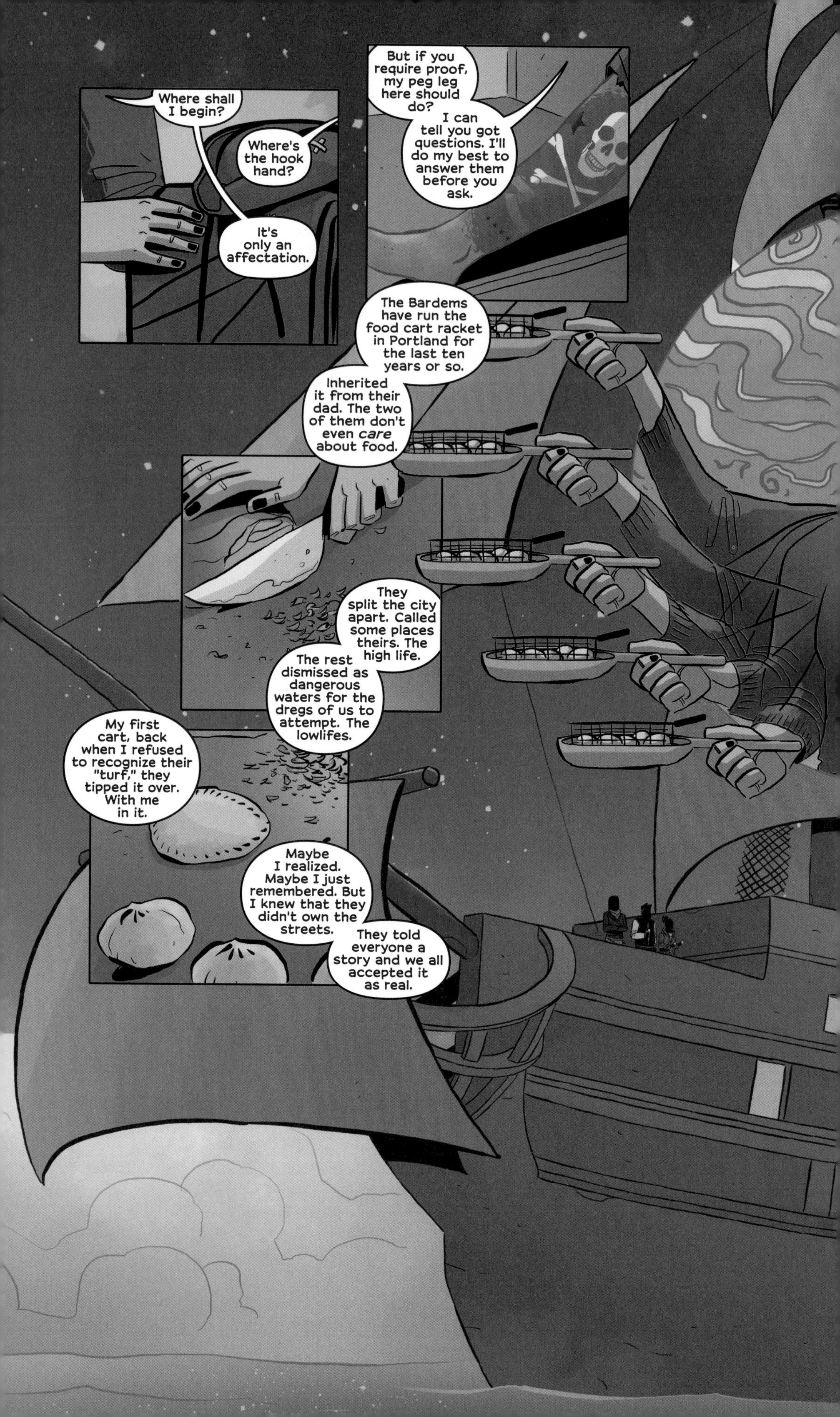
Where shall I begin?
Where's the hook hand?
It's only an affectation.
But if you require proof, my peg leg here should do?
I can tell you got questions. I'll do my best to answer them before you ask.
The Bardems have run the food cart racket in Portland for the last ten years or so.
Inherited it from their dad. The two of them don't even *care* about food.
They split the city apart. Called some places theirs. The high life.
The rest dismissed as dangerous waters for the dregs of us to attempt. The lowlifes.
My first cart, back when I refused to recognize their "turf," they tipped it over. With me in it.
Maybe I realized. Maybe I just remembered. But I knew that they didn't own the streets.
They told everyone a story and we all accepted it as real.

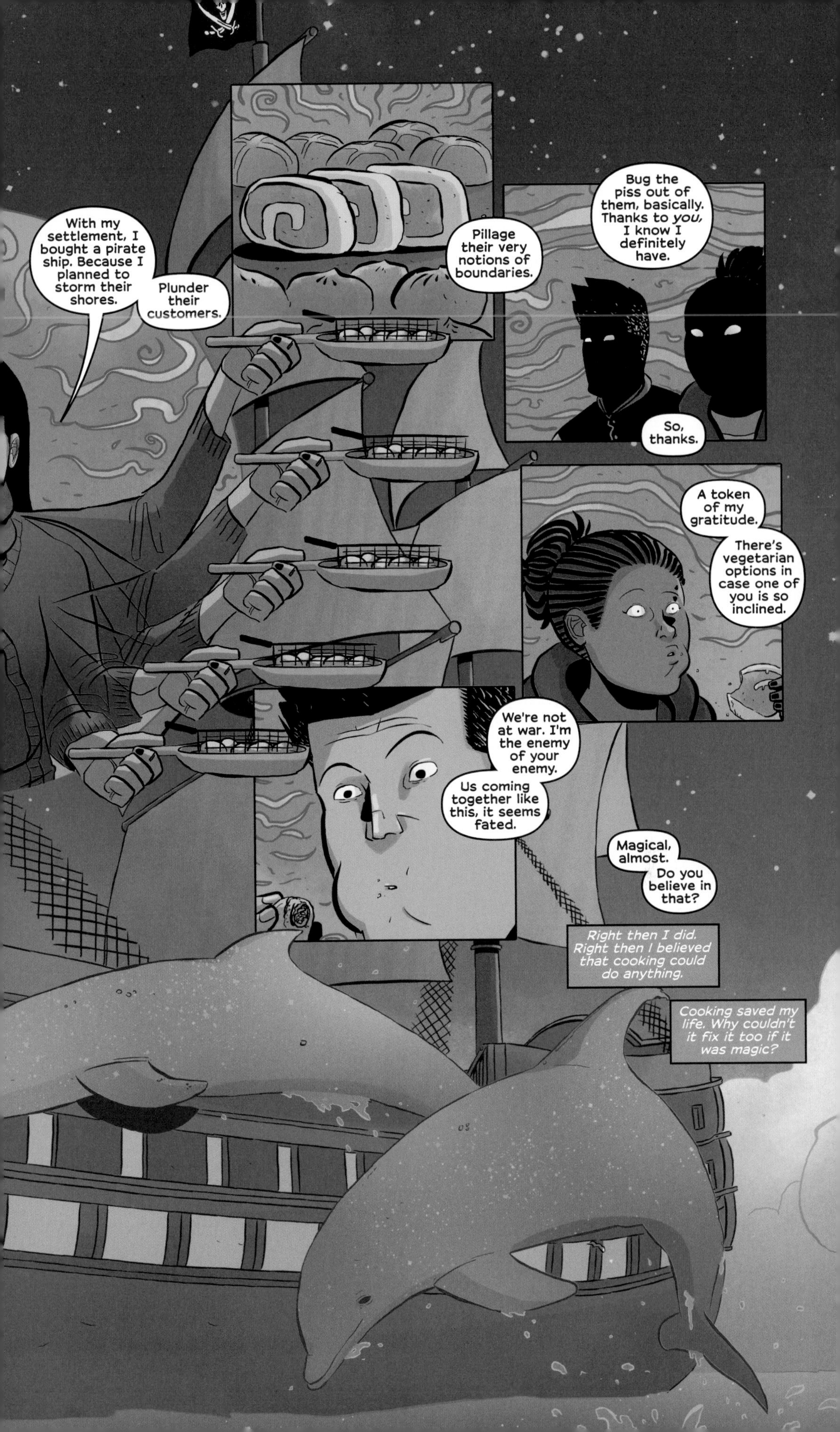
With my settlement, I bought a pirate ship. Because I planned to storm their shores.
Plunder their customers.
Pillage their very notions of boundaries.
Bug the piss out of them, basically. Thanks to *you,* I know I definitely have.
So, thanks.
A token of my gratitude.
There's vegetarian options in case one of you is so inclined.
We're not at war. I'm the enemy of your enemy.
Us coming together like this, it seems fated.
Magical, almost.
Do you believe in that?
Right then I did. Right then I believed that cooking could do anything.
Cooking saved my life. Why couldn't it fix it too if it was magic?

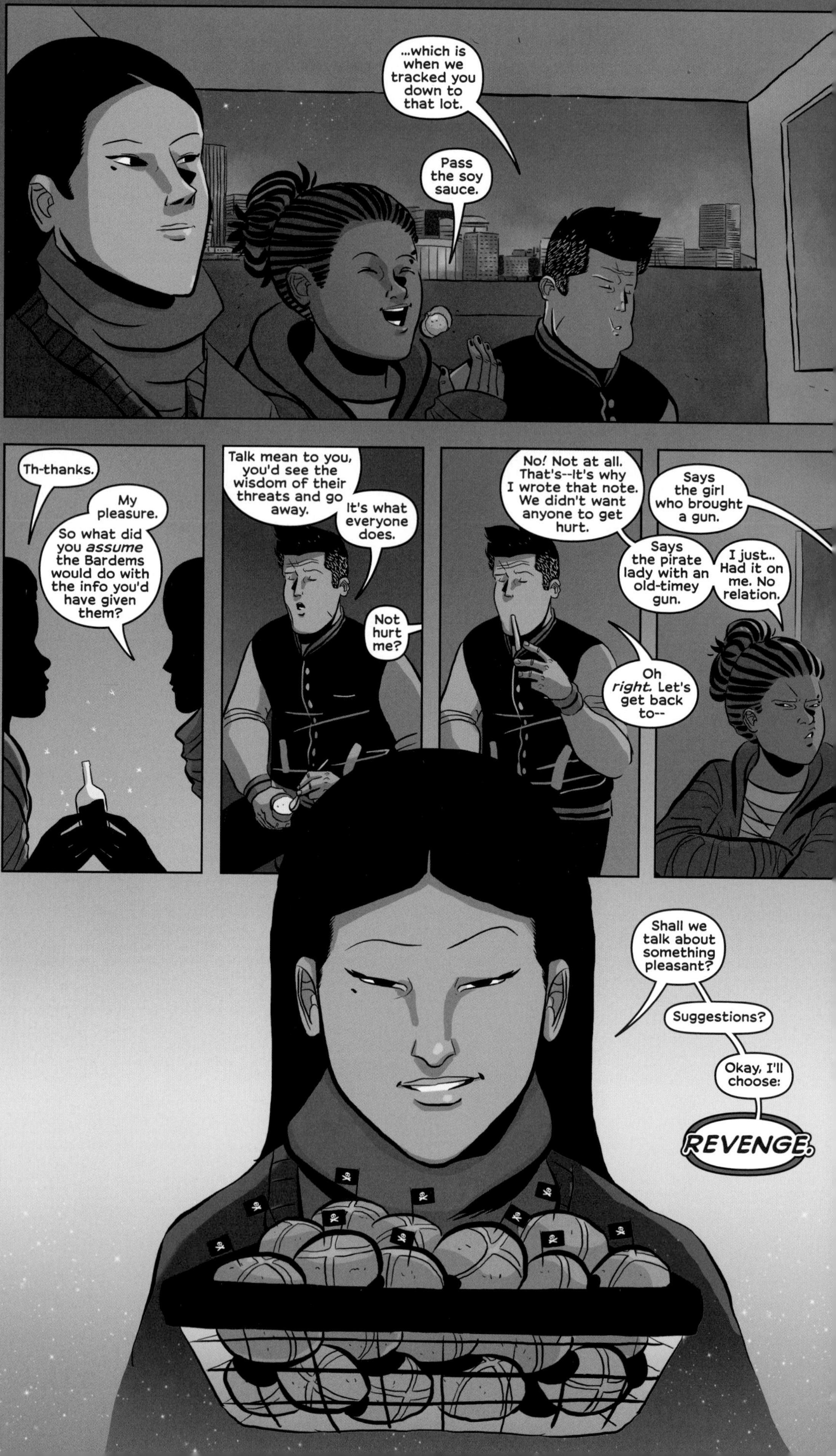

...which is when we tracked you down to that lot.
Pass the soy sauce.
Th-thanks.
My pleasure.
So what did you *assume* the Bardems would do with the info you'd have given them?
Talk mean to you, you'd see the wisdom of their threats and go away.
It's what everyone does.
Not hurt me?
No! Not at all. That's--It's why I wrote that note. We didn't want anyone to get hurt.
Says the pirate lady with an old-timey gun.
Oh *right.* Let's get back to--
Says the girl who brought a gun.
I just... Had it on me. No relation.
Shall we talk about something pleasant?
Suggestions?
Okay, I'll choose:
REVENGE.

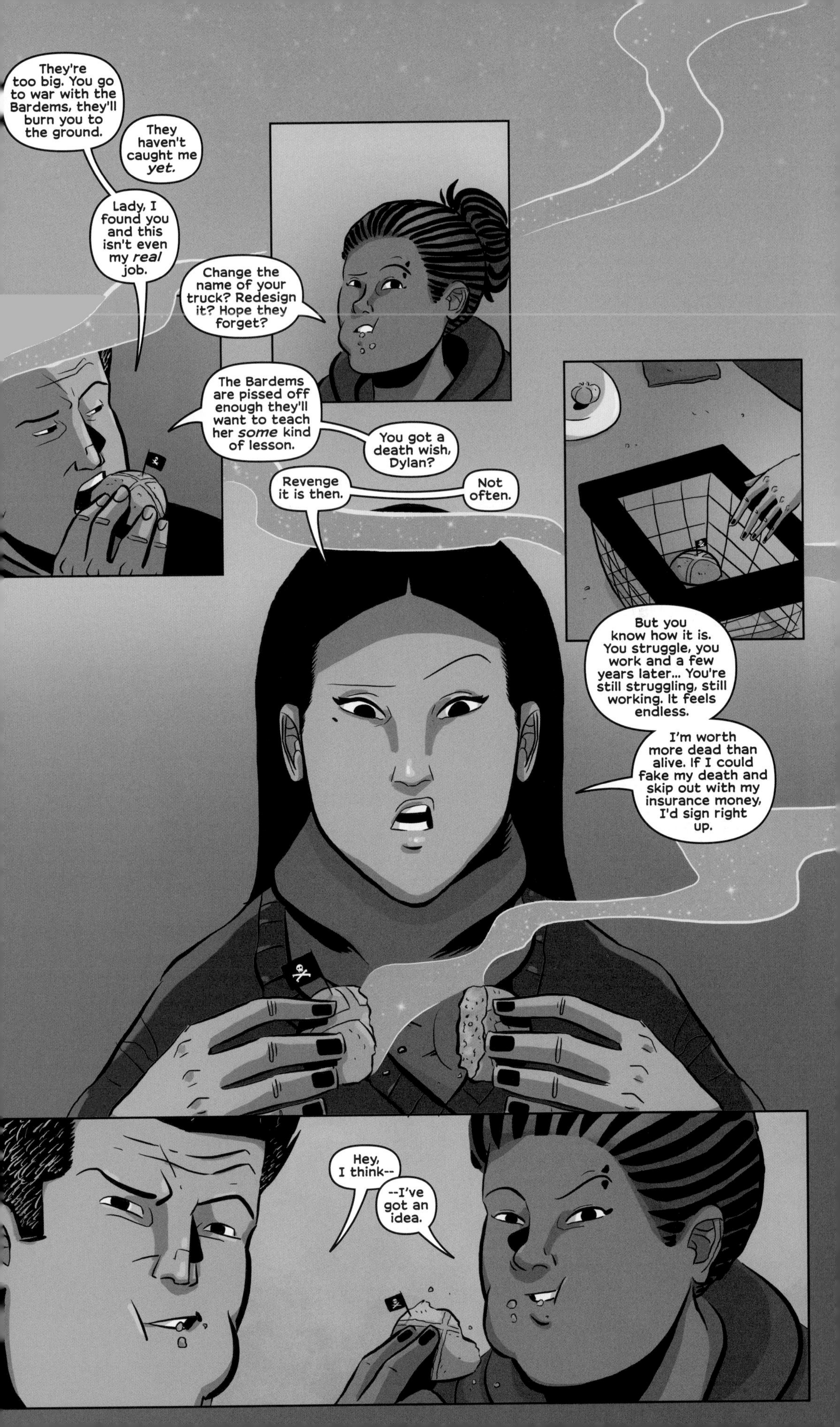
They're too big. You go to war with the Bardems, they'll burn you to the ground.
They haven't caught me *yet.*
Lady, I found you and this isn't even my *real* job.
Change the name of your truck? Redesign it? Hope they forget?
The Bardems are pissed off enough they'll want to teach her *some* kind of lesson.
You got a death wish, Dylan?
Not often.
Revenge it is then.
But you know how it is. You struggle, you work and a few years later... You're still struggling, still working. It feels endless.
I'm worth more dead than alive. If I could fake my death and skip out with my insurance money, I'd sign right up.
Hey, I think--
--I've got an idea.

What time then?

We'll let you know, we gotta talk to a few people. Bring an extra leg.

How romantic.

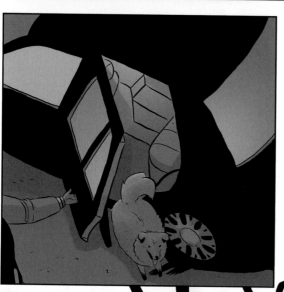

Dylan's amazing, right?

She really is.

I can't wait to see her again. She's... Wow.

Hey, so, about the gun...

Y'know. You could have asked, is all. It's not like I want it, but it's nice to know where your loose gun is.

Why'd you need it?

Protection. There's... There's a lot of stuff in my life I haven't told you about.

So tell me.

If we get through the next few days, okay. But you have to promise you'll still like me after I tell you.

Jeez, Harp. I don't even like you *now*.

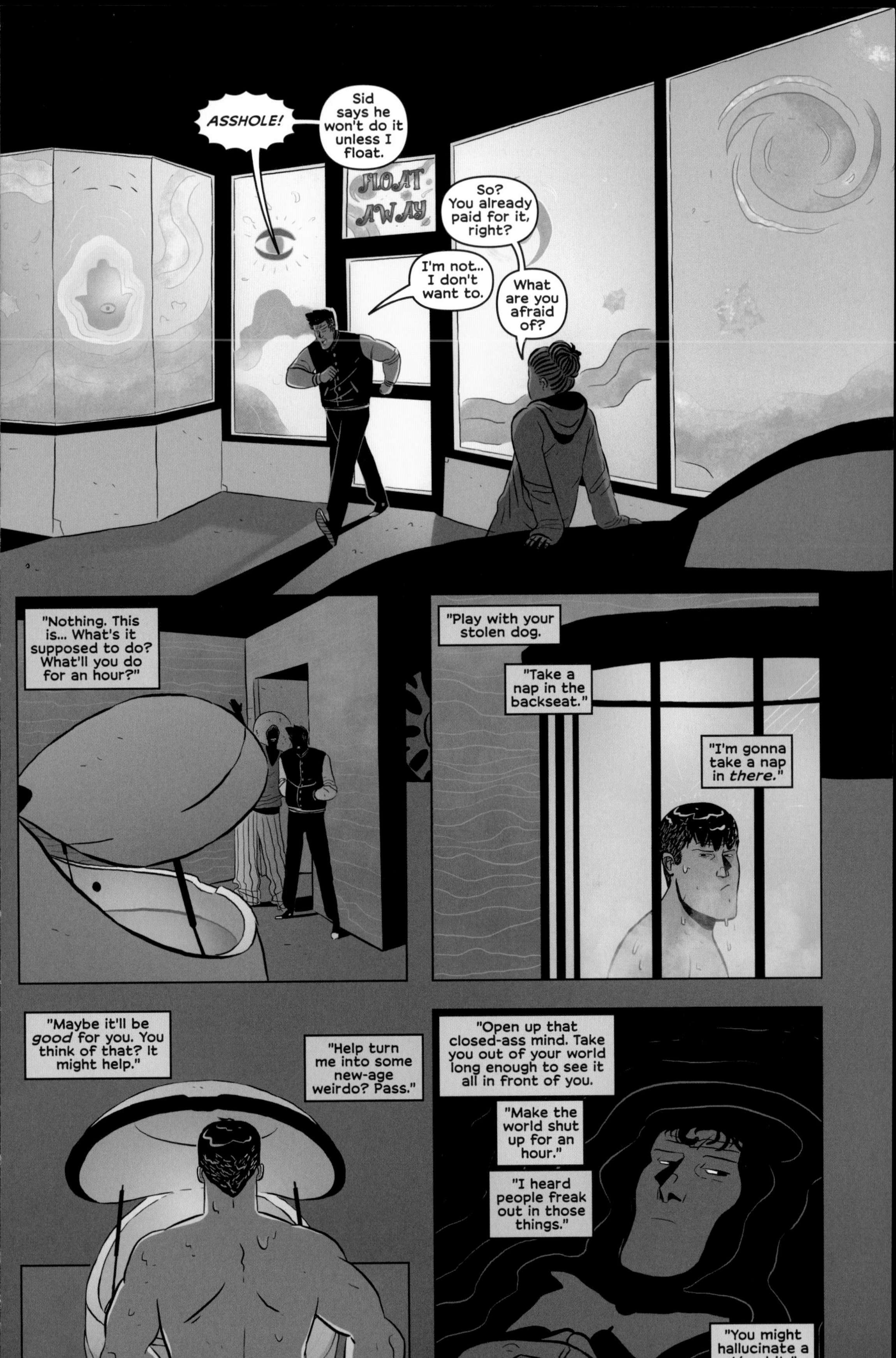
ASSHOLE!
Sid says he won't do it unless I float.
FLOAT AWAY
So? You already paid for it, right?
I'm not... I don't want to.
What are you afraid of?
"Nothing. This is... What's it supposed to do? What'll you do for an hour?"
"Play with your stolen dog.
"Take a nap in the backseat."
"I'm gonna take a nap in *there.*"
"Maybe it'll be *good* for you. You think of that? It might help."
"Help turn me into some new-age weirdo? Pass."
"Open up that closed-ass mind. Take you out of your world long enough to see it all in front of you.
"Make the world shut up for an hour."
"I heard people freak out in those things."
"You might hallucinate a *tiny* bit."

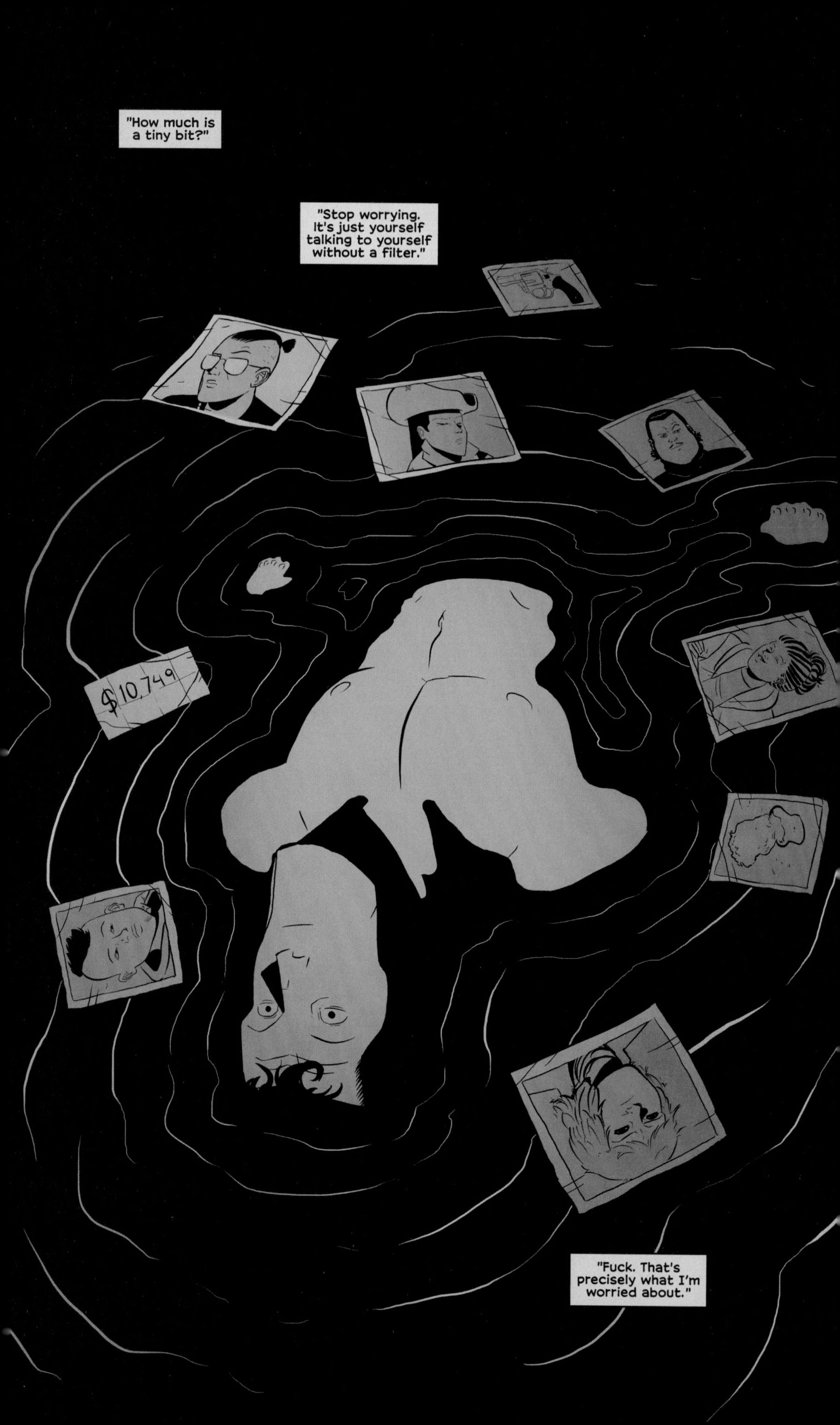
"How much is a tiny bit?"
"Stop worrying. It's just yourself talking to yourself without a filter."
$10,749
"Fuck. That's precisely what I'm worried about."

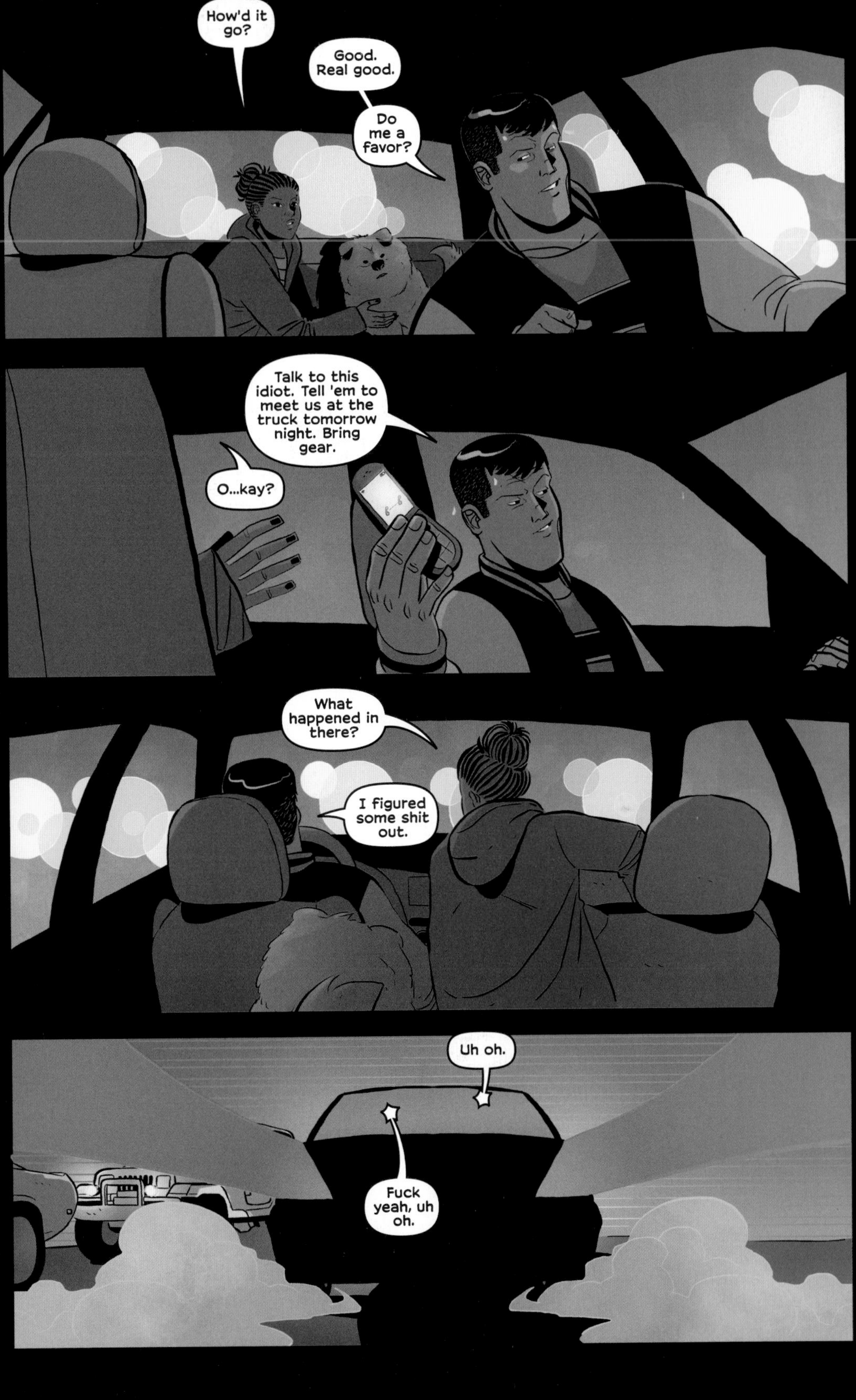
How'd it go?
Good. Real good.
Do me a favor?
Talk to this idiot. Tell 'em to meet us at the truck tomorrow night. Bring gear.
O...kay?
What happened in there?
I figured some shit out.
Uh oh.
Fuck yeah, uh oh.

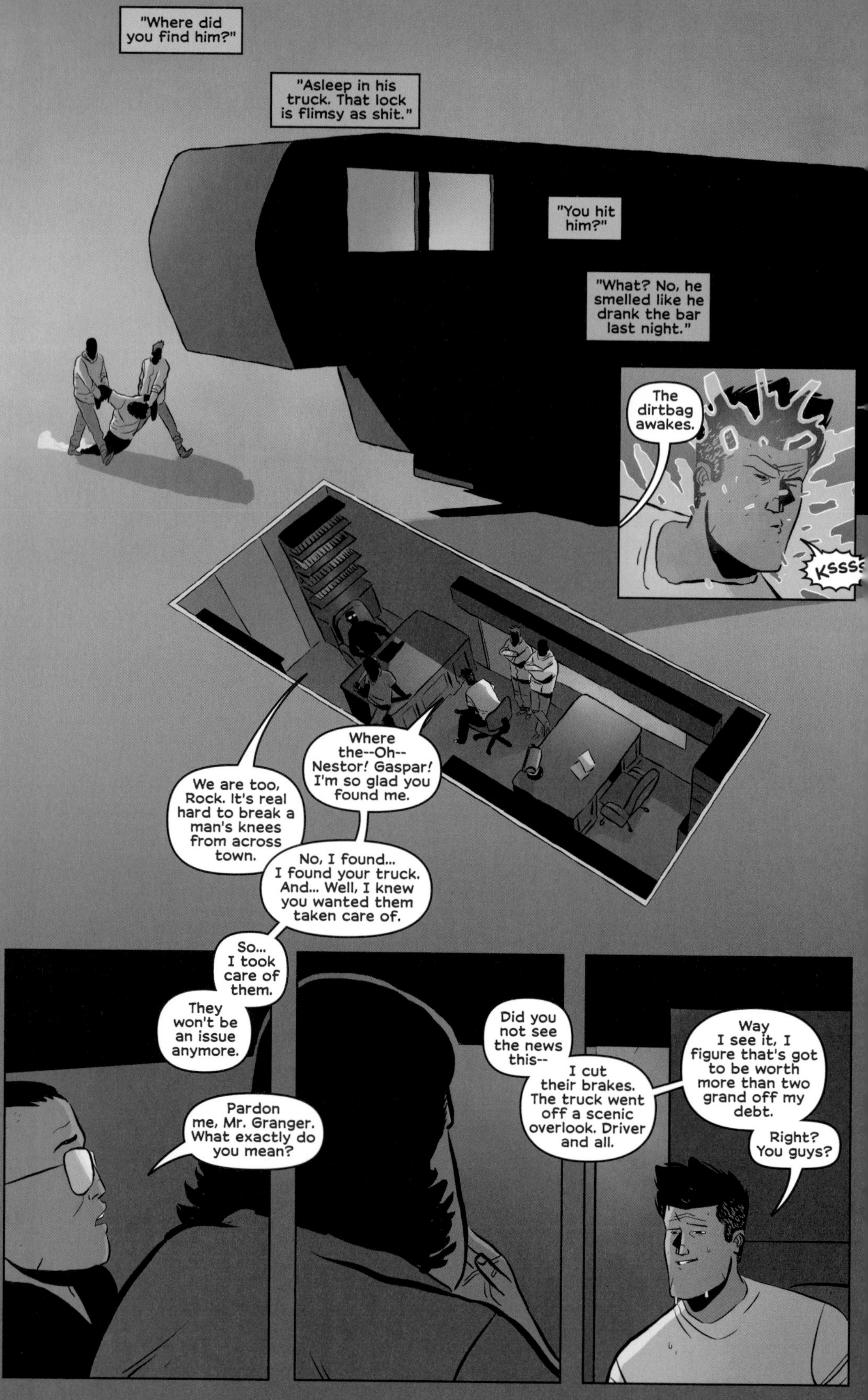

"Where did you find him?"
"Asleep in his truck. That lock is flimsy as shit."
"You hit him?"
"What? No, he smelled like he drank the bar last night."
The dirtbag awakes.
KSSS
Where the--Oh-- Nestor! Gaspar! I'm so glad you found me.
We are too, Rock. It's real hard to break a man's knees from across town.
No, I found... I found your truck. And... Well, I knew you wanted them taken care of.
So... I took care of them.
They won't be an issue anymore.
Pardon me, Mr. Granger. What exactly do you mean?
Did you not see the news this--
I cut their brakes. The truck went off a scenic overlook. Driver and all.
Way I see it, I figure that's got to be worth more than two grand off my debt.
Right? You guys?

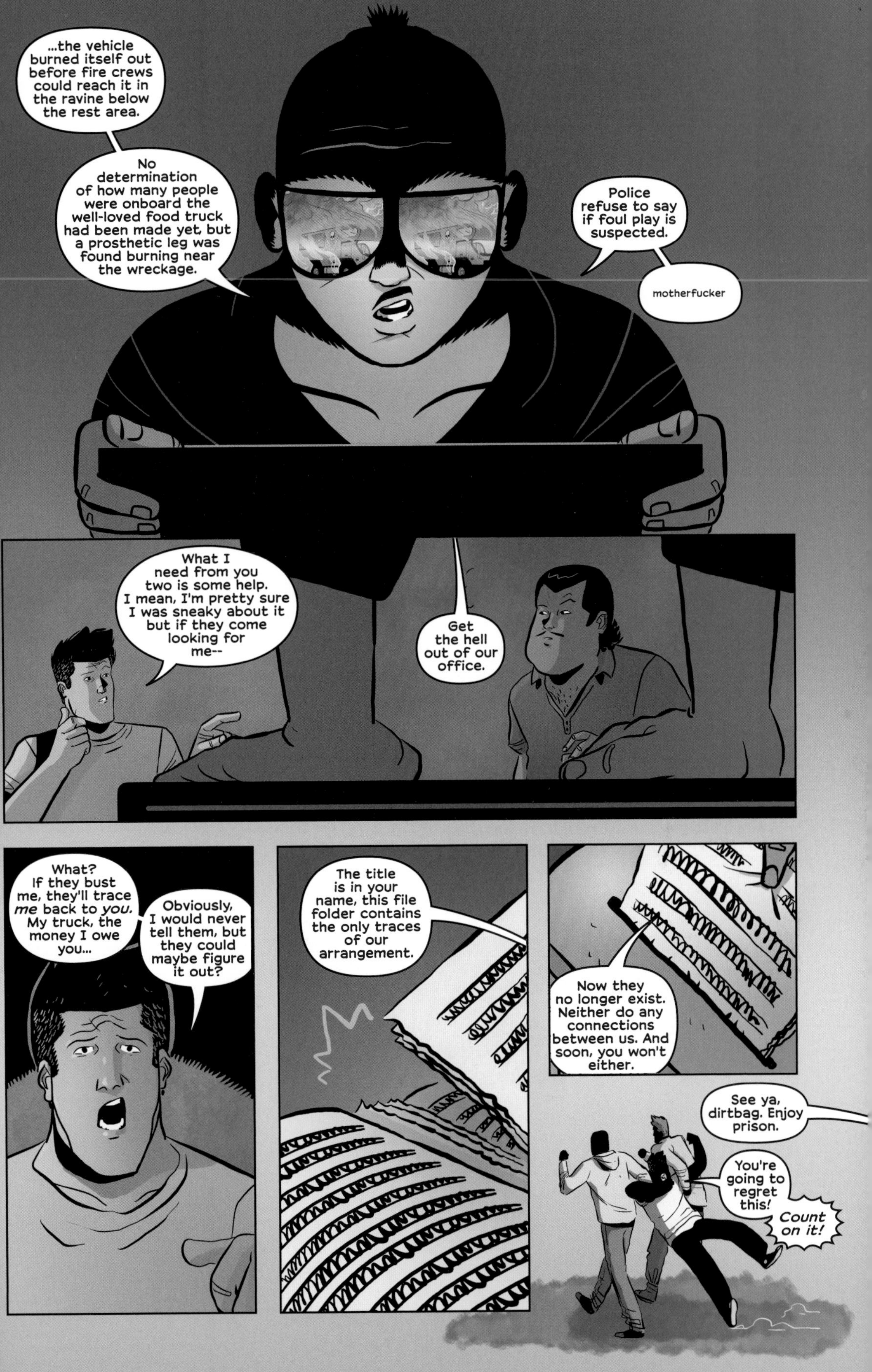
...the vehicle burned itself out before fire crews could reach it in the ravine below the rest area.
No determination of how many people were onboard the well-loved food truck had been made yet, but a prosthetic leg was found burning near the wreckage.
Police refuse to say if foul play is suspected.
motherfucker
What I need from you two is some help. I mean, I'm pretty sure I was sneaky about it but if they come looking for me--
Get the hell out of our office.
What? If they bust me, they'll trace *me* back to *you.* My truck, the money I owe you...
Obviously, I would never tell them, but they could maybe figure it out?
The title is in your name, this file folder contains the only traces of our arrangement.
Now they no longer exist. Neither do any connections between us. And soon, you won't either.
See ya, dirtbag. Enjoy prison.
You're going to regret this!
Count on it!

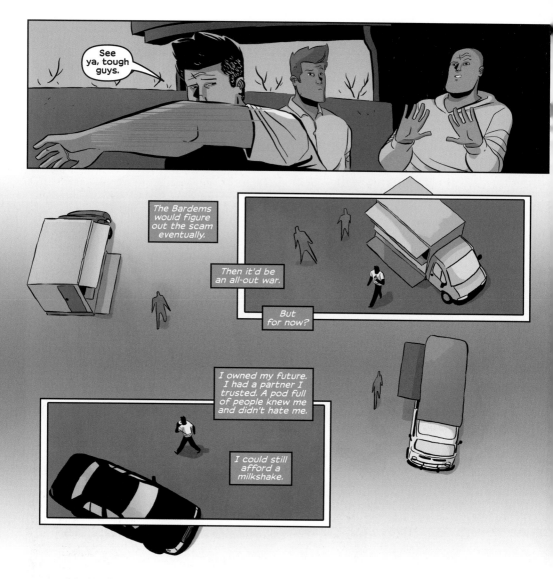

See ya, tough guys.

The Bardems would figure out the scam eventually.

Then it'd be an all-out war.

But for now?

I owned my future. I had a partner I trusted. A pod full of people knew me and didn't hate me.

I could still afford a milkshake.

Tell me they bought it.

I didn't even have to cry.

One more appointment and that's it...

We're free.

Uh huh.

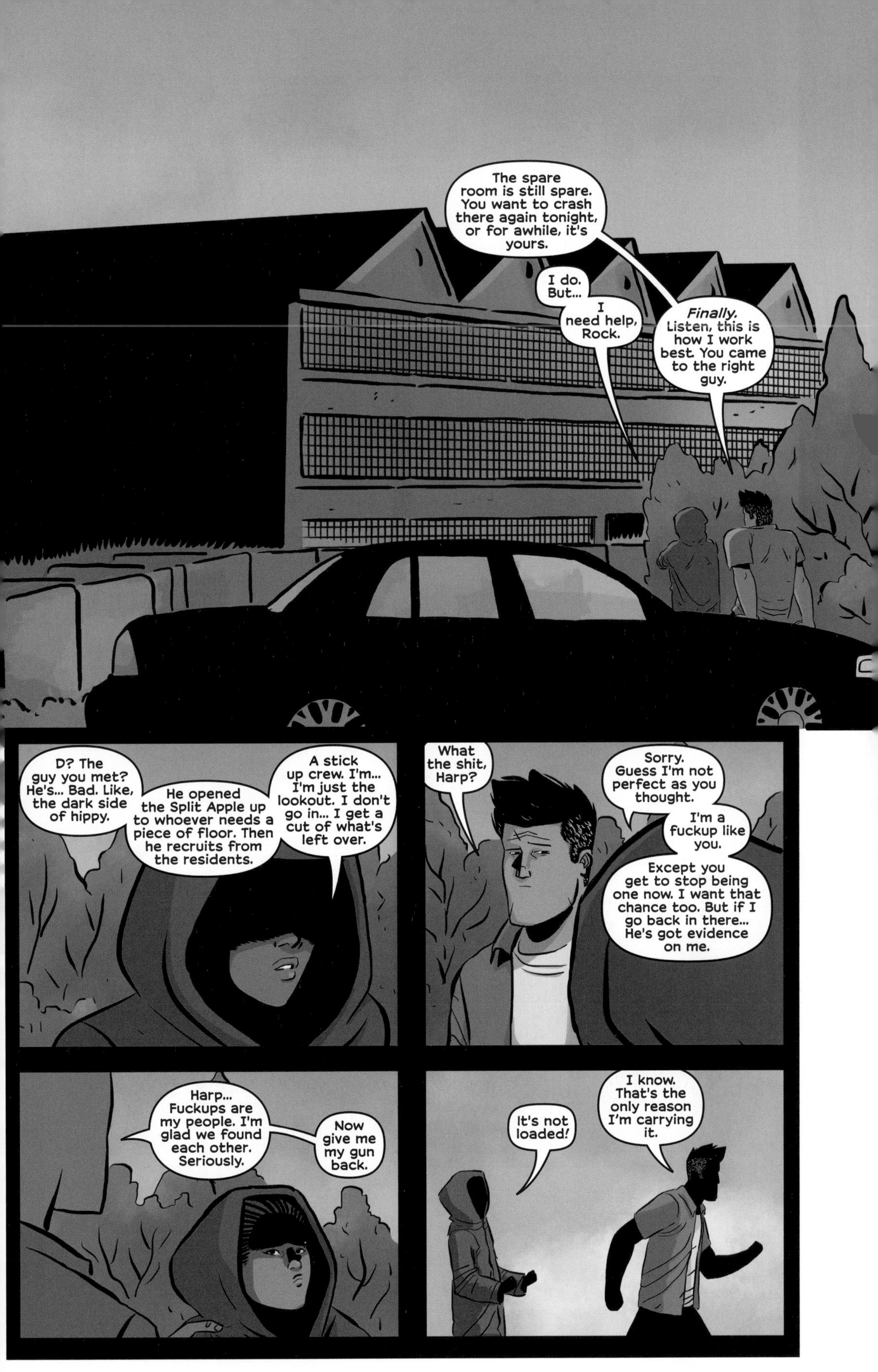
The spare room is still spare. You want to crash there again tonight, or for awhile, it's yours.
I do. But...
I need help, Rock.
Finally. Listen, this is how I work best. You came to the right guy.
D? The guy you met? He's... Bad. Like, the dark side of hippy.
He opened the Split Apple up to whoever needs a piece of floor. Then he recruits from the residents.
A stick up crew. I'm... I'm just the lookout. I don't go in... I get a cut of what's left over.
What the shit, Harp?
Sorry. Guess I'm not perfect as you thought.
I'm a fuckup like you.
Except you get to stop being one now. I want that chance too. But if I go back in there... He's got evidence on me.
Harp... Fuckups are my people. I'm glad we found each other. Seriously.
Now give me my gun back.
It's not loaded!
I know. That's the only reason I'm carrying it.

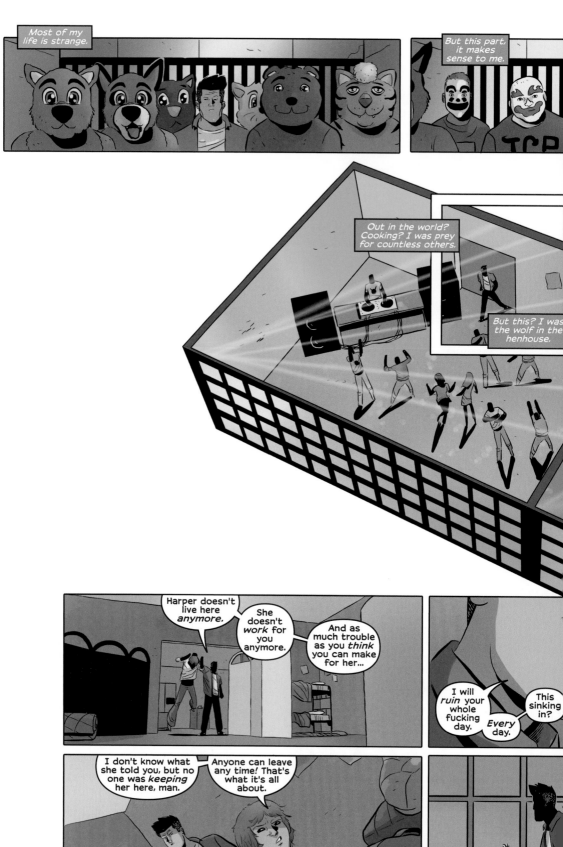

Most of my life is strange.

But this part, it makes sense to me.

Out in the world? Cooking? I was prey for countless others.

But this? I was the wolf in the henhouse.

Harper doesn't live here *anymore.*

She doesn't *work* for you anymore.

And as much trouble as you *think* you can make for her...

I will *ruin* your whole fucking day. *Every* day.

This sinking in?

I don't know what she told you, but no one was *keeping* her here, man.

Anyone can leave any time! That's what it's all about.

Keep packing.

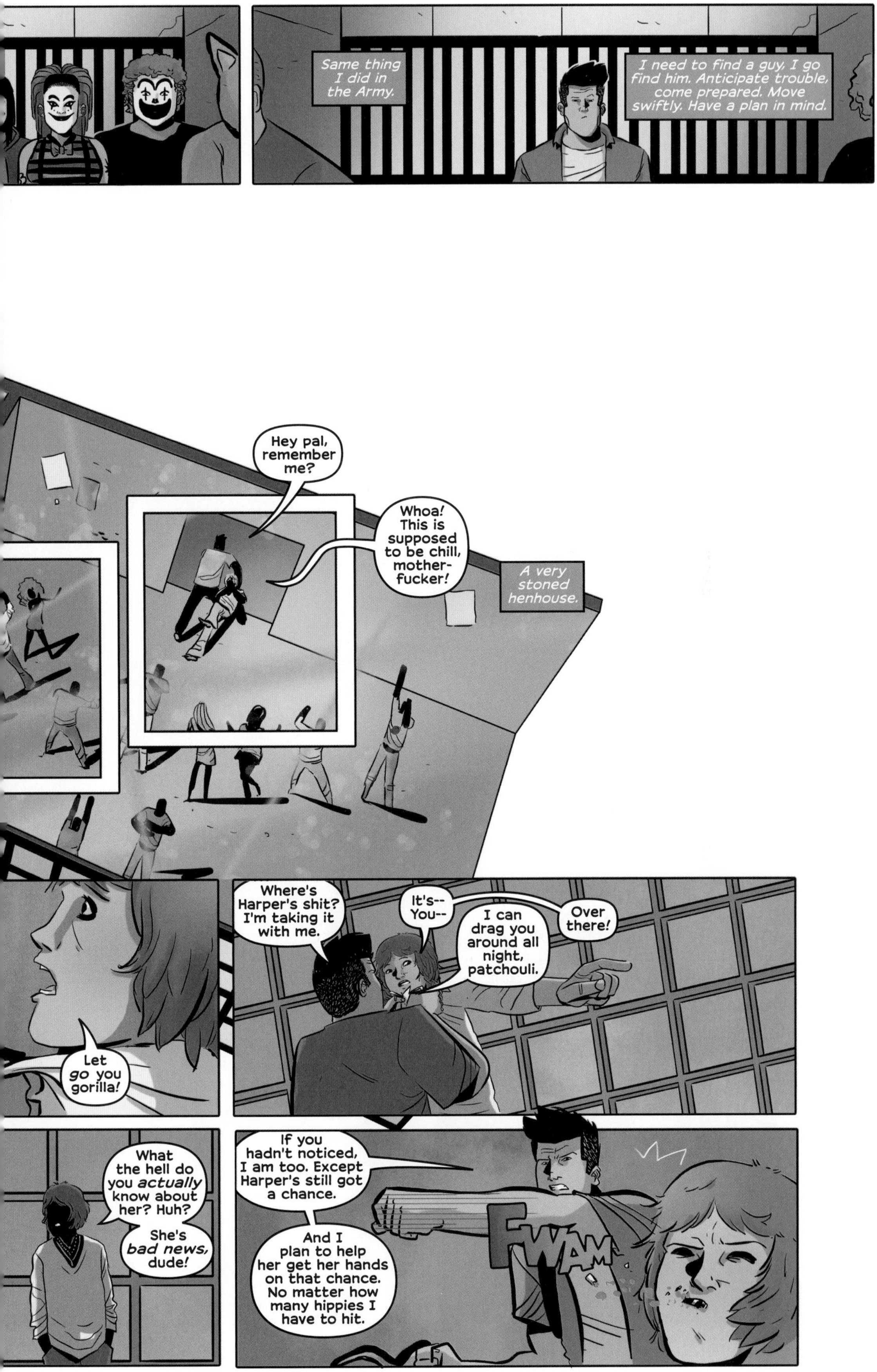
Same thing I did in the Army.
I need to find a guy, I go find him. Anticipate trouble, come prepared. Move swiftly. Have a plan in mind.
Hey pal, remember me?
Whoa! This is supposed to be chill, mother-fucker!
A very stoned henhouse.
Let go you gorilla!
Where's Harper's shit? I'm taking it with me.
It's-- You--
I can drag you around all night, patchouli.
Over there!
What the hell do you actually know about her? Huh?
She's bad news, dude!
If you hadn't noticed, I am too. Except Harper's still got a chance.
And I plan to help her get her hands on that chance. No matter how many hippies I have to hit.
FWAM

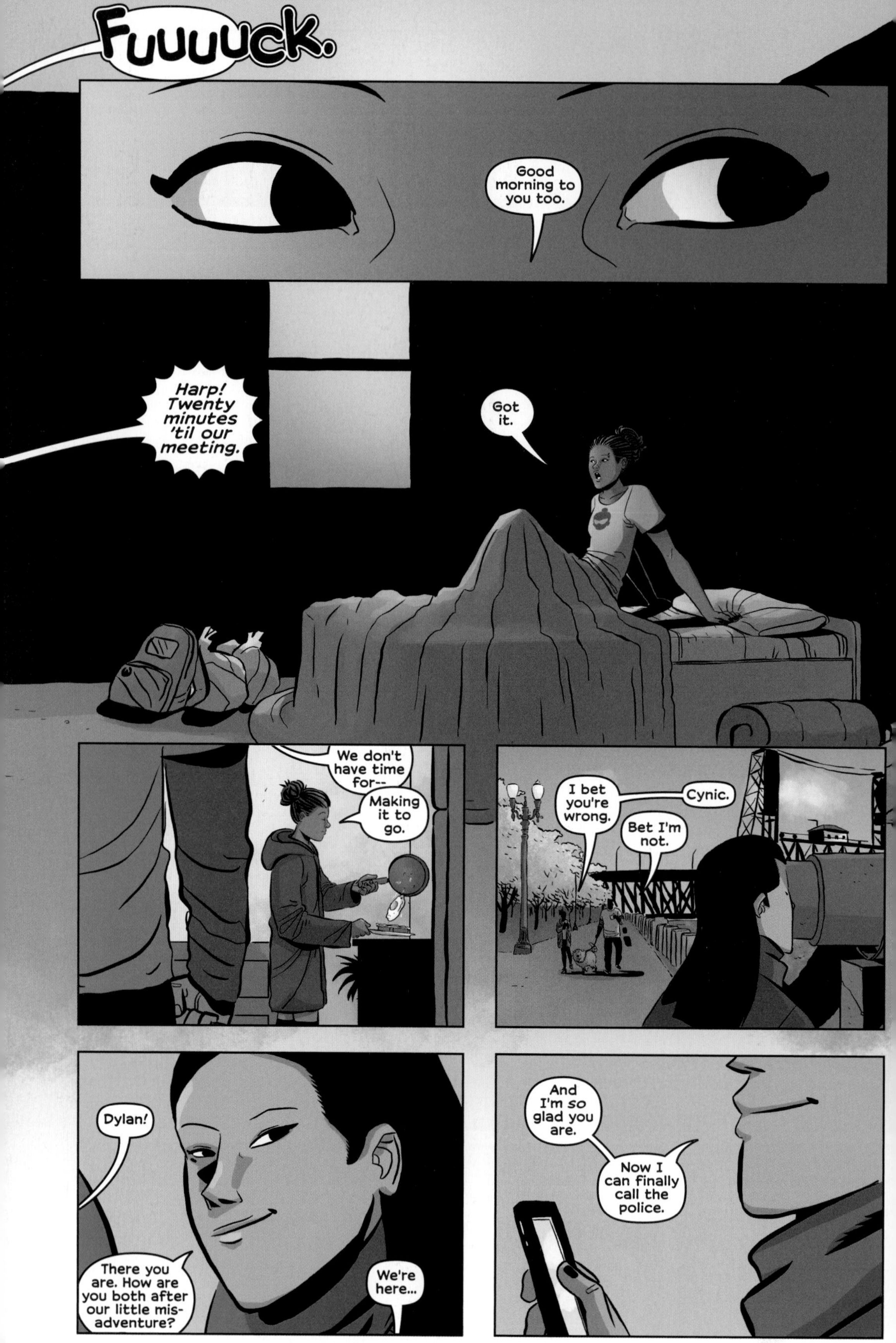
Fuuuuck.
Good morning to you too.
Harp! Twenty minutes 'til our meeting.
Got it.
We don't have time for--
Making it to go.
I bet you're wrong.
Cynic.
Bet I'm not.
Dylan!
There you are. How are you both after our little mis-adventure?
We're here...
And I'm so glad you are.
Now I can finally call the police.

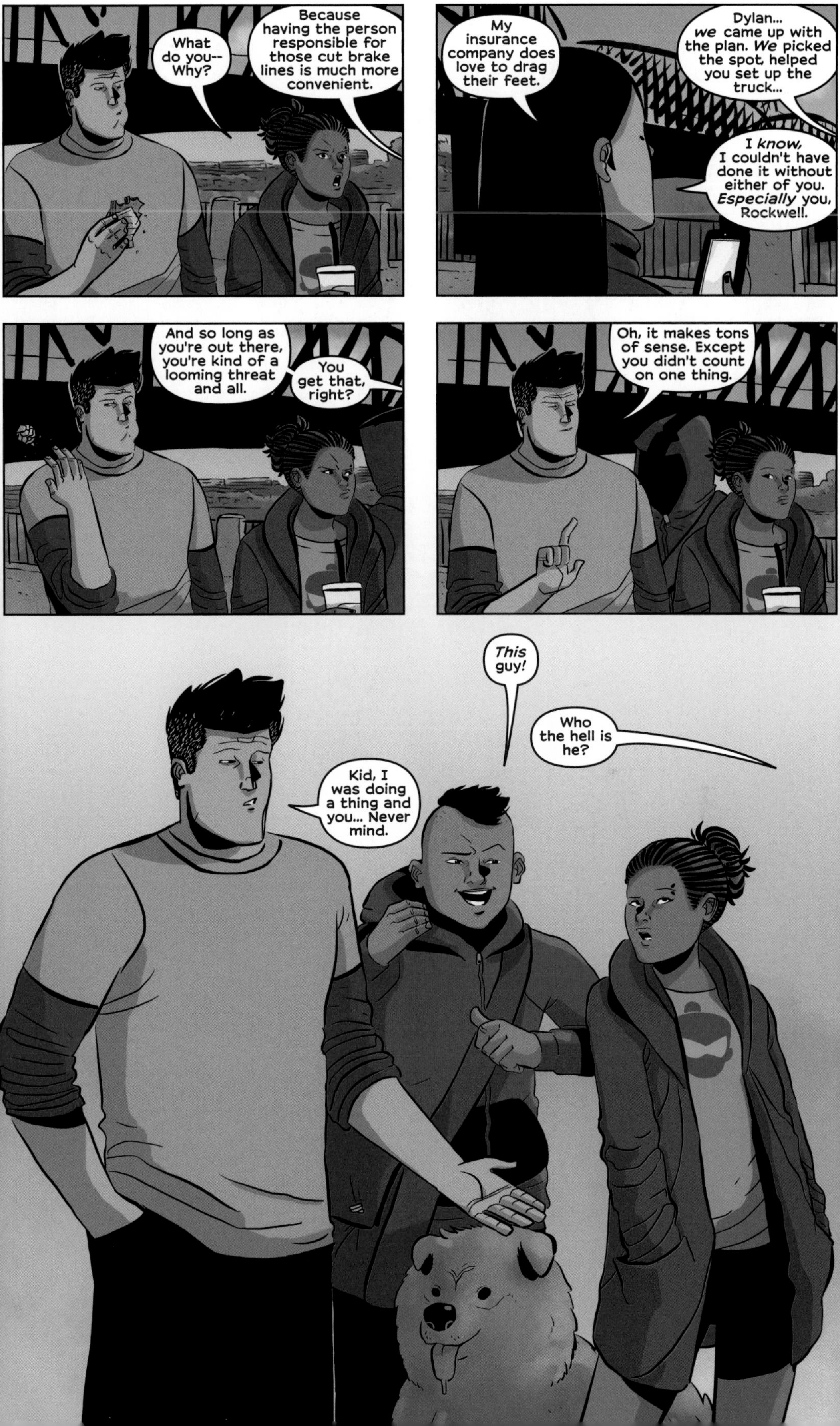
What do you-- Why?
Because having the person responsible for those cut brake lines is much more convenient.
My insurance company does love to drag their feet.
Dylan... *we* came up with the plan. *We* picked the spot, helped you set up the truck...
I *know*, I couldn't have done it without either of you. *Especially* you, Rockwell.
And so long as you're out there, you're kind of a looming threat and all.
You get that, right?
Oh, it makes tons of sense. Except you didn't count on one thing.
This guy!
Who the hell is he?
Kid, I was doing a thing and you... Never mind.

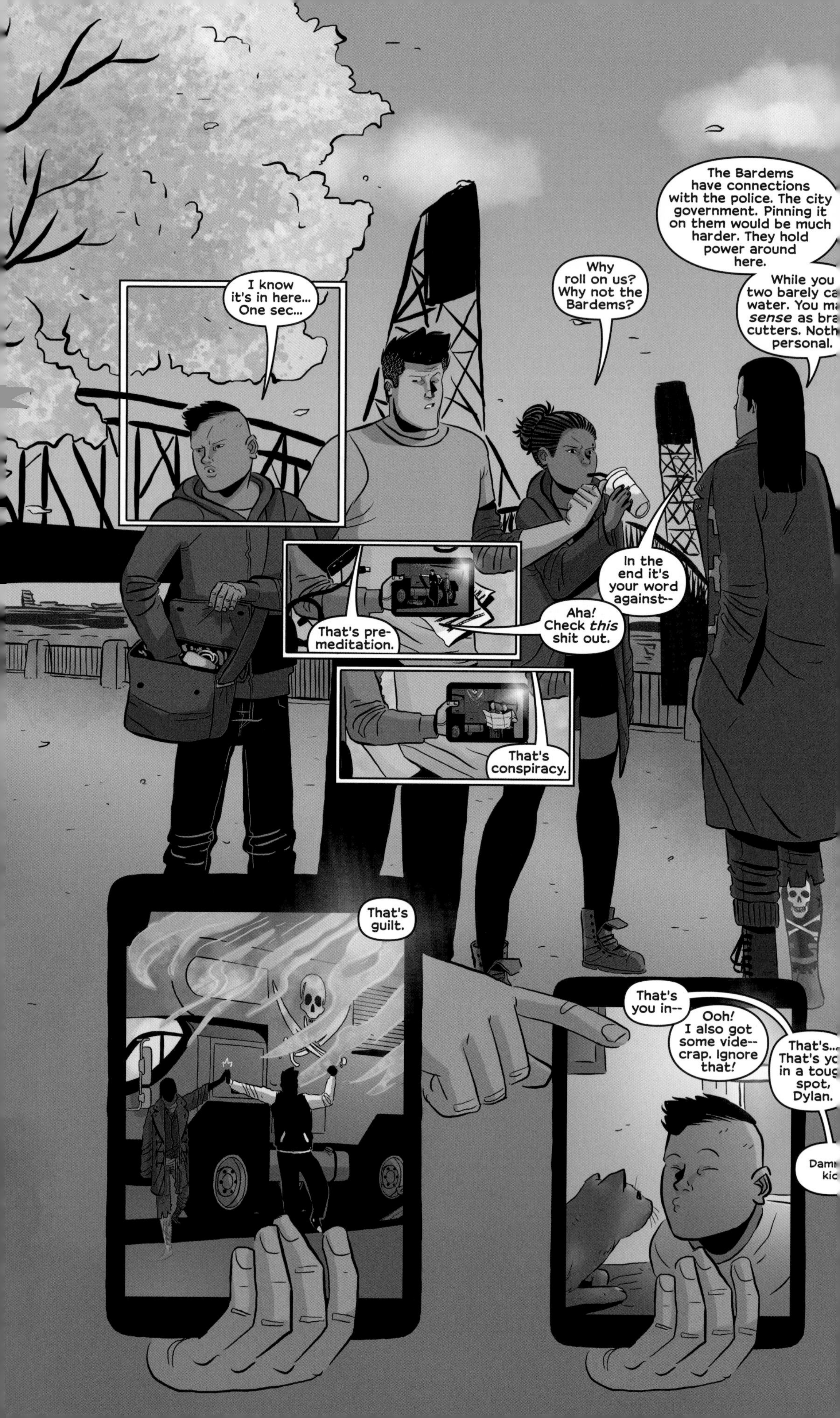

I know it's in here... One sec...
Why roll on us? Why not the Bardems?
The Bardems have connections with the police. The city government. Pinning it on them would be much harder. They hold power around here.
While you two barely ca water. You ma sense as bra cutters. Noth personal.
In the end it's your word against--
Aha! Check *this* shit out.
That's pre-meditation.
That's conspiracy.
That's guilt.
That's you in--
Ooh! I also got some vide-- crap. Ignore that!
That's... That's yo in a toug spot, Dylan.

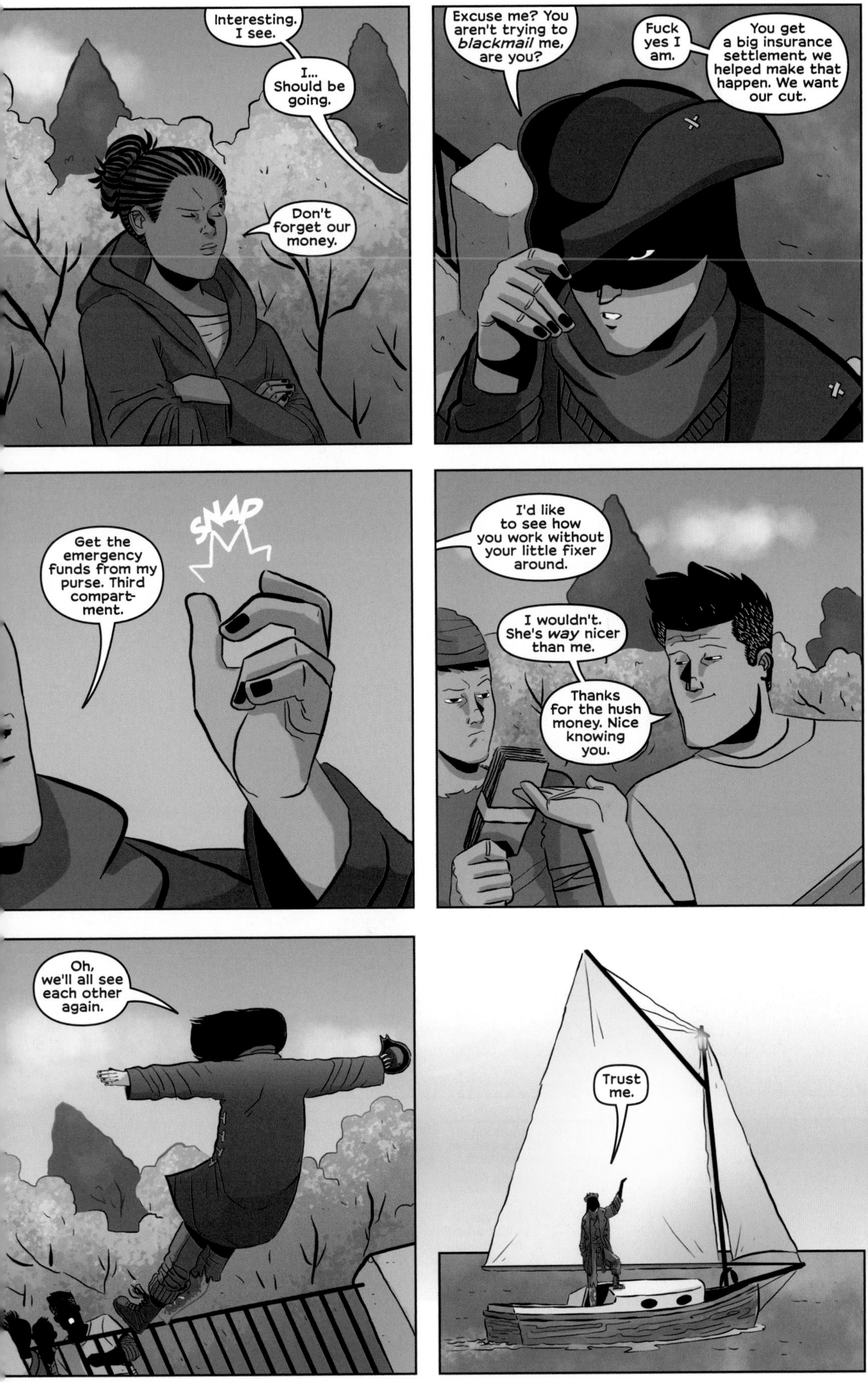
Interesting. I see.
I... Should be going.
Don't forget our money.
Excuse me? You aren't trying to *blackmail* me, are you?
Fuck yes I am.
You get a big insurance settlement, we helped make that happen. We want our cut.
Get the emergency funds from my purse. Third compart-ment.
SNAP
I'd like to see how you work without your little fixer around.
I wouldn't. She's *way* nicer than me.
Thanks for the hush money. Nice knowing you.
Oh, we'll all see each other again.
Trust me.

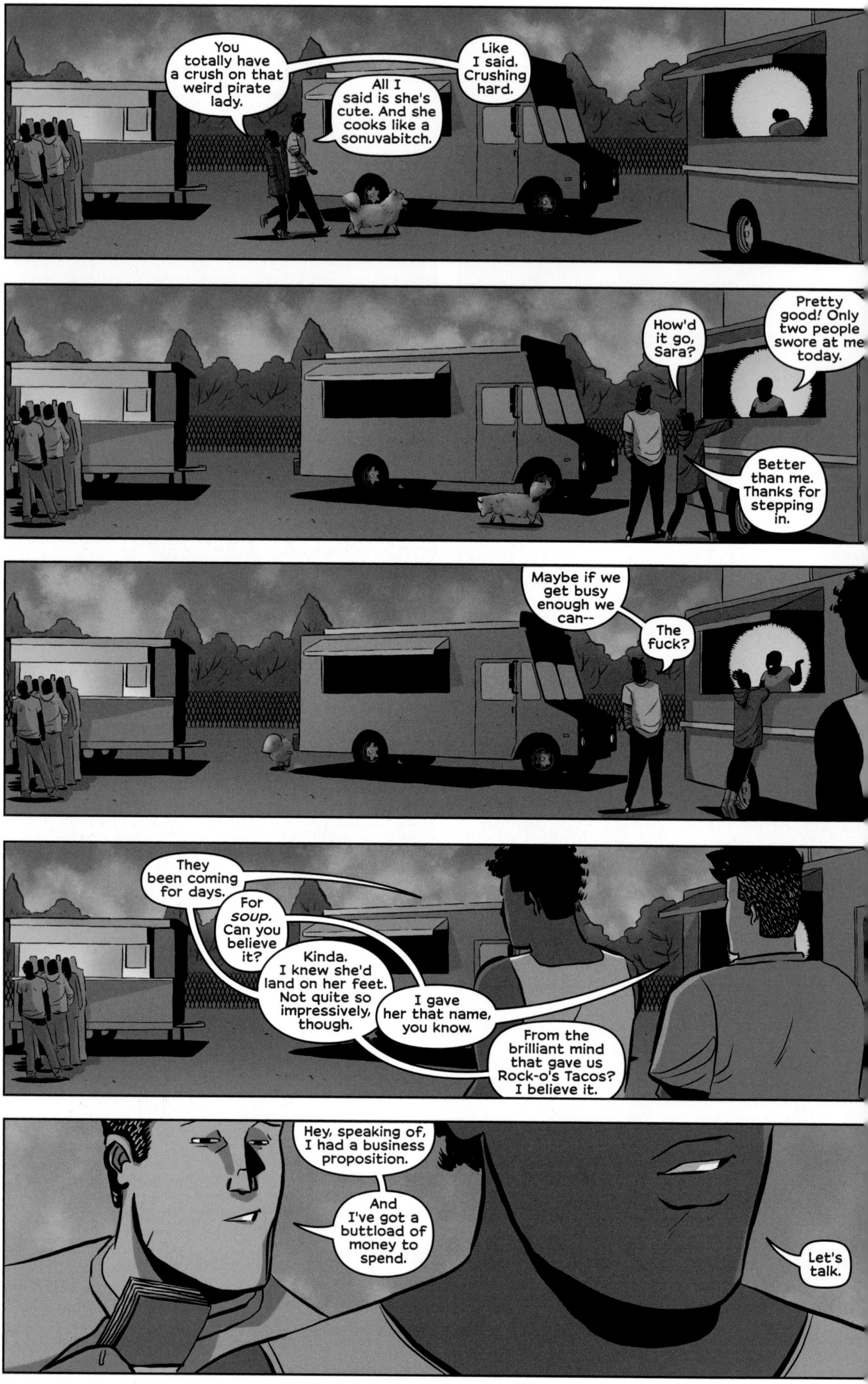
You totally have a crush on that weird pirate lady.
All I said is she's cute. And she cooks like a sonuvabitch.
Like I said. Crushing hard.
How'd it go, Sara?
Pretty good! Only two people swore at me today.
Better than me. Thanks for stepping in.
Maybe if we get busy enough we can--
The fuck?
They been coming for days.
For *soup.* Can you believe it?
Kinda. I knew she'd land on her feet. Not quite so impressively, though.
I gave her that name, you know.
From the brilliant mind that gave us Rock-o's Tacos? I believe it.
Hey, speaking of, I had a business proposition.
And I've got a buttload of money to spend.
Let's talk.

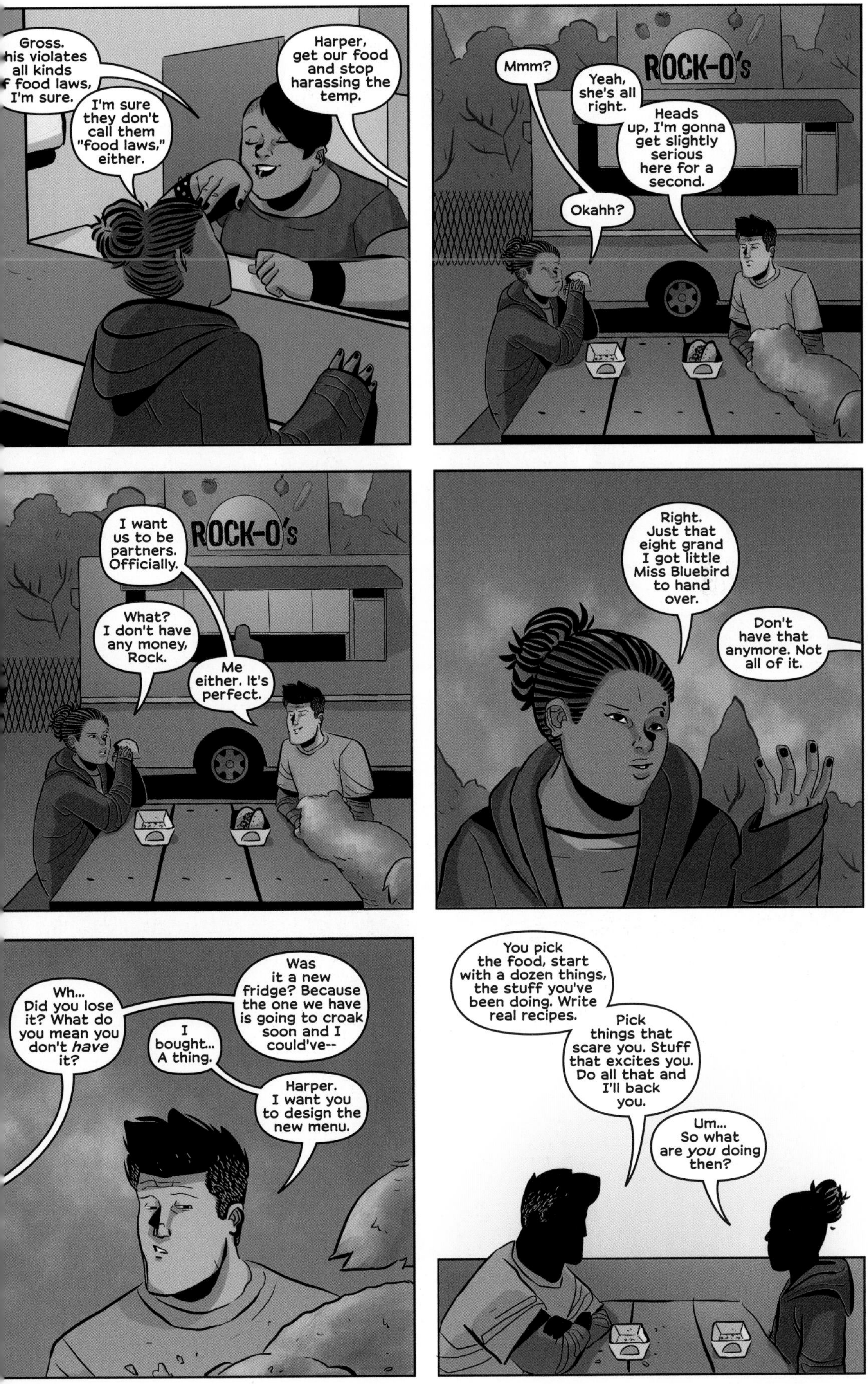
Gross.
his violates all kinds
f food laws, I'm sure.
I'm sure they don't call them "food laws," either.
Harper, get our food and stop harassing the temp.
ROCK-O's
Mmm?
Yeah, she's all right.
Heads up, I'm gonna get slightly serious here for a second.
Okahh?
ROCK-O's
I want us to be partners. Officially.
What? I don't have any money, Rock.
Me either. It's perfect.
Right. Just that eight grand I got little Miss Bluebird to hand over.
Don't have that anymore. Not all of it.
Wh... Did you lose it? What do you mean you don't *have* it?
I bought... A thing.
Was it a new fridge? Because the one we have is going to croak soon and I could've--
Harper. I want you to design the new menu.
You pick the food, start with a dozen things, the stuff you've been doing. Write real recipes.
Pick things that scare you. Stuff that excites you. Do all that and I'll back you.
Um... So what are *you* doing then?

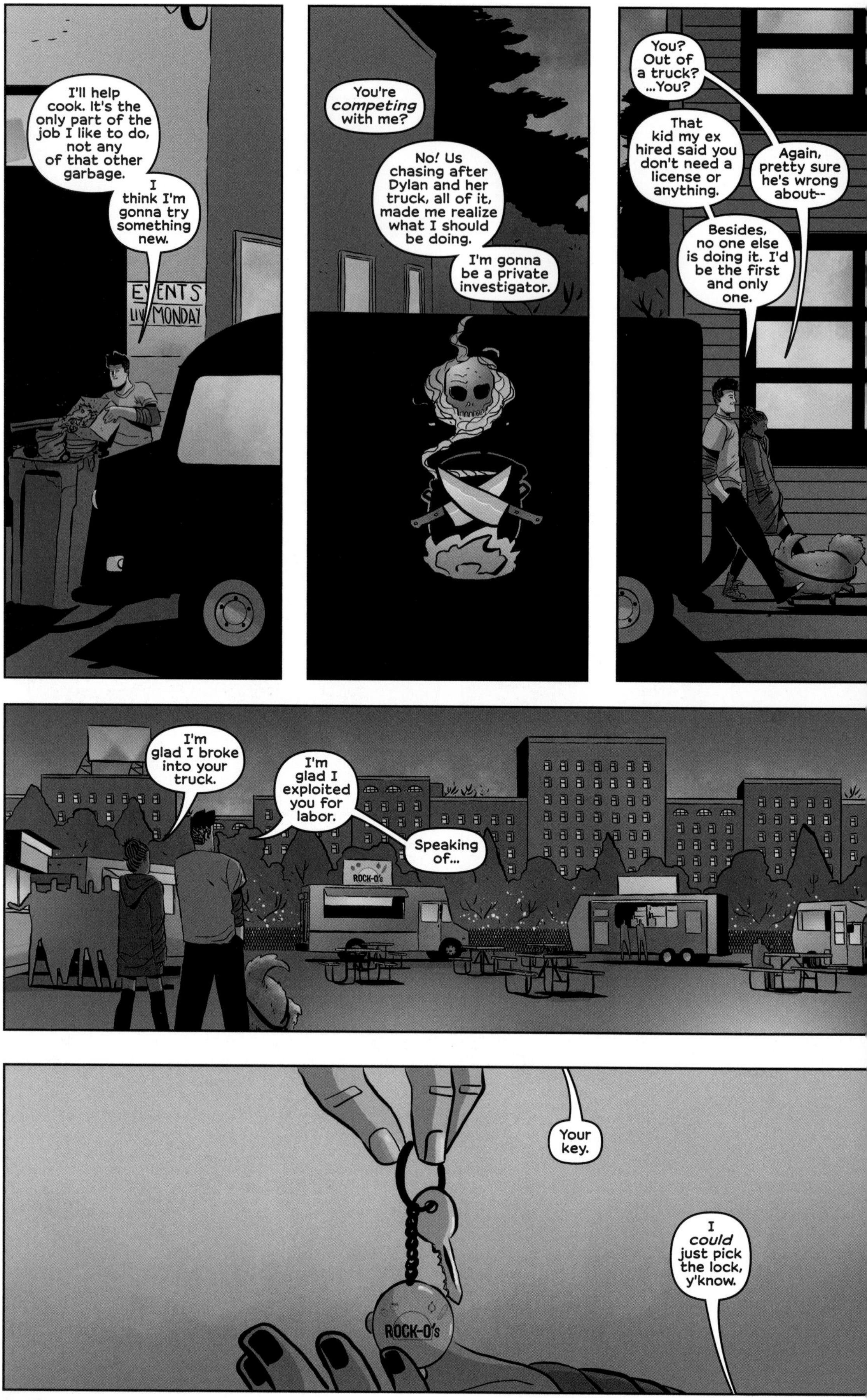
I'll help cook. It's the only part of the job I like to do, not any of that other garbage.
I think I'm gonna try something new.
EVENTS
MONDAY
You're *competing* with me?
No! Us chasing after Dylan and her truck, all of it, made me realize what I should be doing.
I'm gonna be a private investigator.
You? Out of a truck? ...You?
That kid my ex hired said you don't need a license or anything.
Again, pretty sure he's wrong about--
Besides, no one else is doing it. I'd be the first and only one.
I'm glad I broke into your truck.
I'm glad I exploited you for labor.
Speaking of...
ROCK-O's
Your key.
I *could* just pick the lock, y'know.
ROCK-O's

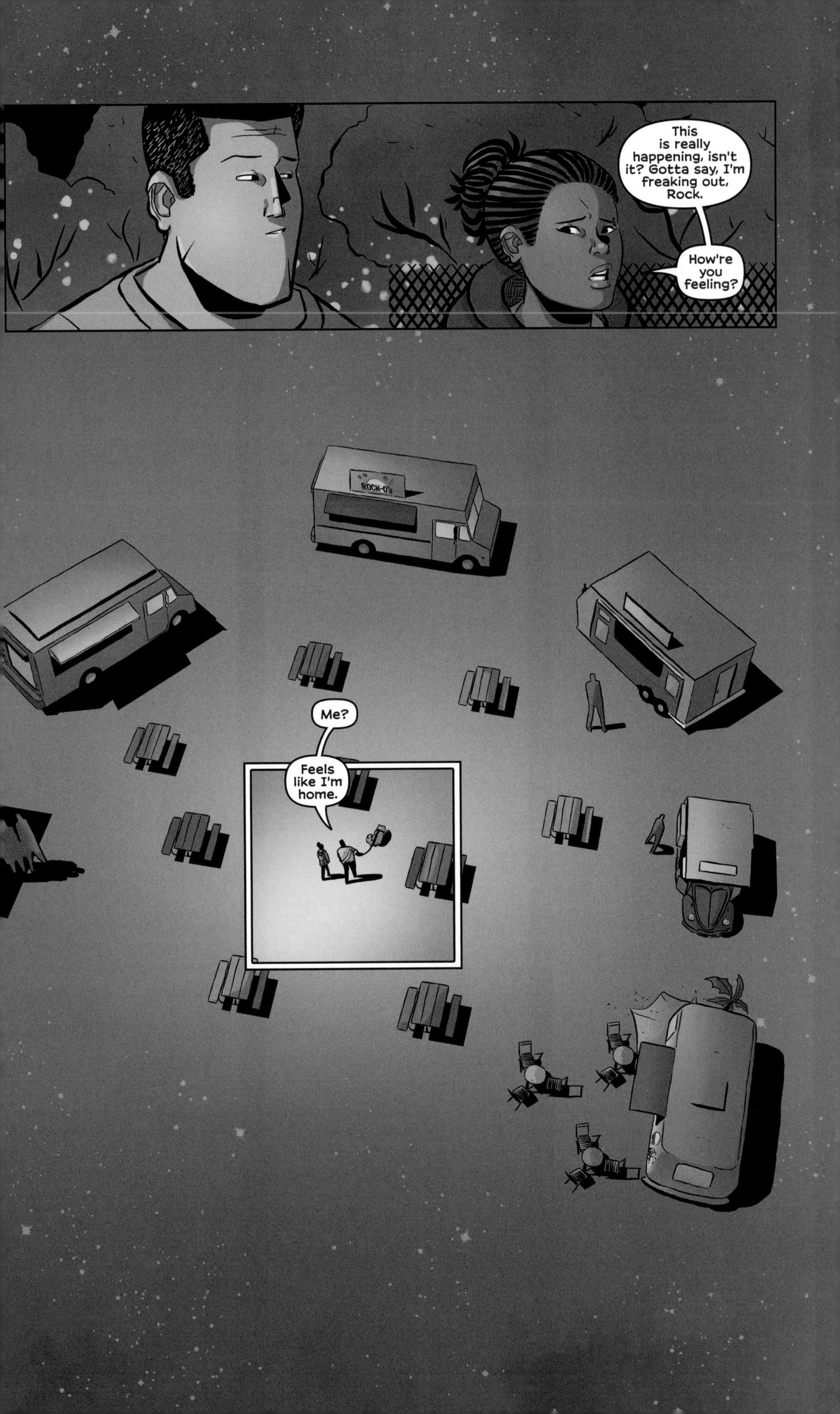
This is really happening, isn't it? Gotta say, I'm freaking out, Rock.
How're you feeling?
ROCK-O's
Me?
Feels like I'm home.

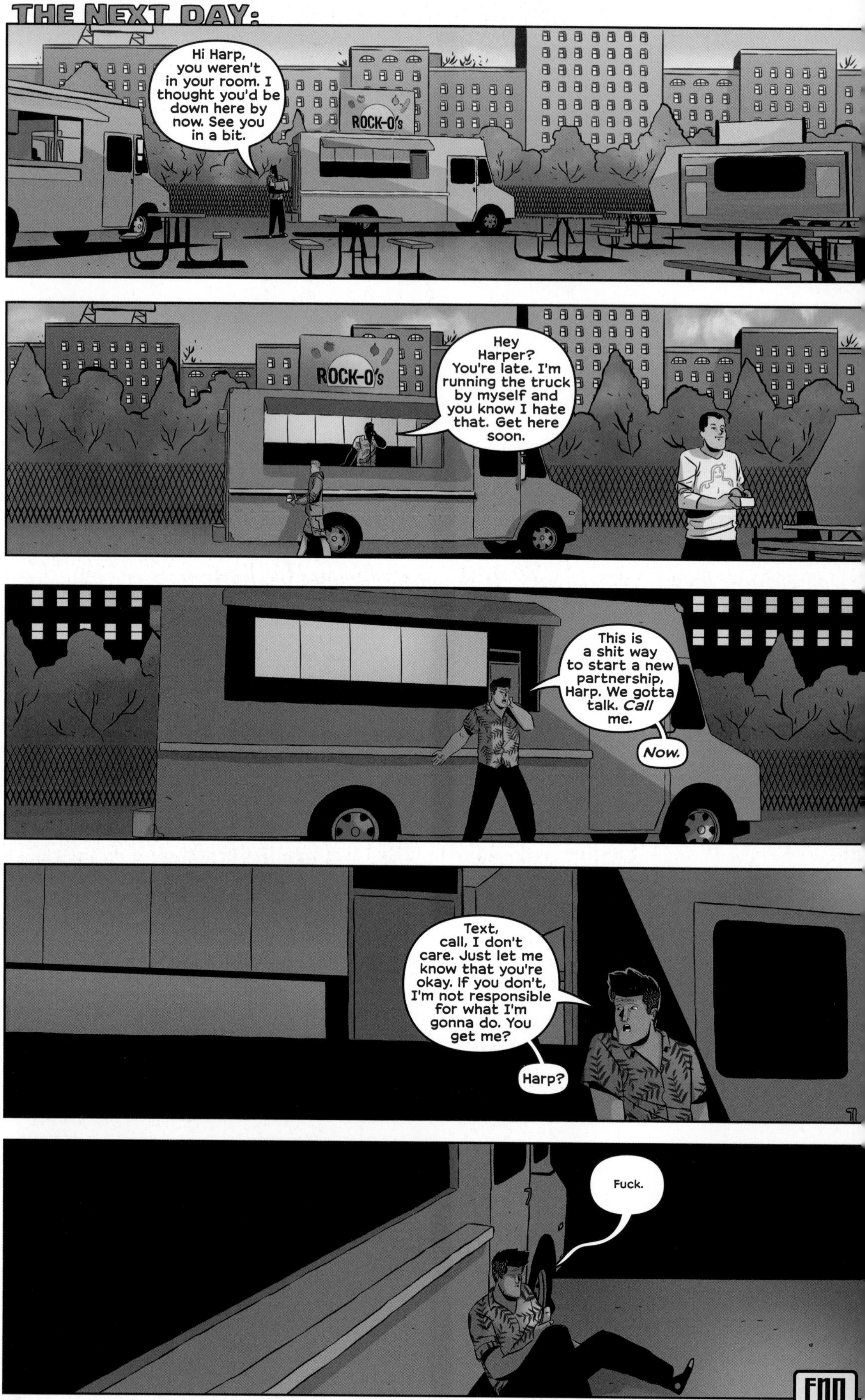
THE NEXT DAY:
Hi Harp, you weren't in your room. I thought you'd be down here by now. See you in a bit.
ROCK-O's
ROCK-O's
Hey Harper? You're late. I'm running the truck by myself and you know I hate that. Get here soon.
This is a shit way to start a new partnership, Harp. We gotta talk. *Call* me.
Now.
Text, call, I don't care. Just let me know that you're okay. If you don't, I'm not responsible for what I'm gonna do. You get me?
Harp?
Fuck.
END

COVER GALLERY

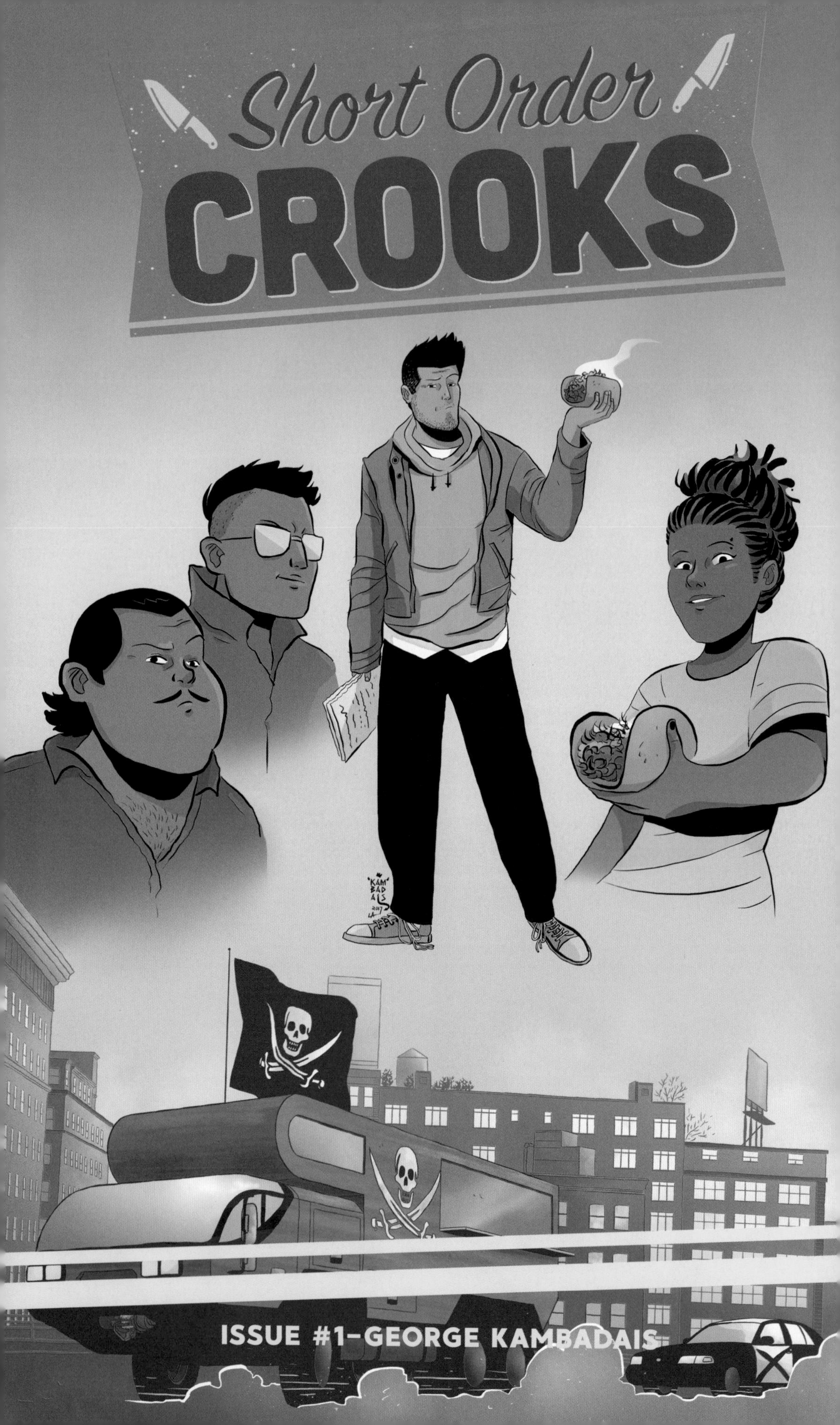

Short Order
CROOKS
ISSUE #1–GEORGE KAMBADAIS

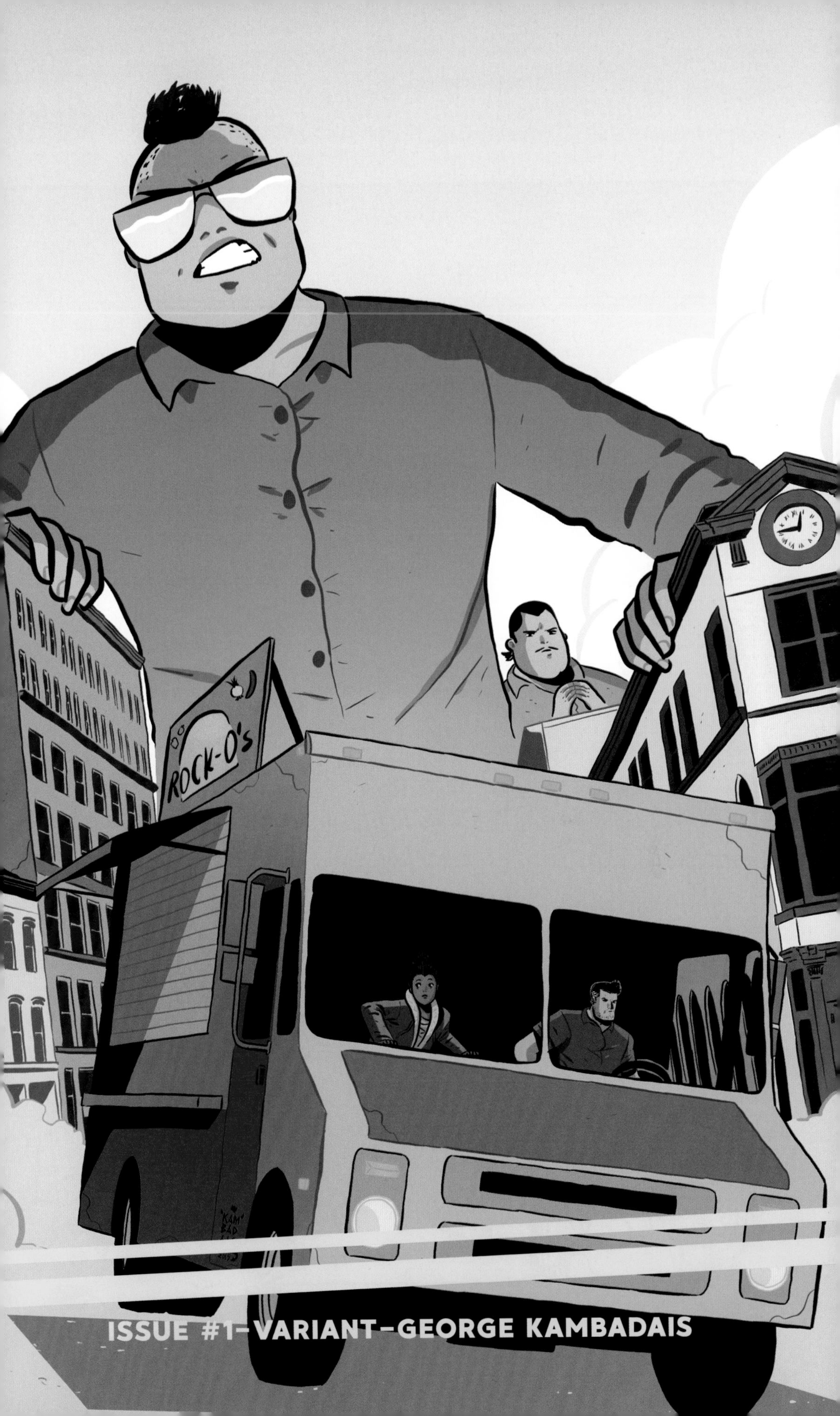
ROCK-O's

ISSUE #1–VARIANT–GEORGE KAMBADAIS

ISSUE #1–VARIANT–KENDALL GOODE

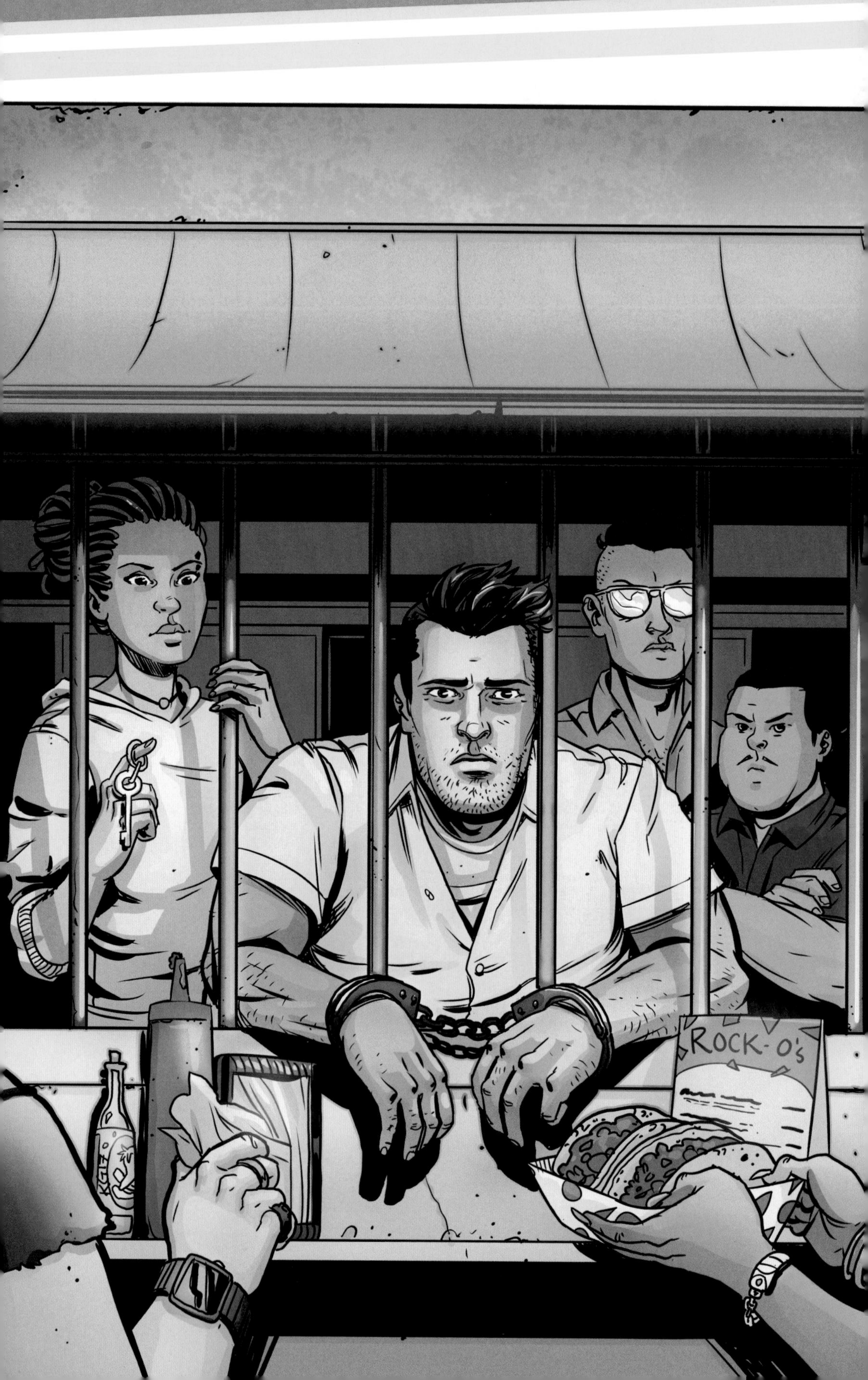
ROCK-O's

ISSUE #2—GEORGE KAMBADAIS

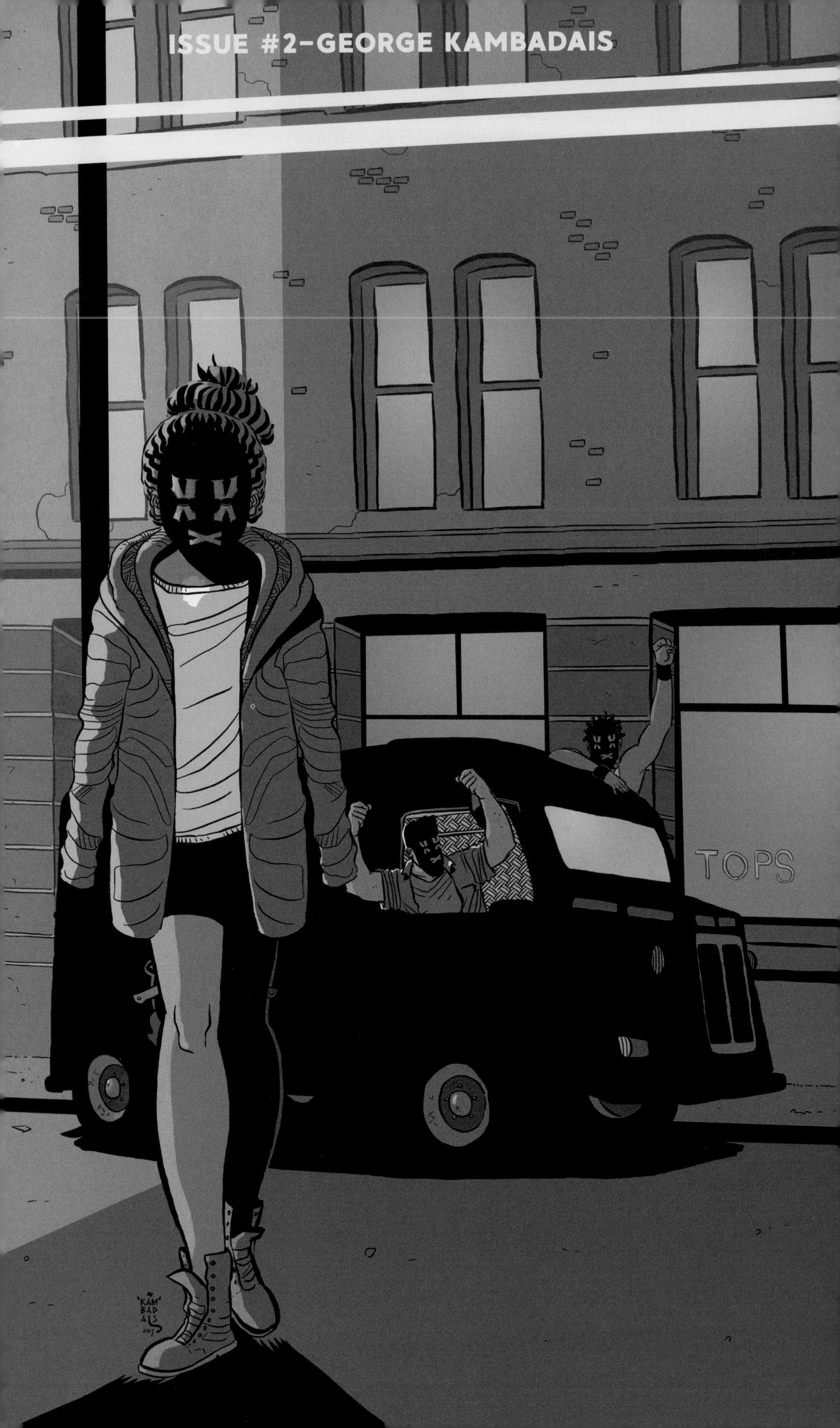
TOPS

ISSUE #2–VARIANT
JONATHAN BRANDON SAWYER & JOSH JENSEN

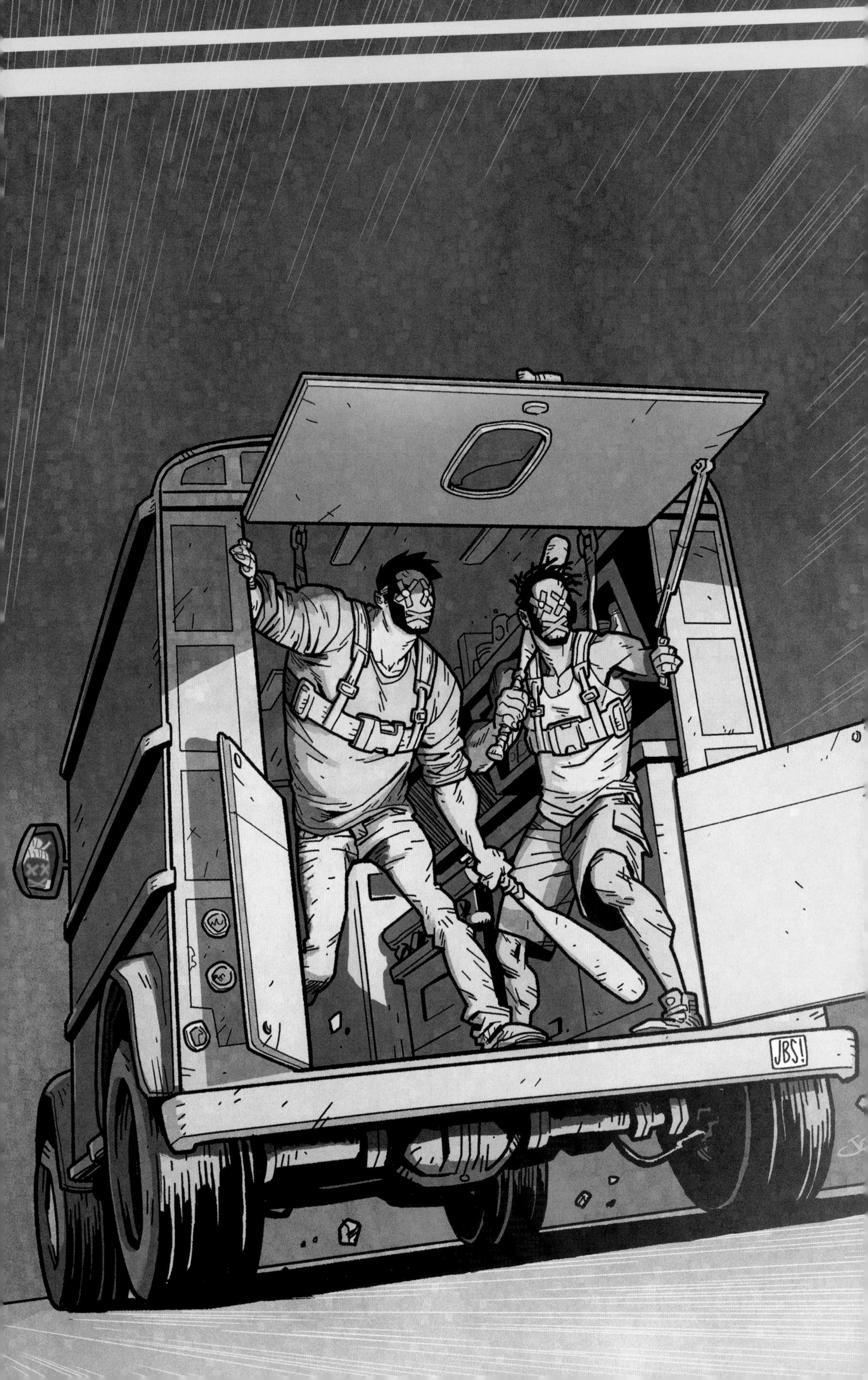
JBS!

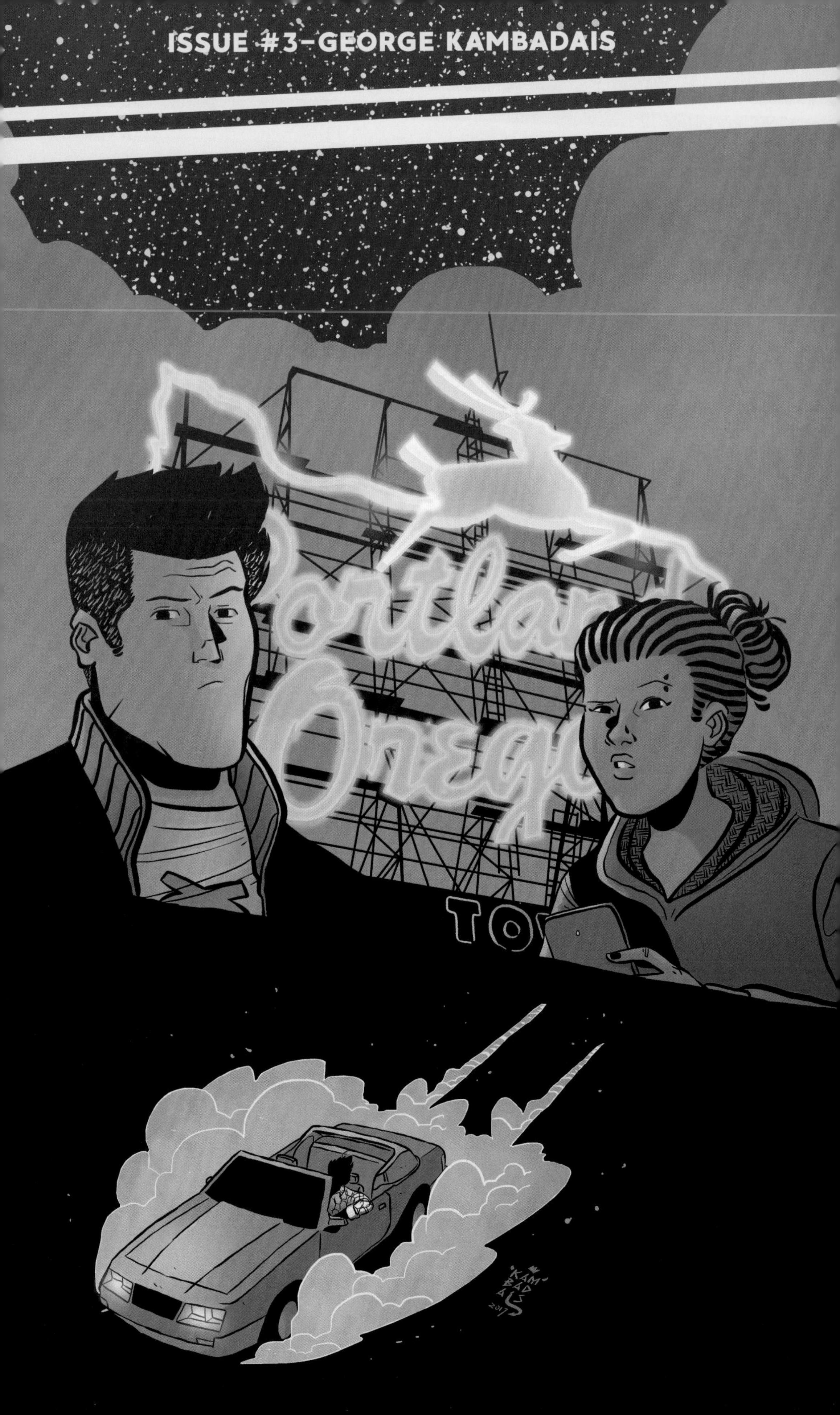
ISSUE #3—GEORGE KAMBADAIS

ISSUE #3–VARIANT–BRIAN LEVEL

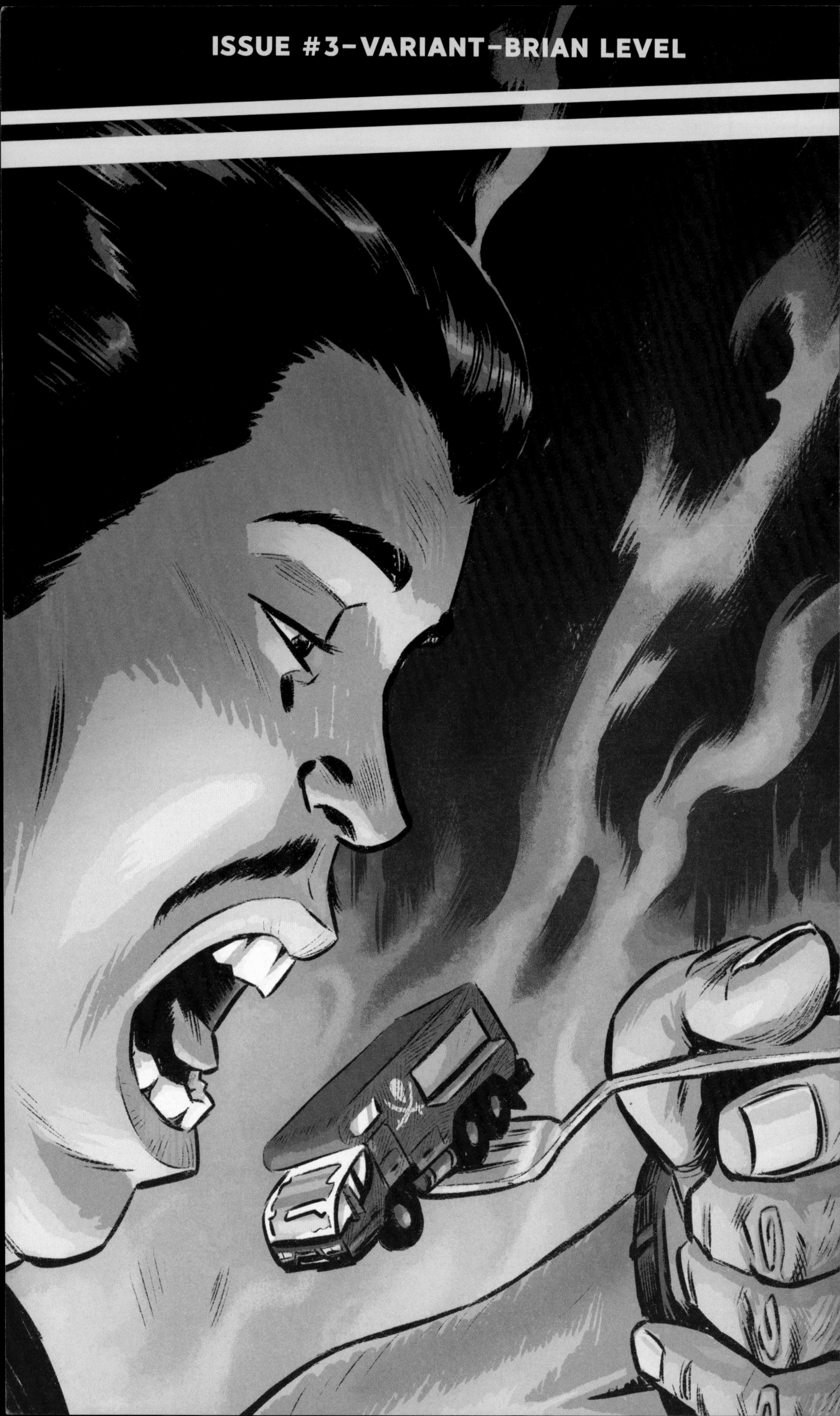

ISSUE #4–GEORGE KAMBADAIS

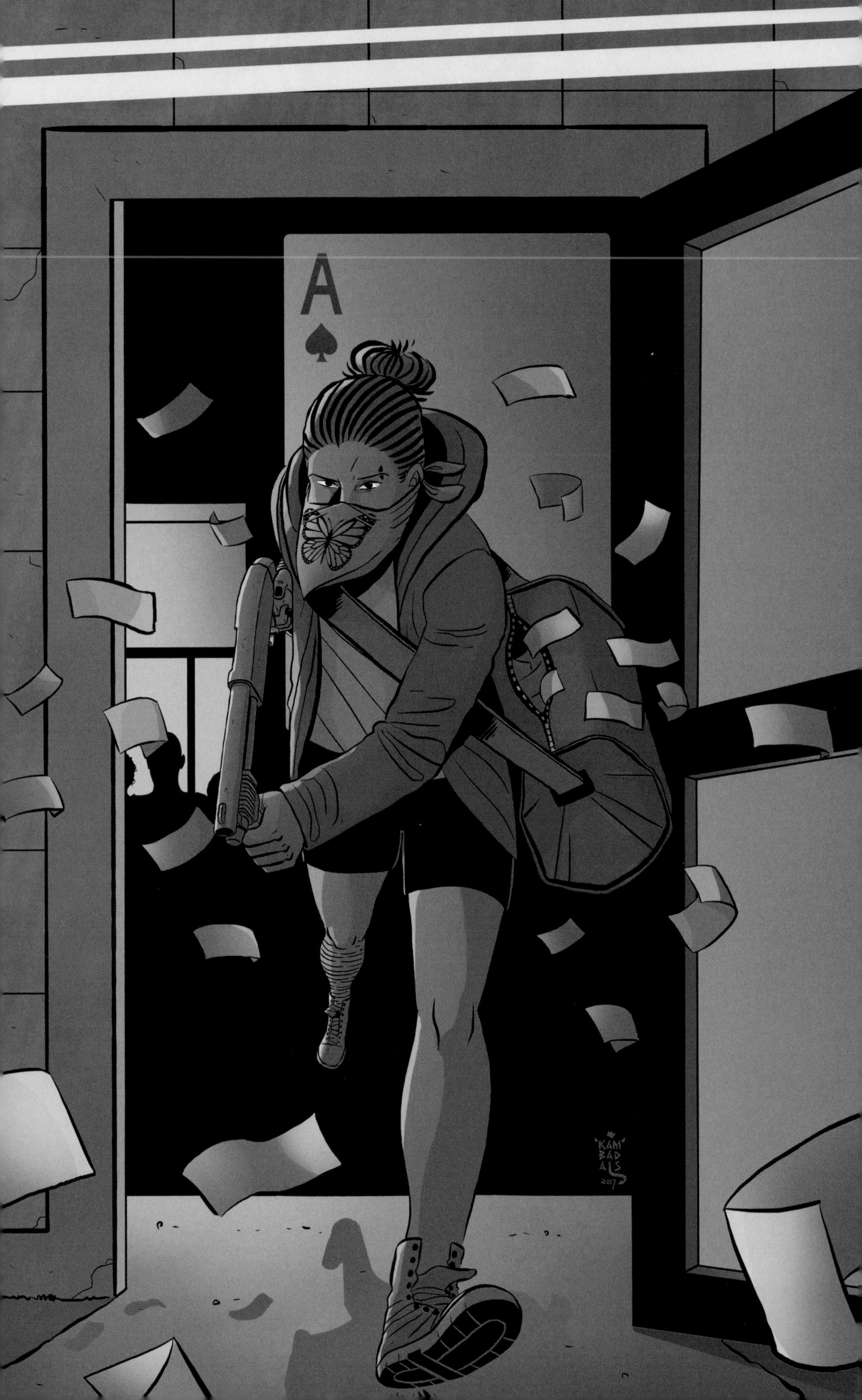
A
KAMBADAIS
2017

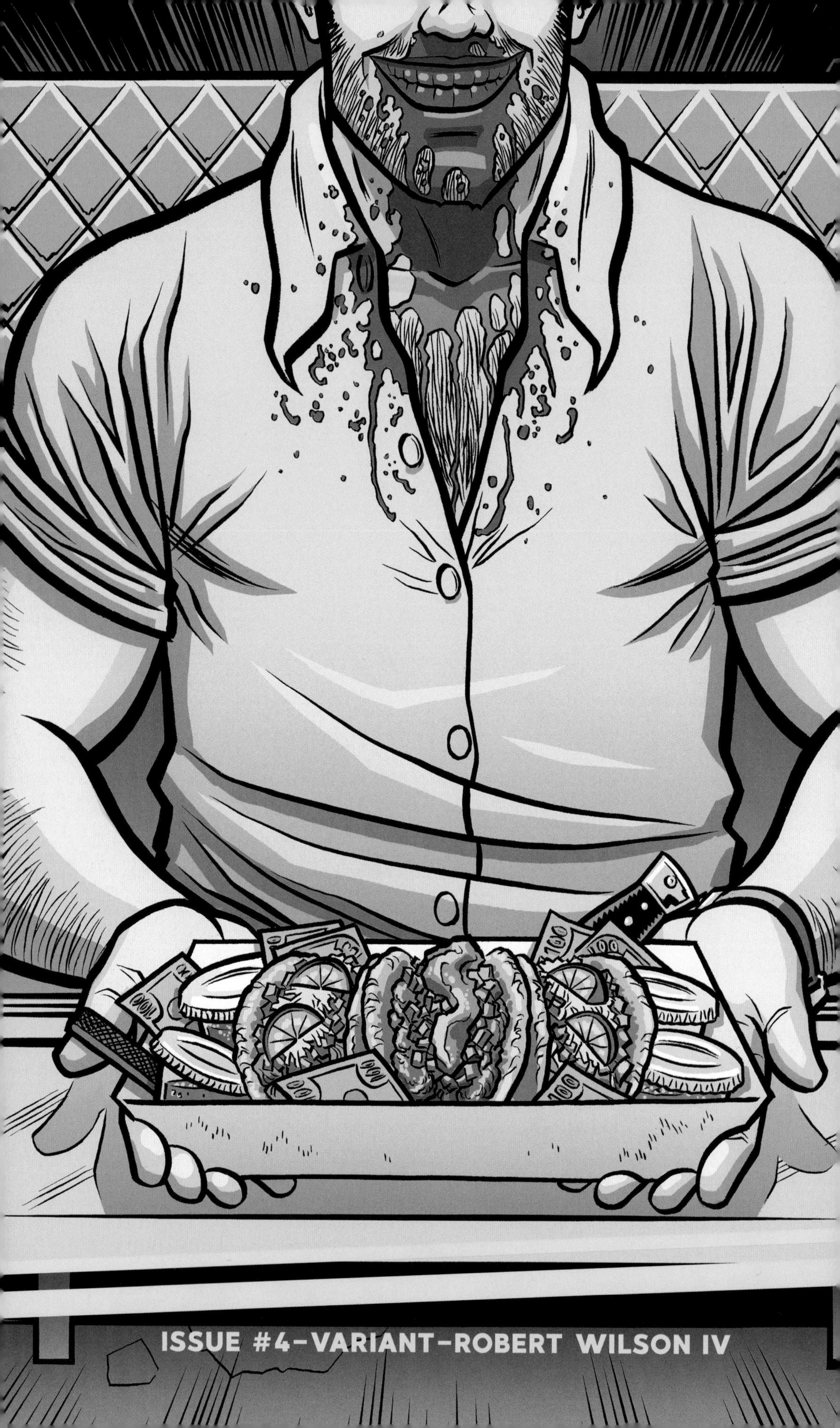
ISSUE #4–VARIANT–ROBERT WILSON IV

ISSUE #5–GEORGE KAMBADAIS

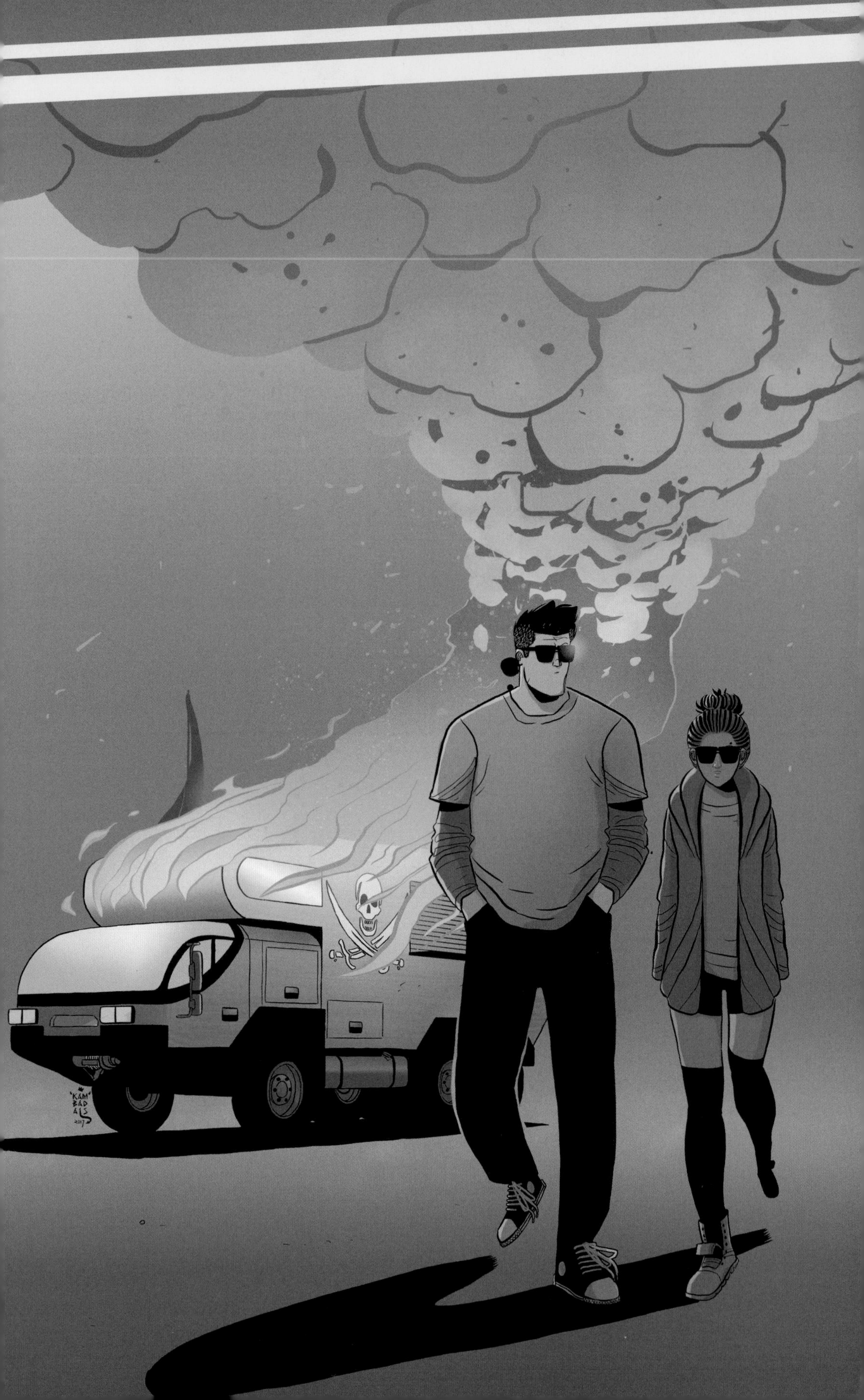

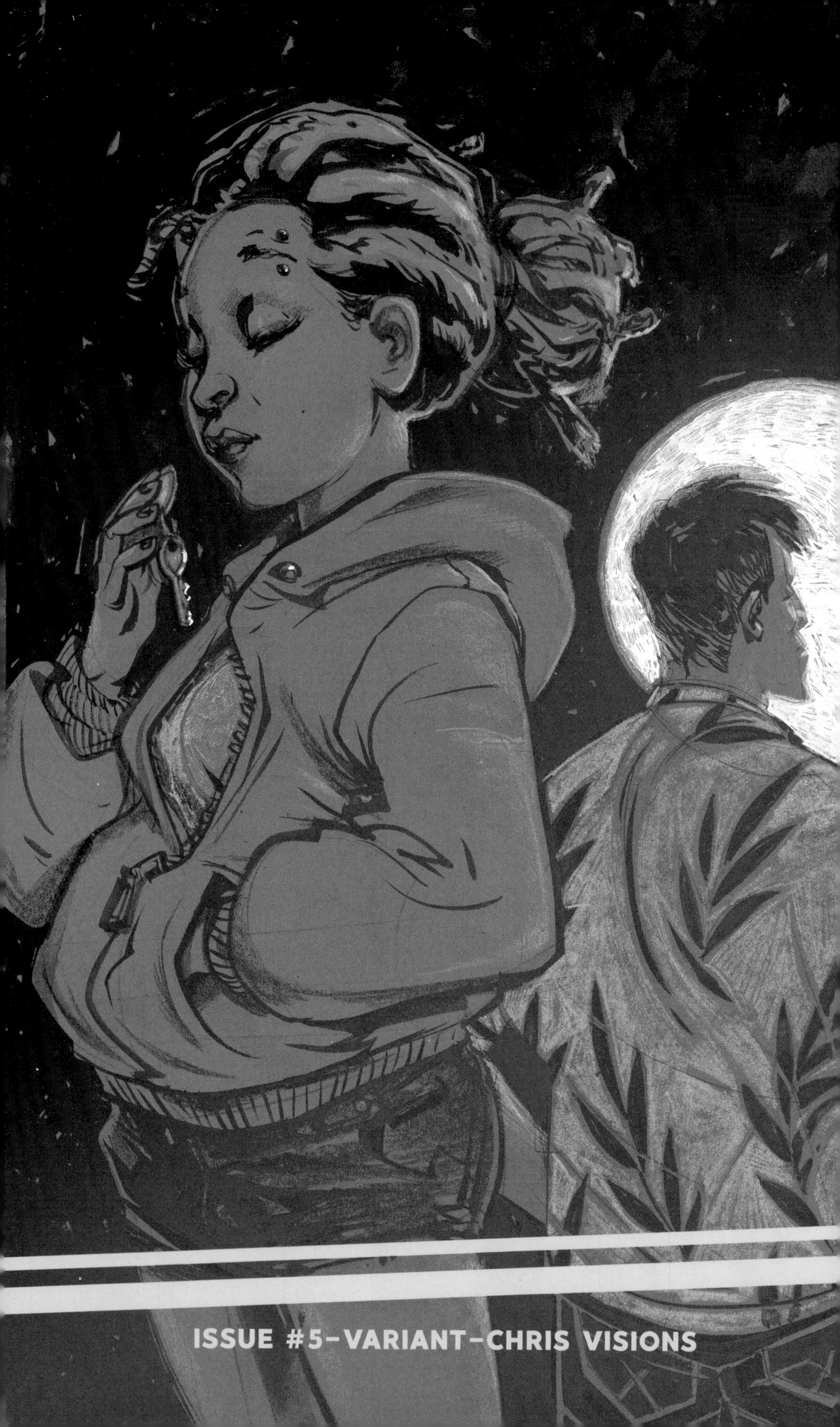

ISSUE #5–VARIANT–CHRIS VISIONS